Knowledge Management
and the Smarter Lawyer

Gretta Rusanow, Esq.

2003

ALM Publishing

New York, New York

The information contained in this book is for informational purposes only and is not intended as legal advice or any other professional service. Persons seeking legal advice should consult with an attorney.

Cover Design: *Michael Ng*

Interior Page Design & Production: *Amparo Graf*

Library of Congress Cataloging-in-Publication Data

Rusanow, Gretta, 1968–
   Knowledge management and the smarter lawyer / Gretta Rusanow.
      p. cm.
   ISBN 1-58852-116-8
      1. Law firms. 2. Knowledge management. 3. Competition. I. Title

   K129.R87 2003
   340'.068--dc21   2003057741

Dedication

To Allan and Ruth, a constant source of inspiration and encouragement, and to Elliott, my first ever management consulting project.

Acknowledgments

I've had the good fortune to work with many talented people throughout my career who have inspired me and have given me some great breaks along the way. Each of them has played a part in helping me write this book. I am indebted to Andrea Bell, who jumpstarted my career by hiring me, a young lawyer at the time, as a project manager in the precedents group of Mallesons Stephen Jaques in Sydney. At Mallesons, I learned about how lawyers work and how the engine of a law firm's business is its knowledge. I am particularly grateful to have worked with the late Howard Schreiber, a true visionary, who ultimately helped me make the switch from law to management consulting. As part of the Law Firm & Law Department Consulting Group at Price Waterhouse (and then PricewaterhouseCoopers) in New York, I worked with a wonderful group of consultants, including Jonathan Bellis and David Horne, who both taught me so much about the business of law.

Over the years, and especially since forming Curve Consulting, I have worked with many delightful clients on their knowledge management initiatives. Their commitment to knowledge management provided me with the opportunity to develop the ideas and concepts described in this book.

Some of the ideas in this book grew out of a study I conducted in 2001 and 2002 of how U.S, U.K. and Australian law firms approach knowledge management. I am grateful to the participants of that study for candidly sharing their thoughts and experiences relating to knowledge management with me. I am also grateful to the legal industry knowledge management professionals I meet in my travels, who are always willing to share their knowledge management stories with me.

My family and friends have listened to me talk ceaselessly about this book for the past year and I thank them for humoring me. I am sure they are as relieved as I am that it is finished!

I thank Jill Margo, Alun Davies, Jamie Wodetzki and Marc Bailin, who each played a role in getting me to the book writing stage.

Finally, a big thank you to the people at American Lawyer Media— Mark Voorhees, Caroline Sorokoff, Pat Rainsford, Maggie Dalla Tana, Amparo Graf, Michael Ng, and in particular, my wonderful editor, Ellen Greenblatt, for guiding me through the writing process, and for transforming my manuscript into this book.

Introduction

Law is a knowledge-based business. Knowledge management is the key to leveraging that knowledge—enabling you to work efficiently, confidently and profitably. Rather than present knowledge management theory, this book demystifies knowledge management and provides a practical guide to applying knowledge management to the practice and business of law.

Each Chapter begins with a hypothetical case study, highlighting many of the issues described in that Chapter. I have developed these case studies based on my own observations throughout my consulting work.

Most Chapters end with a checklist of all the issues described in that Chapter. This checklist is intended as an aid when implementing or critiquing your own knowledge management program.

The Chapters of this book are loosely divided into four parts.

First, Chapters 1 and 2 describe why lawyers need to focus on knowledge management and how they should introduce knowledge management concepts into their practice and business. Chapter 1 describes why knowledge management is a business imperative for lawyers, examining the pressures lawyers face and how knowledge management can help to alleviate those pressures. It describes the broad scope of knowledge management and introduces the concept of the knowledge management strategy. Chapter 2 describes how a law firm can get started in its knowledge management efforts. It describes how law firms should gain management support, understand the knowledge needs of staff, draft a strategy and then implement specific knowledge management initiatives. It effectively summarizes the approach described in Chapters 8, 9, 10 and 11.

Second, Chapters 3-7 describe the critical elements of knowledge management you must address. I have dedicated a chapter to each element.

Before you define a knowledge management strategy or implement knowledge management initiatives, you need to be clear on the knowledge you are trying to manage. Chapter 3 describes the scope of knowledge that a lawyer uses. Lawyers often limit their definition of knowledge to core, explicit, legal knowledge—such as case law, legislation, and best practice documents. This Chapter describes the much broader range of knowledge lawyers use to practice law and to manage their businesses.

Lawyers often think knowledge management is synonymous with technology. However, knowledge management involves many non-technology systems and processes. Chapter 4 considers the scope of knowledge management at a law firm. It breaks down the definition of knowledge management into its parts, then examines the broad scope of knowledge management initiatives in a law firm.

Knowledge management requires significant dedicated resources to do it right. Chapter 5 describes the knowledge management organization in a law firm, including the appropriate size, composition and positioning of the knowledge management organization.

Chapter 6 considers the many cultural barriers to knowledge management in law firms. There are also some elements of the law firm culture that are conducive to knowledge management. This Chapter examines both sides. It also suggests how law firms can overcome cultural barriers and move toward the target knowledge management culture.

Knowledge management may not be all about technology, but it is a critical element of knowledge management. Chapter 7 addresses the technology elements of knowledge management. Since technology changes so rapidly, this Chapter does not provide an inventory of current knowledge management technology solutions. Rather, it focuses on the key principles any law firm should apply to the development of knowledge management technology tools.

Third, Chapters 8–11 focus on how to approach knowledge management at your firm—from developing your strategy through to leveraging your knowledge management efforts with clients. The first three of these Chapters describe how to draft a strategy and implement specific knowledge management initiatives that meet your knowledge management and business objectives. Because knowledge management is so closely tied to the business of law, discussion also includes how to measure and demonstrate the value of knowledge management to your business. Finally, since a law firm is in the business of selling its knowledge, Chapter 11 suggests ways to leverage your knowledge management efforts with clients.

Fourth, Chapters 12 and 13 are intended as primers for lawyers with needs that differ from the law firm. Chapter 12 presents the concept of knowledge management in the context of the corporate law department. Chapter 13 describes how knowledge management concepts apply to the solo practitioner.

I hope you find this book practical, informative and helpful.

Gretta Rusanow

May 2003

Contents

PART 1
Knowledge Management and the Business of Law

PART II

Critical Elements of Knowledge Management

PART III

How to Approach Knowledge Management

289   Chapter 9
Implementing Knowledge Management

337   Chapter 10
The Value of Knowledge Management

PART IV

Knowledge Management for Other Shapes and Sizes

Knowledge Management and the Business of Law

Managing Knowledge
Is About Working Smarter

Chapter Contents

A law firm is number three in its market and aims to become number one within three years. In order to achieve this growth, the law firm develops a strategy to attract the best clients, the best work, and the best lawyers in the market.

To understand which clients it wants to attract, the firm must first understand its existing client base. This enables management to identify opportunities to win more work with existing clients. It also highlights gaps in the existing client base and prompts the firm to target new clients.

To attract the best work, the firm must understand which practice groups differentiate the firm from its competitors and identify opportunities to leverage those practice groups. The firm must examine whether those practice groups operate efficiently. It must also understand where there are opportunities to develop other practice groups into market leaders.

The firm understands that having the best clients and the best work is not enough to attract the best lawyers. Lawyers place strong emphasis, especially in the early years of practice, on professional development. The firm knows it must provide the leading professional development program in order to attract and keep the best lawyers in the market.

To develop and implement its strategy, this law firm will use its knowledge. To understand its client base and develop its client strategy, the firm will use its knowledge of its clients and the industries in which they operate. To identify which practice groups differentiate the firm in its market, the firm will use both its knowledge of the market and the firm's financial position.

Where the firm identifies opportunities for practice groups to work more efficiently, it will develop knowledge tools to aid staff. For a transaction-centric practice, the firm may develop precedent documents. For an advice-centric practice, it may implement a repository of best practice client letters of advice. If a practice group is involved in large-scale projects, it may develop project management tools.

To attract and retain the best lawyers, the firm must be committed to the development of its lawyers. Providing a formal professional development program is common in leading law firms. Ensuring that lawyers are mentored, and have the opportunity to continually move forward is also critical.

Thus, management uses the firm's knowledge to create its business strategy. It also recognizes that leveraging the firm's knowledge is key to achieving its business objectives.

Defining Knowledge Management

Knowledge management is a management concept borne out of the information age we live in. Knowledge is a critical asset of an organization, and in some organizations, is the most important asset. Knowledge is what differentiates one organization from its competitors. In pure commercial terms, knowledge management is therefore about leveraging that differentiating asset so that an organization leads, and breaks away from, its competitors.

"Knowledge management" has been defined in many ways—from the deeply academic to merely a new name for what used to be "information management." Since this book is about applying this very important management concept to your legal practice and your legal business, I have a process and goal oriented definition that will apply throughout this book.

Put simply, *knowledge management is the leveraging of your firm's collective wisdom by creating systems and processes to support and facilitate the identification, capture, dissemination and use of your firm's knowledge to meet your business objectives.* It is about recognizing that practicing law is a knowledge based profession—and managing your knowledge is key to managing your practice—whether you are a large law firm, solo practitioner, in-house counsel or a lawyer in the public sector. In essence, knowledge management is about working smarter.

Since a law firm is a knowledge based business, managing knowledge is about managing your business. There is a direct link between a firm's knowledge and its profitability. Knowledge management is not a short-lived management concept—it is an absolutely critical element of how a law firm manages its business.

For a law department, managing knowledge is key to managing the legal risk exposure of the wider organization it serves. The law department must also carefully manage its costs. There is a direct link between a law department's knowledge and its ability to manage the legal risk exposure of the wider organization. There is also a direct link between how well a law department manages its knowledge and the cost of the law department.

Throughout this book, I refer to how law firms should approach knowledge management. Regardless of where you practice as a lawyer, knowledge management is about working smarter. It's about understanding what knowledge you use in your practice and in your business—and how you can leverage that knowledge—to achieve your business objectives.

While your business objectives vary depending on where you practice law, the elements of knowledge management do not. Whether you practice in a law firm or a law department, in the public or private sector, in a partnership or as a solo practitioner, this book is for you.

More than databases and documents...

Knowledge management is more than databases and broader than legal documents—though both play a role. It is about identifying all the types of knowledge you possess and leveraging that knowledge. Knowledge about your clients, and the industries in which they operate, influences how you deliver your legal services. Knowledge about third parties, such as regulators, opposing counsel and judges, is also key.

Explicit and tacit knowledge...

Knowledge management is about managing the knowledge you have on paper (explicit knowledge) and the knowledge so intrinsic to your daily practice that you cannot quite articulate it (tacit knowledge).

More than information management...

Knowledge management is not another name for information management. Law firms have traditionally implemented information management systems to store data relating to documents, clients, staff and finances. While these systems store important data, and provide critical information in the form of reports and queries, they do not provide knowledge. People take information and turn it into knowledge.

Why Knowledge Management Is Critical

The legal industry has faced significant pressures in recent years. In the past, law firms could depend on long-standing relationships with their clients, lawyers who stayed with the firm throughout their careers, and an unlikely threat of competition beyond the city in which the firm operated. Law departments faced little pressure from their organizations to demonstrate their value to the organization. Lawyers, whether in the public or private sector, did not face the time pressures produced through the introduction of instantaneous communication tools such as e-mail, faxes and mobile telephones. The pressures facing lawyers today make knowledge management a business imperative.

Clients place increasing pressure on law firms to provide efficient, proactive, commercially focused legal services at a lower cost

Law firm clients have become very sophisticated buyers of legal services. The typical Fortune 500 corporate law department has implemented an outside counsel management program, carefully managing the number of firms it uses and defining what it expects from those firms. When a corporate law department reduces the number of law firms it uses, it increases the proportion of work it sends to its smaller panel of law firms.

In providing more work to a law firm, the client expects certain efficiencies including lower costs and a faster turnaround time. In other words, it expects the law firm to work smarter.

When a client negotiates lower hourly rates and flat fee arrangements, the law firm must find more efficient ways to work in order to maintain its profitability. Lawyers must identify ways to leverage the knowledge of its experts. Where a firm negotiates a flat fee arrangement, a partner with the incentive to delegate work to more junior (cheaper) staff can use knowledge management to enable him to confidently make the assignment.

Rather than drafting all the transactional documents, a partner can draft a precedent document and rely on more junior lawyers to produce a first draft. This frees the partner to take on more client work. It also gives the junior lawyer the learning experience he wants without requiring the partner to spend a great deal of time as a teacher.

Meeting client demands for a faster turnaround time can also be achieved through knowledge management. Project methodologies reduce the time it takes to run a matter. A repository of prior work product reduces research time. Precedent documents reduce drafting time.

Clients often talk about the "proactive lawyer." Corporations are looking for their outside counsel to practice preventive law—identifying legal issues before they become high risk, and navigating the corporation through these issues.

Through creating a culture of knowledge sharing, a key component of knowledge management, a law firm ensures that lawyers across different practice groups are working together to identify client needs. The example below illustrates how knowledge management enables lawyers to be proactive.

A litigation partner of a large law firm, having recently handled a case for an airline company, identifies a pattern of high risk behavior in the company which could result in more litigation in the future. A corporate practice group in the firm also handles work for the airline. The litigation partner meets with the corporate practice group to discuss how the firm can provide compliance training to the airline. The litigation partner and a corporate partner meet with the General Counsel of the airline, presenting the identified issue and proposing a solution.

The General Counsel is grateful to the partners for highlighting the issue, and most importantly, for presenting a solution. The airline company retains the firm to provide compliance training to its employees.

Clients also want access to their law firms' knowledge—both knowledge relating to the client, and more. As corporations become more sophisticated about knowledge management, their law departments look to outside counsel to provide access to their knowledge. Implementing knowledge management systems and processes in a law firm creates the opportunity to market these systems and processes to clients. Giving clients access to law firm knowledge management systems and processes builds a stronger client relationship.

Knowledge management therefore supports and facilitates one of the most critical law firm business objectives—the development of client loyalty.

Technology creates an expectation of faster and alternative legal services

In the age of instantaneous communication, lawyers have been forced to find quicker ways to deliver traditional legal services. Knowledge management systems and processes enable lawyers to work more efficiently and provide legal services quicker than ever before.

The Internet has also opened a whole new market for lawyers to sell their services. Lawyers must examine how they will use technology to deliver services to their clients. On-line advisory and drafting tools, developed and managed by law firms, are becoming commonplace. Knowledge management systems and processes provide the foundation of on-line services.

The information age has led to an explosion of information that lawyers must digest

In this age of the Internet and other electronic information services, lawyers face a multitude of information sources, and an exponential increase in the amount of information they must digest.

With the mass of information passing a lawyer's desk, how does he have the time to focus on the information that is critical to his practice? Consider the risk implications of missing a critical piece of information. Lawyers must be able to access accurate information when they need that information. The aim of knowledge management is to present the knowledge lawyers need when they need it. Knowledge management involves identifying what knowledge a lawyer needs and where that knowledge can be found, and then delivering that knowledge to lawyers in an easily digestible form.

Lawyers can pursue alternative career paths

It is not unusual for a lawyer to spend fewer than three years in a law firm. Many choose not to practice at all. To attract and retain lawyers, law firm salaries have risen dramatically in recent years. The result is that lawyers need to be trained in a significantly shorter time frame than before in order to become profitable for the firm because they cost so much, and because they may generate a profit for only a short period. Professional development programs are therefore critical.

Fighting the trend is another goal of law firms. The traditional large law firm environment of exceedingly long hours does not hold much charm for a lawyer with options. Law firms are no longer competing only with other law firms to keep the best staff. Law firms have been forced to examine their work environment, and create ways to improve retention rates.

Creating a work environment where lawyers are intellectually stimulated and challenged is very important. Enabling lawyers to do their work and go home at a reasonable hour is also important. Minimizing the low value added work in a lawyer's practice is just one way knowledge management creates a more rewarding work environment. No matter how specialized a lawyer's practice is, there will be some element of low value added work in his practice. For example, consider how much time lawyers spend:

- ♦ drafting common documents from scratch because no firm precedent document exists.

- ♦ researching a question of law using poor research tools.

- ♦ searching for the correct form[1] to use in a matter because there is no single form library.

----

[1] This refers to a form created by a third party, such as a court or a regulatory body. This is different from a "form document," a term used by many law firms to refer to a precedent document, created by a law firm as a starting point for client-specific documents.

Knowledge management involves identifying low value added work and developing systems and processes to minimize the time spent on those elements. This results in lawyers having more time to spend on intellectually stimulating and challenging work. They may also be able to work fewer hours and lead a more balanced life.

Consolidation of law firms has led to multi-office, multi-practice organizations, and many associated diseconomies of scale

The size of law firms has grown exponentially in recent years. Firms based in one city have formed associations with firms in other cities. Some have then formed national firms. In turn, national firms have merged with firms in other regions to create global, mega-firms. The aim has been to grow the firm's profitability by leveraging the firm's expertise in certain markets and by expanding its client base by associating with other firms. The result has also been certain diseconomies of scale.

A large firm may find that there is little sharing of knowledge across practice groups and offices. There are a number of cultural reasons for this. Where the partner compensation model rewards the individual rather than the firm, practice groups tend to operate as separate business units, focused only on growing their own practices. There is no incentive to share work with others, since there may be no reward for referring work to colleagues. Indeed, there may be overlap in areas of practice between lawyers in different practice groups. These groups may be competing with each other in the market. Lawyers may also believe that their knowledge base is their power base, and that sharing that knowledge would dilute their value. This lack of knowledge sharing between individuals and practice groups means that the firm is not leveraging its multi-practice, multi-office infrastructure. Practice groups are not looking at cross selling opportunities with other practice groups. These inefficiencies and lost business opportunities may directly impact the firm's revenue.

> Consider my earlier illustration of the airline company with a pattern of high-risk behavior. This time, the litigation partner does not consult with his corporate group. This is because the firm does not reward knowledge sharing across practice groups. If the litigation partner referred work to his corporate group, he would not derive any financial benefit from the referral. Indeed, despite working for a common client, the partners in these different practice groups rarely speak to one another. Instead, a smaller firm, offering compliance training services, is focused on growing its client base. The firm tracks the litigation cases associated with the airline company and targets the company as a potential client of the firm's services. The smaller firm presents its proposal to the General Counsel of the airline company and wins the work.
>
> The large law firm misses out on this substantial piece of work—simply because the partners did not share knowledge about the client.

Lawyers may also not be referring work to other more appropriate practice groups. This creates a high risk situation for the firm. Consider the following example:

A corporate lawyer is advising a developer on the disposition of property. The corporate lawyer does not consult the firm's tax lawyers on this matter. Due to a recent tax ruling, there are significant tax implications to the proposed structure of the transaction. The corporate lawyer's decision not to consult a tax expert ultimately costs the client $100,000 and the firm has lost the confidence of the client. This could have been avoided if the corporate lawyer had sought assistance from his colleagues in the tax group.

Without knowledge management, the larger the firm, the greater the danger that this vast infrastructure will not be leveraged.

Global consolidation and the entry of multidisciplinary practices has increased competition

As firms grow beyond their traditional local market, they have created new markets for themselves. Conversely, they face increased competition from others. This places enormous pressure on the law firm to differentiate itself in multiple markets and from multiple competitors.

Firms need to have a thorough understanding of their business and take a strategic approach to their future growth. To understand their business, law firms must manage knowledge about their firms' market position, competitors, key clients and market trends. With this knowledge, firms can develop a business strategy to build upon its market strengths, address its market weaknesses and differentiate itself from its competitors.

Law departments must demonstrate their value to the organizations they serve

A law department cannot demonstrate its value in terms of increasing revenue and profitability. It must demonstrate its value by controlling its organization's legal costs. This means managing its organization's legal risk exposure, so that litigation and settlement costs are minimized. It also means controlling the costs associated with operating an internal law department. This includes managing the number of staff, finding the right mix of inside and outside counsel, and managing costs associated with using outside counsel.

A law department must use its knowledge about legal matters impacting its organization to manage the organization's legal risk exposure. It must use knowledge about its staff, workload and outside counsel to manage the operation of the law department. It can work more efficiently through the use of precedents and best practice documents.

★ ★ ★ ★

This combination of pressures forces law firms and law departments to rethink their traditional business models. Because law firms and law departments are knowledge-based organizations, knowledge management is critical to their continuing success. This is not about a management fad. This is about how well you run your business and how well you use your knowledge to address these ever-increasing pressures.

A Brief History of Knowledge Management
in Law Firms

Knowledge management is not a new concept for lawyers. Lawyers have always managed their knowledge in one form or another.

Work product repositories

Databases of legal opinions and best practice documents are key examples of capturing and disseminating a law firm's knowledge. While there are differences in how firms approach the scope and quality control of these databases, the objective is the same. Firms recognize that the work performed for a specific client may have much greater application. Its value extends beyond the specific client engagement to future, similar engagements.

Precedent or form libraries

The firm-wide precedent (or form) document library has long been established in many law firms. Maintained by a team of lawyers and administrators, this library contains partner-approved template documents that lawyers must use as the basis of new client documents. Precedent documents enable lawyers to save time in creating the first draft of a document. They also ensure that a consistent level of quality is applied to drafting—a critical element of the firm's risk management process.

Professional development

The professional development programs of law firms are critical to the development of their lawyers, and, thus, to the future success of the firm. Law firms make a major investment in developing their lawyers. While a law graduate possesses the basic tools to practice law, it takes many years to become an expert practitioner. Law school graduates know this—and will be influenced by a law firm's approach to professional development in deciding which firm to join.

The Opportunities for Knowledge
Management

Lawyers intuitively "get" knowledge management because it is consistent with how a law firm operates. However, while several components of knowledge management already exist in law firms, lawyers tend to take a narrow approach. The emphasis is on capturing explicit legal knowledge. Generally, law firms have not focused adequately on addressing who will build and maintain knowledge management systems and processes. Lawyers have not yet addressed the many cultural barriers to knowledge management, such as the time based billing model and the partner compensation model. There has also been little exploration of how a law firm's knowledge management systems and processes can be leveraged with clients.

A narrow approach to knowledge management can undermine the value knowledge management can bring to a law firm:

Lawyers place a strong emphasis on managing legal knowledge, without acknowledging the importance of managing knowledge about clients and their industries, the skills and expertise of staff, or knowledge about third parties. Lawyers should take an expanded view when determining what exactly is "the knowledge" they use to practice law.

Law firm knowledge management initiatives have often focused on collecting best practice documents and precedents, without providing the context in which these documents may be used. A junior lawyer, asked to draft a loan agreement, may not know which of the many loan agreement precedents to use. Drafting the document is only one component of the loan agreement negotiation process. Law firms should examine ways to contextualize precedents and best practice documents—for example, by providing the relevant documents in the context of a methodology.

Lawyers focus on managing explicit knowledge and pay little attention to tacit knowledge. Although lawyers apply tacit knowledge to every aspect of their work, such knowledge is hard to articulate. However, there are steps lawyers can take to identify and share tacit knowledge. For example, developing a methodology based on a common work process or implementing a skills and expertise locator enables an inexperienced lawyer to access the tacit knowledge known to the experienced members of the firm. Law firms should examine how tacit knowledge can be identified and shared.

Law firms limit their knowledge management initiatives to technology. Having a solid technology platform is critical to the successful capture and delivery of knowledge. However, it is not enough. Knowledge may be captured and delivered without technology. Professional development programs and communities of interest are just two examples of effective knowledge management initiatives that may not involve technology. There must also be a strong culture of knowledge sharing and an organization to develop and maintain knowledge management initiatives.

While discrete data repositories exist, there has been little focus on how to integrate these systems to leverage the firm's knowledge. The financial, document and client relationship management systems are typical discrete elements of a firm's technology platform. Information stored in those systems would be even more valuable if the systems were integrated to provide a true "lawyer desktop" where staff could integrate all knowledge about a matter, a client or a subject through one access point.

Law firm knowledge management initiatives are often the domain of an isolated department. If the library or IT department is responsible for knowledge management, initiatives tend to be narrow in scope. It may be appropriate for the library or IT to be responsible for specific components of knowledge management—but neither can be responsible for ensuring that lawyers and staff contribute to knowledge management systems and programs. Neither group can be responsible for developing content.

Knowledge management requires the involvement of all staff—in all practice groups and administrative functions.

The law firm culture does not reward contribution to knowledge management. In a firm where compensation is based almost solely on revenue generated, and where revenue is generated based on number of hours billed, lawyers hear a strong message that time invested in knowledge management initiatives is not valued.

At a firm where lawyers are not rewarded financially for referring work to colleagues, there is no incentive to promote knowledge sharing across practice groups.

In some law firms, the "knowledge is power" culture means that lawyers believe their career prospects largely depend on their ability to amass a unique base of knowledge. Sharing that knowledge with others would dilute the value of that knowledge.

Law firms need to address cultural barriers to knowledge management in order to build a successful knowledge management environment and reap the rewards of knowledge management. Territoriality is the antithesis of knowledge management.

Achieving Business Objectives Through
Knowledge Management

In this knowledge-based market, there is a direct relationship between a law firm's knowledge and its profitability. It is not just about having the best experts. It is about how your firm leverages those experts. Do you take an *ad hoc* approach to managing client relationships and winning work, or do you use your knowledge strategically to grow your business and give the best advice in the most efficient manner to your client?

Put simply, for a lawyer, knowledge management is about how well you use your knowledge to both define and meet your business objectives. Even in defining its business objectives, your firm should leverage its knowledge. Once those business objectives have been defined, you should look to develop a knowledge management strategy to achieve those objectives.

Typically, lawyers define an information need and approach their IT department to build a database. One lawyer may think there is a very good reason to build the database, but does not consult with his colleagues to define the business need. Nevertheless, the IT department builds the database. With great fanfare, the database is launched. Lawyers soon discover that the database does not meet their business needs. They don't use the system, and consequently do not contribute content to the database. Each department has its own knowledge which is not shared with the rest of the firm. Over time, the content becomes outdated and of unreliable quality. The lawyers quickly lose confidence in the database and stop using it.

While the firm invested significantly in the database, there has been little return on this investment. This is understandable. The database simply had no value to lawyers.

Lawyers should approach knowledge management with the question, "What am I trying to achieve and how does knowledge management help me achieve it?"

Defining Knowledge Management
Objectives

Once your firm's management determines its business objectives, it can define its knowledge management objectives. In order to succeed, knowledge management objectives should be closely tied to your business objectives. Indeed, they are so closely aligned that there will likely be overlap between what is a business objective and what is a knowledge management objective. The main distinction is that knowledge management objectives are more specific to leveraging the knowledge of the firm. The following illustrates how business objectives can be translated into knowledge management objectives:

BUSINESS OBJECTIVE	KNOWLEDGE MANAGEMENT OBJECTIVE
Increase profitability	Work more effectively: ♦ Leverage expertise ♦ Improve productivity ♦ Stop reinventing the wheel ♦ Make available the necessary resources to support the needs of the firm
Attract and retain the best clients	Improve client service: ♦ Improve the speed of delivery of client service ♦ Improve the quality of client service
Attract and retain the best staff	Create a more satisfying work environment: ♦ Enhance professional development ♦ Decrease the time spent on low value added work
Attract and retain the best work	Improve the quality of legal knowledge: ♦ Raise the bar of legal excellence in the firm ♦ Improve the level of expertise and knowledge within the firm ♦ Encourage innovation

Defining Knowledge Management
Initiatives

Once you are clear on your knowledge management objectives, you should define specific knowledge management initiatives to help you achieve these objectives. Let's look at the law firm I described at the start of this Chapter and see how knowledge management supports its business objectives.

> The law firm aims to be the number one firm in its market in three years, through achieving the following business objectives:
>
> - ♦ having the best lawyers
> - ♦ having the best clients
> - ♦ having the best work.
>
> The firm can achieve its objectives through knowledge management.
>
> *Business Objective 1—Attracting and Retaining the Best Lawyers*
>
> To attract the best lawyers, the firm might focus on the knowledge management objectives of:
>
> - ♦ creating a market leading professional development environment
> - ♦ providing the tools the associates need to confidently practice law
> - ♦ creating a balanced work life for its staff

Creating the market-leading professional development environment

Developing a market-leading professional development program and introducing a mentoring program for junior lawyers are two specific *knowledge management initiatives* that support the knowledge management objectives of developing the market-leading professional development environment. This, in turn, facilitates achieving the business objective of attracting and retaining the best lawyers.

Providing the tools the associates need to confidently practice law and creating a balanced work life

Developing a first rate precedent document library, repositories of best practice documents and current awareness services are specific *knowledge management initiatives* that provide young lawyers with the tools they need to confidently practice law, while reducing the time spent on low value added work. As lawyers focus on value added work, a challenging work environment is created. Reducing time spent on low value added work may also enable lawyers to work fewer hours and lead a more balanced lifestyle.

These specific initiatives meet the knowledge management objective of creating a more satisfying work environment by decreasing the time spent on low value added work and focusing on providing lawyers with the tools they need. This in turn, should help achieve the business objective of attracting and retaining the best lawyers.

Business Objective 2—Attracting the Best Clients

To attract the best clients, a firm must demonstrate its expertise. The *knowledge management objective* is to identify and leverage the firm's expertise. Specific *knowledge management initiatives,* such as developing precedent documents and creating repositories of work product, ensure that expertise is not contained within the minds of a few. Rather, all staff will benefit from that expertise. In turn, the clients benefit.

Delivering legal services more efficiently is another *knowledge management objective* that directly supports this business objective. There are a number of *knowledge management initiatives* that enable efficient delivery of legal services. Precedent documents enable lawyers to significantly reduce the time involved in creating a first draft of a document. Since clients are continually looking for high quality work in a shorter timeframe, any means of reducing drafting time enhances a lawyer's ability to meet client demands.

Business Objective 3—Attracting the Best Work

Attracting the best work rests largely on the firm demonstrating its proven track record in managing similar matters. Again, the *knowledge management objective* is to leverage the firm's expertise. One specific *knowledge management initiative* is the creation of a credentials database. If this firm records its credentials based on past projects, it is able to promptly demonstrate its track record.

Another *knowledge management initiative* may be the creation of project methodologies or a skills and expertise locator. These initiatives enable the firm to establish a team of experts, and manage the matter in a smooth and efficient manner.

The Scope of Knowledge Management

Knowledge management is not just about documents and databases. The mistake that many law firms have made is to treat knowledge management as a technology initiative, or to limit knowledge management initiatives to the management of core legal knowledge. To succeed at knowledge management, lawyers must take a broad view of knowledge management, and consider both the strategic and operational elements of knowledge management.

The scope of knowledge—legal knowledge and beyond (Chapter 3). Taking a broad view of the knowledge a lawyer uses to run a practice and a business is the first step in ensuring that knowledge management supports the business, as well as the practice.

As a lawyer, you must manage your core legal knowledge sources to operate your practice:

◆   Case law, commentary and interpretation

◆   Legislation and commentary

◆   Best practice (or model) documents

◆   Precedents (or form) documents

You may also use certain categories of knowledge to operate your business, such as:

- ◆ Firm and practice area knowledge

- ◆ Client knowledge

- ◆ Business and industry knowledge

- ◆ Staff skills and expertise

- ◆ Methodology and processes

- ◆ Past projects and lessons learned

- ◆ Third party knowledge (e.g., regulators, judges, counsel, experts, external consultants and competitors).

- ◆ The firm's market position

- ◆ The firm's revenue, costs and profitability

The scope of knowledge management initiatives—beyond technology (Chapter 4). While a database is an effective tool to capture and disseminate knowledge, there are many non-technology means of managing knowledge. Professional development programs, mentoring programs and communities of interest are some common examples of knowledge management initiatives that do not involve technology. Even office design, such as creating open plan offices, team rooms and a café space, can be a knowledge management initiative—by creating a physical environment that encourages knowledge sharing.

Knowledge management needs an organization to support it (Chapter 5). Managing the process of identifying, capturing, disseminating and using knowledge is labor-intensive. A law firm needs central leadership to direct and implement its knowledge management strategy. Since knowledge needs differ across practice groups, a law firm also requires knowledge management staff at the practice group level. Existing functions, such as the library, intranet, and precedents group, should become part of a wider knowledge management organization. Since knowledge management touches upon all areas of a law firm, careful attention must be paid to positioning the knowledge management organization so that it has the authority to implement knowledge management across all practice groups and administrative functions.

Knowledge management needs a culture to facilitate it (Chapter 6). There are some fundamental clashes between the law firm culture and the objectives of knowledge management. Perhaps the greatest impediment to knowledge management in a law firm is the time-based billing model. This model offers no incentive to work more efficiently, while knowledge management is all about working more efficiently. With the focus on the billable hour, lawyers also have no incentive to focus on investment work, such as contributing to knowledge management. In some law firm cultures, lawyers believe that knowledge is power, and amassing a unique knowledge base is key to their future success. Knowledge management, on the other hand, is all about leveraging knowledge by sharing it with colleagues. Law firms need to build a culture of knowledge sharing. To achieve this, firms must first address cultural barriers by building knowledge management into the firm's business processes, such as the compensation system, career progression model and budgeting system.

Knowledge management needs a solid technology platform (Chapter 7). While knowledge management is not just about technology systems, technology does play an important role in the capture and dissemination of knowledge. Law firms must have core technology tools, and use them well, to support knowledge management.

The Value of Knowledge Management to Lawyers

Since knowledge management has such a direct relationship to the achievement of a lawyer's business objectives, you should focus on the value any knowledge management initiative brings to your business. Before any knowledge management initiative, lawyers should have a good business reason for pursuing the initiative. Ask yourself: How will this initiative help us achieve our business objectives? Do the benefits justify the investment?

Lawyers should create a business case for every knowledge management initiative which articulates the business reason, demonstrable benefits, investment, critical success factors, timing and criteria for measuring value.

As you develop a solid business case for the specific knowledge management initiative, you should also develop a project plan. This will help you to understand: Are you clear on the effort required? Do you have resources available to progress the initiative? What is the deadline for implementing the initiative?

Measuring the value of knowledge management is key. If a lawyer has defined demonstrable benefits at the outset, the lawyer can measure the outcome of the initiative. Every knowledge management initiative should be judged on how well it meets a knowledge management objective and a business objective.

The Role of Management

Law firm management support for, and involvement in, knowledge management is key to its success. The message that management sends to your firm conveys the importance of knowledge management to your firm. If law firm management sends a message that knowledge management is critical to the future growth of the firm, lawyers will start to pay attention to knowledge management. If management addresses the cultural barriers to knowledge management, such as rewarding lawyers for contributing to knowledge management initiatives, lawyers will begin to adopt knowledge management into their daily work practices.

The Results of Knowledge Management

Knowledge management, like any other initiative, requires significant investment—so it must deliver results. The best way to justify investment in knowledge management is to ensure that knowledge management is directly tied to your business objectives. Where a law firm is clear on its business objectives, and how knowledge management can drive the achievement of those business objectives, justifying knowledge management is easy.

If knowledge management is done well, leveraging the knowledge that differentiates you from your competitors will lead to reduced costs, increased revenue, increased profitability, a more satisfying work environment—and the best lawyers, the best clients and the best work.

How Does Our Firm Get Started?

A law firm has five major practice groups. Each practice group has developed its own databases to capture and disseminate knowledge used by staff in the practice group. In all cases, the practice group has requested the IT department to build the databases. No business cases are submitted and the IT department builds databases based on instructions from their clients—the practice groups.

The formats and contents of the databases vary widely across the five groups. For example, the corporate group seeks to capture every letter of advice and transactional document drafted by the group. The real estate group only seeks to capture best practice documents. In some groups, partners determine database format and content. In other groups, paralegals define database format and content.

Responsibility for maintaining the content of the databases also differs across the groups. The banking and finance group assigns a paralegal to regularly collect and publish documents. The corporate group relies on every lawyer to add content to the database. The real estate group has a partner responsible for controlling the quality of content placed in the database.

The outcomes of this approach are as follows:

♦ Since practice groups are responsible for defining and implementing knowledge management systems, without any firm-wide coordination, it is likely that practice groups will implement duplicative databases. This creates a number of inefficiencies. The IT department is pulled in multiple directions as it caters to the different, yet strikingly similar needs of the five practice groups. While there are some differences in the content and format of each database, the purpose of the databases is similar—to store the work product of a practice group. There would be many opportunities to leverage the work already done by practice groups. However, rather than leverage existing databases, lawyers and paralegals spend significant time defining the format and content of each new database.

♦ Without a business case, it is likely that the practice group has not adequately defined how the database supports the practice group's knowledge management and business objectives. It is also likely that the practice group has not adequately considered the costs associated with developing the database. It is unclear about the resources needed to build and maintain the database. This results in significant investment in a database that often does not meet the business needs of the practice group.

- The differing approaches across practice groups to quality of content create risk management issues for the firm. Where a practice group stores all of its documents on the database, placing the emphasis on quantity over quality, lawyers cannot be confident of the quality of content. Over time, lawyers lose confidence in the database and simply stop using it.

- Lawyers have a narrow, reactive approach to knowledge management. Their focus is on storing documents in a database. They do not have a wider understanding of "knowledge" or knowledge management. While accessing best practice documents is important, it may not fully address the knowledge and business needs of the group.

The practice groups in this law firm understand that knowledge is key to their practice. This has motivated lawyers in each practice group to invest in the development and maintenance of databases to store documents. While the lawyers may intuitively link their knowledge needs to their business objectives, they have not taken a strategic approach to knowledge management. The result is an uncoordinated, inconsistent, duplicative and narrow approach to knowledge management. It is unlikely that these databases will have a direct impact on achieving the firm's business objectives.

Knowledge management is more than an academic concept—it is key to your business. As a lawyer, you are in the business of applying your knowledge to your client's specific needs; managing that knowledge is at the heart of managing your practice and your business. Therefore, the first step is defining knowledge management in the context of your firm's business objectives. You must gain the support of law firm management as well as build awareness throughout the firm about knowledge management and its benefits. The firm can then adopt a knowledge management strategy which addresses the knowledge needs of the law firm while driving the achievement of business objectives.

This Chapter examines how to get started with knowledge management in your firm—from gaining management support to implementing knowledge management concepts and initiatives.

Who Will Lead the Charge?

In a law firm with no one responsible for knowledge management and no structured approach to knowledge management, someone has to take the lead. Often, the Director of IT or the head librarian plays the role of the knowledge management champion in its initial stages. The Director of IT is often involved since technology is so inextricably linked to the capture and delivery of information and knowledge at many law firms. The librarian is involved because of the library's role in packaging and delivering information and knowledge for lawyers. Both the IT department and library are critical functions for knowledge management—though neither should be leading knowledge management. Since knowledge management is so inextricably linked to the business of the law firm, it is critical that the partners get involved as champions very early on.

Gain Management Support

Management support is critical to the success of knowledge management in a law firm. However, since knowledge management is a relatively new concept, senior partners of a law firm probably will not know what knowledge management actually is. At best, they may think it means the document management system. A law firm's initial interest in knowledge management may be limited to a few senior people who recognize the value of knowledge management and believe strongly in the firm's need to focus on this area. These people must, with the help of the Director of IT, the head librarian or the head of professional development, explain to the firm's management how knowledge management is more than an academic concept.

At the outset, management needs to understand how knowledge management can drive the achievement of the firm's business objectives. If you are responsible for raising awareness about knowledge management among your firm's management, you should illustrate how knowledge management can achieve your firm's business objectives. You should be as specific as possible. The following two examples illustrate how a specific business objective can be achieved through knowledge management.

A firm identifies that its real estate group could operate more efficiently. Senior partners spend too much time drafting common documents but do not feel confident about delegating work to junior lawyers or paralegals. Unfortunately, the partners cannot charge their clients full partner rates for much of this work. Consequently, 20% of partner time billed to drafting documents must be written off. By drafting precedent documents and creating a professional development program to train junior staff in drafting key transactional documents, the senior partners can feel confident about delegating work to junior lawyers. This enables the real estate group to fully recover fees for the time billed by junior lawyers and frees the senior partners to pursue other work.

* * * *

In response to new legislation to reform the financial services industry, a law firm creates a new practice group with the goal of becoming the market leader in this field. Since this is an emerging area of law, lawyers must be current with industry developments. Lawyers will use media monitors and on-line services to keep up to date. Given the sheer volume of industry developments, lawyers will soon become inundated with material they must digest. Delivering the updates will not be enough. The firm will also need to filter and package information in a digestible manner.

Along with actual legal knowledge, the practice group will begin to amass firm knowledge in this area through applying the law to each client situation. It will also need to address the best ways to capture and disseminate this firm knowledge.

The above examples illustrate how knowledge management directly links to the business of the firm.

Management also needs to see knowledge management in broad terms. This is not just about how lawyers do their legal work. This is also about how management uses its knowledge to operate the firm. You will get management's attention by drawing the lines connecting knowledge management and business objectives. Knowledge about clients, the firm's financial position, projects, and market strengths are all critical to management as it plans for the future. Knowledge management extends to capturing and leveraging the knowledge that management uses to manage the firm and plan for the future.

Management support will build over time. To some degree, initial support for knowledge management requires a leap of faith by management since knowledge management involves a fundamental shift in the culture of a law firm and daily lawyer work processes.

Without management support for knowledge management, you may have databases or a great professional development program, but none of these will ever be leveraged.

Form a Knowledge Management Team

Your firm should create a knowledge management team consisting of senior people who understand the firm's business, have a good understanding of knowledge management and are well respected in the firm. In the absence of a head of knowledge management, the knowledge management team should include senior staff from IT, the library and professional development. The team should ideally include the managing partner, or at least a well respected partner. The purpose of the team is to build awareness about knowledge management throughout the firm and draft a knowledge management strategy.

Management Sends a Clear Message

Once management understands the importance of knowledge management to its law firm's success, it must send a clear message to the firm about its support. Knowledge management requires a fundamental shift in a law firm's culture. The rhetoric of management regarding knowledge management will set the tone for the firm's approach to knowledge management. People are more inclined to adopt change if they understand why they need to change and feel a sense of ownership in the change process. Staff need to understand how knowledge management will not only improve the firm's overall performance, but will also make their work lives better.

Understand the Knowledge Needs of the Firm

Now that everyone in the firm is curious about knowledge management, it's time to stop talking and start doing. You cannot implement knowledge management without first understanding the knowledge needs of the firm and looking at how staff currently address those needs.

At this early stage, engaging staff in the development of the firm's approach to knowledge management is crucial to successful implementation. If staff are involved in planning the firm's approach to knowledge management, they will be more support-ive as the firm implements knowledge management initiatives.

Conducting a "knowledge audit" enables the firm to under-stand the knowledge needs of the firm—and to identify what knowledge management systems and processes the firm already has. An effective way to understand the knowledge needs of the firm is to conduct focus sessions with representative staff from all practice groups and administrative functions. In focus sessions with lawyers, you should find out about how lawyers work and how they use knowledge to do their work. Given that the knowledge needs of lawyers vary across different practice groups, it is more effective to conduct focus sessions for each practice group. These focus sessions will help the knowledge management team to iden-tify existing knowledge management practices. Some of these may represent knowledge management best practice and should be rolled out across the firm. Some current practices may have poten-tial and could be improved upon. Other practices may simply rep-resent worst practice and should be actively discouraged. Consider the following illustration:

BEST PRACTICE	POTENTIAL BEST PRACTICE	WORST PRACTICE
The banking group has developed a set of precedent docu-ments that form the basis of all new transactional docu-ments.	The corporate group has begun to conduct informal debriefing sessions at the conclusion of a matter. The sessions are attend-ed by members of the matter team.	The insurance group has a reposi-tory of all prior letters of advice drafted for clients. The group does not review letters to ensure high quality of content.

BEST PRACTICE	POTENTIAL BEST PRACTICE	WORST PRACTICE
	Debriefing sessions could involve a wider group and more formal processes surrounding the capture of lessons learned could be created.	The group does not regularly review the repository to ensure currency of content.

In sessions with administrative staff, the focus should be on understanding how specific systems and processes supporting knowledge management are maintained. For example, secretaries can provide insight into how the practice group uses the document management system, manages content in the work product repository, or maintains client contact information.

The knowledge management team should also conduct focus sessions or interviews with representatives of administrative functions—including the library, human resources, IT, finance, marketing and professional development. Administrative staff, who are focused on the business aspects of a law firm, are well placed to comment on the law firm from a business perspective.

Since the knowledge management strategy focuses on the business of law, as well as the practice of law, it should address the knowledge needs of all staff—both legal and non-legal. It is critical to understand how non-legal staff at the firm work, and how they use knowledge to do their work.

Finally, asking clients what they think about knowledge management, and their expectations regarding how their outside counsel work, is also important. As clients become more sophisticated about knowledge management, they will have expectations about how their outside counsel approach knowledge management. In Chapter 1, I described how clients want their law firms to be proactive. In Chapter 11, I describe how law firms should promote their knowledge management efforts to clients as a means of demonstrating a strong focus on client service delivery.

To make sure the knowledge management team has a clear understanding of how the firm currently uses knowledge to operate, it should test its findings with the practice groups and administrative functions. For example, for each practice group, the knowledge management strategy team should present a picture of:

- ♦ core work processes
- ♦ existing knowledge management tools and processes
- ♦ how staff share knowledge
- ♦ how lawyers are trained
- ♦ what staff know about clients and their industries
- ♦ contact with other practice groups

In analyzing how the firm currently uses knowledge to operate, the knowledge management team should look at industry best practices. This will help the team establish whether any knowledge management best practices are evident in the firm and where there may be knowledge management opportunities in the firm.

In addition to identifying the specific knowledge needs of staff, the focus sessions and interviews also identify any barriers to knowledge management which need to be addressed. These may be cultural impediments, such as the time-based billing model. They may be organizational barriers, such as lack of resources. They could be technological impediments, such as insufficient systems and applications to manage knowledge.

With the firm's confidence that the knowledge management strategy team understands its knowledge needs, the team should develop a knowledge management strategy.

Draft a Knowledge Management Strategy
(Chapter 8)

The knowledge management strategy should reflect the knowledge needs and work processes of all staff, as well as your firm's culture and its business strategy. The strategy will thus provide a blueprint for the development of knowledge management processes and tools. It should define the scope of knowledge management at your firm. It should also address the technology elements of knowledge management, though technology is only one component of knowledge management. It must focus on building a culture of knowledge sharing, creating an organization to support and facilitate knowledge sharing, and ensuring that knowledge management initiatives reflect the work processes of all staff.

The strategy should describe the firm's knowledge management objectives and highlight its current approach to knowledge management. The strategy should contain recommendations to move the firm from its current approach to knowledge management to the achievement of its knowledge management objectives, but be flexible enough to enable practice groups to develop knowledge management processes and tools that meet their needs.

Following are the key issues your firm should address in its knowledge management strategy:

♦ **What are the firm's business objectives?**

Since knowledge management is a key business driver, the knowledge management strategy should align with the firm's business strategy.

♦ **What are the firm's knowledge management objectives?**

The firm's knowledge management objectives should articulate exactly how knowledge management will support the firm's business objectives.

♦ **What is the scope of knowledge you will manage?**

The firm should define the scope of knowledge it intends to manage. Is the focus on managing legal knowledge or all knowledge used at the firm? Will the firm manage only explicit knowledge, or examine ways to address tacit knowledge?

♦ **What is the scope of knowledge management initiatives you will pursue?**

Will these initiatives be purely technology driven, or will the firm implement technology and non-technology systems and processes to manage knowledge? Will the firm focus only on implementing systems to capture and share knowledge, or will it focus on building a knowledge management organization and addressing cultural barriers to knowledge sharing?

♦ **What are the strengths of your culture?**

Since knowledge management becomes part of the way your firm works, it should reflect your firm's culture. If a key strength of your firm is its culture of encouraging the individual, your firm's approach to knowledge management must place strong emphasis on the knowledge management needs of individuals and their practice groups.

♦ **What are the cultural barriers to knowledge management you need to address?**

Will the time-based billing system discourage lawyers from contributing to knowledge management? Do the partner compensation system and career progression model encourage knowledge hoarding? Do practice groups operate as separate businesses or as one firm?

♦ **What is the target culture you want to establish?**

Will your culture encourage sharing knowledge with others? Will staff think like a firm, not like a practice group? Will staff seek out ways to work more efficiently? Will your firm value investment in the future?

◆ **What approach will your firm take to knowledge management?**

Will knowledge management be managed centrally? Will it be completely decentralized? Will your firm adopt a hybrid model?

◆ **What will your knowledge management organization look like?**

Who will lead it? How many knowledge management staff will there be? What will be the roles of knowledge management staff? Which existing functions will form part of the knowledge management organization?

◆ **How will the knowledge management organization be positioned in the firm?**

Who will the head of knowledge management report to? What is the relationship between the knowledge management organization and administrative functions? What is the relationship between the knowledge management organization and the practice groups?

◆ **What will your knowledge management technology system[1] look like?**

Will the firm develop a single user interface into multiple applications? Will the firm focus on developing a firm-wide, heavily vetted, work product repository?

....

[1] Throughout this book, the knowledge management technology system is referred to simply as the "knowledge management system."

♦ **What technology tools do you have?**

Does the firm have the fundamental components of its knowledge management technology platform? Is each tool already leveraged, or are there opportunities to improve use of the existing tools?

♦ **What tools do you need?**

Are there clear gaps in your firm's technology platform? Do you have an enterprise wide search engine? Do you need a document management system? Has the firm implemented a contact management system? Will the intranet serve as the firm's portal?

♦ **How will knowledge management support business development?**

How will your firm employ knowledge management concepts in how it wins work? How will your firm manage its knowledge of clients and past work? Since clients are increasingly focused on knowledge management, how will your firm promote knowledge management to its clients?

♦ **What is the relationship between knowledge management and e-business?**

If your firm offers e-business solutions based on the firm's knowledge, how will knowledge management support and facilitate them?

♦ **Will your firm give its clients access to its knowledge management initiatives?**

Increasingly, clients are looking to their law firms to provide access to law firm knowledge. Will your firm give clients access to its work product repositories? Will your firm develop client specific precedent documents? Will you offer tailored training sessions for clients?

♦ **What are the critical success factors?**

What are the key cultural, organizational, and techno-logical factors that may affect the success of knowledge management at the firm?

♦ **What will knowledge management cost?**

Consider the cost of creating a knowledge management organization, implementing or developing technology tools, developing professional development programs, or changing the compensation system and career progression model. Consider also the cost of not doing knowledge management.

♦ **What value will knowledge management bring to your firm?**

How will you measure the value of knowledge management to your firm? What hard measures, such as financial data and usage data will you use? What soft measures, such as anecdotal feedback about value, will you use?

Management Adopts the Knowledge Management Strategy

While management has articulated knowledge management as a key business driver, adopting the knowledge management strategy drafted by the knowledge management team and investing in knowledge management demonstrates its ongoing commitment to knowledge management.

Implementing Knowledge Management
(Chapter 9)

The strategy sets out the firm's strategic approach to knowledge management. Implementing the strategy requires the knowledge management steam to identify specific initiatives that enable the firm to achieve its strategic goals. Some recommendations in the strategy will be simple to implement. For example, a recommendation to appoint a Director of Knowledge Management merely requires the human resources department to draft a position description (see Chapter 5) and hire the best candidate. On the other hand, a recommendation to address lack of interaction between practice groups may require a series of initiatives.

Knowledge management is not a project with a completion date. This is about adopting new ways to work that, over time, become deeply ingrained in the work processes within your firm. It takes several years to achieve the desired knowledge management environment—even with a well thought through knowledge management strategy. The key is to take a phased approach.

Take a Phased Approach to Implementation

As knowledge management takes several years to implement, your firm should examine the recommendations within its knowledge management and identify short term, mid term and long term goals.

From the beginning, your firm should focus on building a strong foundation for knowledge management. This means agreeing on the scope of knowledge management (and the scope of knowledge to be managed). It involves developing a culture to facilitate the sharing of knowledge in your firm. It means creating a formal knowledge management organization to direct knowledge management at your firm, and develop programs and systems to support knowledge management. It also means implementing knowledge management technology tools to support the capture and dissemination of knowledge.

Agreeing on the firm's definition of the scope of knowledge management at your firm is a critical first step in the implementation of knowledge management. It provides a common language to define specific knowledge management initiatives throughout the firm and paves the way for the smooth implementation of knowledge management initiatives.

Implementing knowledge management initiatives requires strong direction and significant resources. While a knowledge management organization will evolve over time, at a minimum, your firm must appoint a dedicated resource to lead the implementation of your firm's knowledge management strategy.

Developing a solid technology platform is also an iterative process. In the initial stages of implementing knowledge management, the firm should focus on leveraging the systems and technology tools it already has, before acquiring new tools. For example, where a firm has a document management system, it should examine whether that system is working well. Can lawyers find what they are looking for? Do people categorize documents appropriately when they save documents? If there are problems with the system, can they be rectified?

In the short term, (a period of 12 to 18 months), your firm should focus on simple knowledge management initiatives that are easy to implement and provide high value to the firm. This "quick win" approach is an effective way to build understanding of, and support for, knowledge management.

A typical first step is to have practice groups define their knowledge needs, and help those groups define knowledge management initiatives to address their needs. Consider the following example:

A practice group has difficulty sharing knowledge about current matters within the group. Practice group members feel uninformed and frustrated. Introducing regular meetings and posting information on the practice group intranet page will help address this issue. The practice group meetings provide a formal structure to communicate important knowledge about current matters, while providing a forum for sharing tacit knowledge. For staff who cannot attend the meeting, the same information communicated in the meeting is posted on the intranet.

Simple, high value knowledge management initiatives include drafting precedents, building a repository of best practice documents, developing a professional development program and creating a practice group intranet site.

There will be a wide range of knowledge needs across different practice groups. In a transaction-centric practice, knowledge management initiatives will probably focus on precedents and best practice transaction documents. In a tax practice, knowledge management initiatives may focus on providing lawyers with access to the most current tax rulings.

The short term goal should be to build a solid foundation for more sophisticated knowledge management in the firm. Addressing some of the basic cultural barriers to knowledge management, creating a formal organization to lead knowledge management, and looking at ways to leverage the firm's technology platform, enables you to begin building support for knowledge management—and paves the way for the successful implementation of more complex, higher value knowledge management.

In the short term, your firm may have focused on developing a precedent system, building a repository of best practice documents, creating a leading professional development program, and implementing its intranet. The focus will probably be on initiatives to capture and share explicit knowledge. In the mid term (18 to 36 months), your firm should focus on building upon the basic systems and processes introduced in the short term. With this strong foundation, your firm can focus on more complex knowledge management initiatives.

During its first year, a law firm concentrated on implementing discrete knowledge management systems and processes. Among its short term initiatives, the firm developed a firm-wide professional development program. It built upon its repository of best practice documents. It developed a library of precedents. Having built these discrete knowledge management tools, the firm recognizes that using the repository of best practice documents and the library of precedents assumes that lawyers possess a certain level of knowledge they may not necessarily have.

The purpose of the best practice document repository and the precedent library is to help junior lawyers draft documents. However, if the junior lawyer does not know what to search for, or when to use a particular document, the best practice documents and precedents have limited value. The firm therefore identifies a need to build some context around the best practice and precedent documents.

The firm builds a series of know-how files by integrating the content of professional development programs with the firm's best practice and precedent documents. Each know-how file focuses on one core process, leading a novice through the steps of the process. Within each step of the process, there is a link to the relevant best practice or precedent document. Developing a know-how file contextualizes the best practice and precedent documents. In doing so, it ensures that these important knowledge management resources are not just used by the people who drafted the documents. Now, the documents make sense to people who had no knowledge of the context in which these documents apply.

By building upon the basic knowledge management systems and processes, and analyzing how lawyers would use those systems and processes, the firm has developed a sophisticated knowledge management initiative, which really does leverage the firm's knowledge. This initiative could only be implemented in the mid term, since it relied upon the development of each discrete system in the short term.

Mid term projects should largely focus on leveraging the achievements of the short term. The above example illustrates how a firm can build more complex, and more valuable knowledge management initiatives, by building on its initial systems and processes.

Since the focus in the short term is typically on managing explicit knowledge, your firm should broaden its focus in the mid term to managing tacit knowledge. Developing know-how files involves capturing some tacit knowledge about the use of a document and making that knowledge explicit. There are many other mid term projects that address capture and sharing of tacit knowledge. These may include developing a debriefing process, drafting project methodologies, implementing a skills and expertise locator and creating communities of practice.

There should also be a shift away from the heavy practice group focus evident in the short term. By the mid term, your firm should be clear on which initiatives are best managed at the firm-wide level.

In reviewing the short term knowledge management initiatives of each practice group, the knowledge management organization will have a clear picture of the varying standards of knowledge management across the practice groups. To ensure a consistent firm-wide approach, the knowledge management organization might identify core knowledge management standards that should be achieved and maintained by every practice group.

Many of the cultural barriers to knowledge management can be best addressed in the mid term. By this stage, the firm has already seen the value of simple knowledge management. It should also see the limitations of knowledge management at the firm caused by cultural barriers. Since knowledge management is no longer a theoretical concept, demonstrating the cultural barriers to knowledge management should be straightforward. It should also be relatively easy to identify how best to address these cultural barriers.

The resources required to implement knowledge management should also become clearer in the mid term. While the focus in the short term is on leadership of the knowledge management organization, in the mid term, your firm should examine whether it has adequate knowledge management resources to build more complex, higher value knowledge management systems and processes.

The increased understanding of knowledge management typically leads to an increased appetite for knowledge management initiatives. This typically involves looking at more sophisticated use of a firm's technology platform. In the short term, your firm should be leveraging its existing technology platform. In the mid term, the limitations of your existing technology platform will be evident. This will be the appropriate stage to identify gaps in the knowledge management technology platform, and examine new systems that fill those gaps.

In the long term (3 to 5 years), your firm should focus on implementing initiatives to develop sustainable best practice knowledge management. By this stage, the firm should have created a culture that supports and promotes knowledge sharing. It should have built a knowledge management organization to direct and facilitate the development of knowledge management programs and systems through the firm, consistent with the firm's knowledge management strategy. It should have built a technology infrastructure to support capture and delivery of knowledge.

Over time, some knowledge management initiatives may best be implemented as a firm-wide initiative. Other initiatives may only ever apply to a specific practice group. The key is to be aware of all initiatives, and constantly examine their applicability to the wider firm.

Specific initiatives should expand beyond an internal, practice group focus to providing a more commercially focused, client and industry-centric view of knowledge. In the long term, the firm should be looking to leverage its knowledge management initiatives with clients—both through providing knowledge management services to clients, and in simply applying knowledge management to the firm's business development efforts.

Apply Business Rigor to Every Phase and Every Initiative

The key to succeeding at knowledge management is not only defining your knowledge management objectives. It is also ensuring that every knowledge management initiative meets those objectives.

Implementing a knowledge management strategy means defining specific initiatives to achieve the firm's knowledge management and business objectives. Drafting project plans and business cases is critical at the start of any initiative. Conducting pilot initiatives gives the knowledge management organization the opportunity to get initiatives right. Measuring the value of each initiative is fundamental to demonstrating how knowledge management drives the achievement of your firm's business objectives.

Write a Project Plan

The knowledge management strategy will, at best, contain recommendations to address specific issues relating to knowledge management. Turning those recommendations into task oriented projects is the next step. Once the firm has adopted its strategy, the knowledge management organization needs to identify the tasks involved in implementing a recommendation. Planning a project also involves identifying the resources needed to undertake each task, the time involved and associated costs. The project plan will also help the firm understand the critical success factors that may affect the progress of the project.

Your firm should draft a project plan for every knowledge management initiative—whether it originates out of a specific recommendation in the strategy, or comes from a specific isolated practice group knowledge need.

The project plan provides the firm with a clear picture of the effort involved in undertaking a knowledge management initiative and helps the firm to decide whether the initiative is justified.

Draft a Business Case

Along with the project plan, the business case is a critical tool in the implementation of specific initiatives that achieve the firm's knowledge management and business objectives. The business case contains a description of the proposed initiative, the business need, the current situation, benefits, and criteria for measuring value. It also describes the investment and critical success factors involved in implementing the initiative, drawing upon the project plan.

Since the purpose of knowledge management is to support and facilitate the achievement of the firm's business objectives, each knowledge management initiative should be directly linked to the achievement of those objectives. Without a demonstrated business need, and a justifiable investment, the firm is simply wasting its money pursuing a knowledge management initiative. Sooner or later, the firm finds this out. It is much better to assess the potential value of the initiative before any investment is made.

Run a Pilot

Many knowledge management initiatives involve a complete departure from the firm's traditional approach. Some initiatives will come out of a very good idea that may or may not work in practice. Some knowledge management initiatives need time to demonstrate their value. Taking a conservative approach to knowledge management will typically mean a narrow approach to knowledge management. Firms need to take risks with their knowledge management initiatives. The best way to manage this risk is to implement a pilot initiative, with very clear guidelines about the scope of the pilot. The pilot approach gives a firm the opportunity to test risky ideas in a managed fashion—and gives potentially high value knowledge management initiatives a chance to succeed.

Measure the Value of Every Initiative (Chapter 10)

Knowledge management is all about driving the achievement of your firm's business objectives. To do it well requires significant, ongoing investment by the firm. Demonstrating the value of knowledge management to the firm is critical to securing the ongoing support necessary to implement knowledge management initiatives. It is simply not possible to demonstrate value, without first measuring value. This is not just about hard numbers. Value can also be measured in soft terms. The key question to ask is, "How does this knowledge management initiative specifically achieve our knowledge management objectives—and support the achievement of our business objectives?" Consider the following example:

> The partners of a corporate mergers and acquisitions group see a wide variance in the quality of work produced by its pool of junior lawyers dispersed across several offices. Partners only feel confident delegating work to lawyers they have personally trained. With a surge in mergers and acquisitions work in the New York office, partners need to delegate work to junior lawyers in other offices. If they don't delegate, they face a resourcing crisis. If they do delegate, they know they will have to spend more time supervising lawyers in other offices.

The partners design a professional development program to train junior lawyers in the core processes surrounding mergers and acquisitions. The program ensures that all lawyers take a consistently high standard approach to their work.

Partners soon notice a marked improvement in the quality of work generated by junior lawyers across different offices, and feel more confident delegating work to junior lawyers across all offices. This solves the group's resourcing issues and reduces the supervision time of partners.

Leveraging Knowledge Management with Clients (Chapter 11)

Knowledge management is increasingly becoming a market differentiating factor for law firms. Clients want to know about their law firm's approach to knowledge management and expect to derive the benefit from the firm's knowledge management efforts. As clients develop their own sophisticated knowledge management systems and processes, they will come to expect that their law firms will match this level of sophistication.

As a firm implements specific knowledge management initiatives, it should consider how it could ultimately leverage those initiatives with its clients. This may include giving clients access to client-related firm knowledge, or the firm's broader knowledge management systems and processes. It could include developing client tailored knowledge management systems and processes or even developing market products based on the firm's knowledge management efforts. In the longer term, knowledge management may directly generate revenue for law firms.

Critical Elements
of Knowledge
Management

Defining the Scope of Knowledge

3

A medium size commercial law firm focuses its knowledge management strategy on the capture of its best practice transactional documents and letters of advice. The firm builds a firm-wide repository of these documents. It implements a stringent manual review process to ensure that content meets a high standard of quality. The firm encourages lawyers to contribute content to the database through reward and firm recognition.

The work product repository provides a solid foundation to share key explicit knowledge within the firm. However, at best, the work product repository captures core explicit legal knowledge. Because the system only stores explicit knowledge, it does not provide a means of sharing tacit knowledge. For example, the repository does not provide a roadmap to the experts among its staff. It does not store knowledge about the firm's clients or the industries in which they operate.

> Lawyers don't just read legal texts and draft documents; they must interpret the law in the context of their client's specific situation. The knowledge lawyers use to practice law extends well beyond black letter law. The work product repository only meets a fraction of the lawyers' knowledge needs.

Before a law firm can develop its knowledge management strategy, it must be clear about the knowledge it should manage. Understanding and defining the scope of knowledge used in a law firm is fundamental to developing a knowledge management strategy that reflects the business of the firm.

Legal knowledge is often the focus of law firm knowledge management initiatives—knowledge relating to the **practice of law.** Even in the practice of law, lawyers use non-legal knowledge, such as knowledge about their clients and the market. A law firm also uses many categories of non-legal knowledge to operate—knowledge relating to the **business of law.** Both elements must be considered in defining the scope of knowledge to be managed.

Law firms have also traditionally focused on capturing and leveraging the **explicit knowledge** of the firm, such as precedent and best practice documents. However, the intellectual capital of a law firm includes both explicit knowledge and **tacit knowledge.** While the work product of a lawyer is extremely valuable, it only represents a small portion of the knowledge and experience of its author.

A broad, all-encompassing approach will ensure that knowledge management initiatives reflect the work practices of law firm staff and drive the achievement of your firm's business objectives. Once your law firm has a clear picture of the scope of knowledge it possesses and uses, it is able to develop a strategy for managing that knowledge effectively in order to provide real value to the firm.

This Chapter defines knowledge, considers explicit knowledge and tacit knowledge in the context of a legal environment, and describes the broad categories of knowledge used within a law firm.

Knowledge, Information and Data

Before defining the scope of knowledge, it's helpful to understand the meaning of data, information and knowledge. The terms are often used interchangeably, and while they overlap, there are differences in their meanings. Knowledge management is not a new name for information management. It is much more than information management.

Here are some basic definitions:

Data refers to unstructured, objective facts. Data can be in the form of numbers, words or symbols. The meaning of data will depend on the context in which it is used.

Information is data presented in a particular context. Information attaches meaning to data.

Knowledge is value added by people—context, experience and interpretation—to information. Knowledge is therefore human effort applied to information.

The following illustrates the differences between data, information and knowledge in the legal services context.

As an employment lawyer, you are asked to advise your client on the legal ramifications of dismissing an employee who was drunk and abusive at your client's holiday party.

Having never dealt with this specific issue, you enter the terms "employee dismissal" and "drunken conduct" into your firm's information systems to identify any references to this subject. In other words, you are searching for occurrences of the *data*, "employee dismissal" and "drunken conduct."

Your research leads you to eight cases dealing with this issue. The case law provides you with *information* about this question of law, by placing the data in context.

Your analysis of the case law and its application to your client's specific set of circumstances is the *knowledge* you have created.

There is a strong human element to knowledge. Since knowledge requires the application of human experience to information, there is an inherent **value** attached to knowledge that does not apply to information. Because of this, knowledge is often referred to as the "intellectual capital" of an organization. Viewing

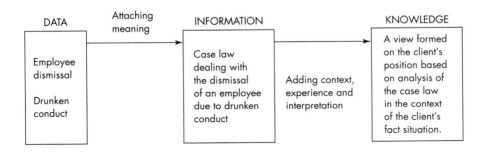

DATA	Attaching meaning	INFORMATION		KNOWLEDGE
Employee dismissal Drunken conduct		Case law dealing with the dismissal of an employee due to drunken conduct	Adding context, experience and interpretation	A view formed on the client's position based on analysis of the case law in the context of the client's fact situation.

knowledge as intellectual capital is particularly relevant to an organization where knowledge is its key asset—such as a law firm.

In defining the scope of knowledge a lawyer uses, data and information play a role—but the real focus must be on the knowledge created through the application of experience to that data and information. Any law firm can provide information systems to access external and internal information. The key is understanding how that information is applied to create knowledge—and capturing and presenting that knowledge in a way that supports the creation of more knowledge in your law firm.

Tacit and Explicit Knowledge

The knowledge or intellectual capital of a law firm consists of both explicit knowledge and tacit knowledge. Traditionally, law firms have focused on managing explicit knowledge. Little attention has been paid to tacit knowledge. This means that law firms are not leveraging this valuable component of their intellectual capital.

What is explicit knowledge?

Explicit knowledge is formal and systematic. It can be easily communicated and shared.[1] Typically, it has been documented. Lawyers use many examples of explicit knowledge in their practices—created externally or internally.

Legal texts, legislation, case law and commentary are the most common examples of externally created knowledge. Lawyers also create many categories of explicit knowledge. Letters of advice,

---

[1] Nonaka, "The Knowledge Creating Company," Harv. Bus. Rev. on Knowledge Mgnt. 31 (1998).

legal briefs, and transactional documents such as deeds and agreements are common examples.

Traditionally, law firms have focused their knowledge management activities on the management of external explicit knowledge (through library and on-line services) and internally generated explicit knowledge (through precedent collections and work product databases).

What is tacit knowledge?

Tacit knowledge on the other hand, is not so easily expressed. It is highly personal, hard to formalize and difficult to communicate to others.[2] It may also be impossible to capture. The challenge is to identify which elements of tacit knowledge can be captured and made explicit—while accepting that some tacit knowledge just cannot be captured. For tacit knowledge that cannot be captured, the goal is to connect the possessors of tacit knowledge with the seekers of that knowledge. An illustration follows.

> The major projects practice group in the London office of a global law firm has been highly successful in its market and wants to expand its practice. Since the group is relatively small, and few outside the group have experience in managing major projects, the group must find ways to leverage its knowledge with other lawyers in the firm.

....
2 *Id.*

So far, the partners have focused their knowledge management efforts on developing precedent documents. Senior partners have developed these documents by identifying best practice transactional documents and drawing upon their experience in managing these transactions. These precedents form the basis of any new major projects transaction.

Precedent documents are very helpful to a lawyer who is familiar with the process of a major project transaction. However, without knowledge of the process of how to manage a major project and when to use a particular document, the precedents on their own are not useful to others in the firm. The precedents only represent a very small part of the senior partner's knowledge—and on their own, have limited value.

The partners of the group possess an enormous amount of tacit knowledge about major projects acquired over years of managing these transactions. At the same time, it is highly likely that a partner could describe the key steps involved in managing a major project. By developing a methodology based on the partner's approach to managing major projects, the firm places context around the precedent documents. Inexperienced lawyers assigned to a major project can refer to the methodology, and consequently understand the process. With this context, the lawyer can confidently access the relevant precedent documents. For example, the partners develop a methodology for managing the construction of a shopping mall. The partners define the major steps of this project as:

- ◆ Acquiring land
- ◆ Seeking public authority approval for land development
- ◆ Constructing the shopping mall
- ◆ Leasing space in the shopping mall to retailers

For each step in the process, the partners describe which documents to use, and in which context to use those documents, as well as the relevant legislation and case law lawyers must consider.

A methodology sets out the basic steps in a matter—and provides context for the precedent documents—but what of the nuances of running a major projects matter? For example, in what circumstances should lawyers use one form of document over another? How should lawyers deal with public authorities? Are there negotiating tips for lawyers? The partners develop a training module on how to manage a major project—sharing their lessons learned with less experienced lawyers joining their team.

Acknowledging that not all tacit knowledge can be made explicit, the firm builds a "know-who" system to capture information about who possesses expertise. This system enables less experienced lawyers to identify the expert. Rather than memorializing every element of the partners' knowledge, a know-who system, such as a skills and expertise locator, contains staff skills, a record of previous deals, client relationships and references to key documents or methodologies authored by staff. Most importantly, it contains contact details. When an inexperienced lawyer is asked to work on a major project, he knows to contact one of the partners in the London based major projects group.

The combination of a skills and expertise locator, training sessions, methodology and precedent documents, leverages both the explicit and tacit knowledge of the major projects group.

Knowledge for the Practice of Law

Core explicit legal knowledge

In defining the scope of knowledge used in a law firm, lawyers typically place a heavy emphasis on core explicit legal knowledge, such as:

- ♦ Case law, commentary and interpretation
- ♦ Legislation and commentary
- ♦ Best practice (or model) documents
- ♦ Precedent (or form) documents

The first two categories—case law, commentary and interpretation, and legislation and commentary—are externally created and are typically made available by the library either electronically or in hard copy. The latter two categories—best practice documents and precedent documents—are internally created knowledge.

Best practice documents are matter specific documents that a firm has identified as a good example of its work product and could be used again in a similar fact situation. These documents, however, remain specific to the matter and cannot be applied broadly to multiple situations. Typically, these documents have been examined by a firm committee, which judges the quality of the work product before publishing it on the firm-wide work product repository. This process of quality control assures staff that the work product can be re-used.

Precedent documents are generic documents that the firm has typically invested in developing for use in many matters. Precedent documents ensure a baseline level of quality in the documents generated using the precedent. Drafting a document based on a firm-approved precedent saves time, eliminates duplication, ensures consistency and enables drafting to be delegated to junior lawyers.

While best practice documents and precedents are traditionally the focus of knowledge management initiatives, and are indeed important, there are two key limitations to this approach. First, using a precedent system or a work product repository assumes that lawyers know what they are looking for. However, if you are an inexperienced lawyer (the most likely person to use a precedent or a best practice document), this may not be the case.

Second, lawyers do not just draft documents. You do not provide legal advice in a vacuum. You listen to your clients and advise them on the law in the context of their specific circumstances. You consider black letter law and apply it to your clients' unique situation. The document tells only the end of a long story.

Non-legal knowledge

The categories of knowledge described above are critical to a lawyer's practice, though it is not an exhaustive list. There are many categories of non-legal knowledge that are critical to a lawyer's business. This knowledge may be either explicit, or so deeply ingrained in the work practices of staff that it remains as tacit knowledge. Many law firms overlook these broader, and sometimes tacit, elements of knowledge so important to its business.

For example, in a commercial law firm, lawyers must know about their clients and the industries in which they operate. This knowledge enables lawyers to give commercially sound advice to serve the unique needs of the client. Knowledge about clients and their industries is therefore a key component of the knowledge used in a law firm.

Similarly, a litigation lawyer must often apply strategy in progressing a matter. In addition to knowledge about case law and legislation, a litigation lawyer also knows about the likely mindset of a judge, the tactics of opposing counsel and the most appropriate expert or external consultant. Knowledge about third parties therefore forms an essential part of the knowledge of a litigation lawyer.

Knowledge for the Business of Law

Like any business, a law firm must have a clear understanding of its market position and its business strategy. The categories of knowledge described above are used by lawyers in the practice of law. However, lawyers use a broader range of knowledge in managing their legal services businesses—knowledge relating to the business of law.

A law firm possesses knowledge about:

♦ Relative market strengths and weaknesses of its practice groups

♦ Clients

- Past projects
- Competitors
- Industry trends
- Market opportunities

In finding better ways to manage the knowledge used in the practice of law, lawyers should not exclude knowledge applied to the business of law.

Define the Broad Categories of Knowledge

To ensure that your firm's knowledge management strategy reflects your firm's business objectives, consider the broad categories of knowledge used by all staff in your law firm, for both the practice of law and the business of law—and both tacit and explicit knowledge about:

- The law
- The firm and its practice areas
- Clients
- The commercial market and specific industries
- Staff skills and expertise
- Methodology and processes
- Past projects and lessons learned
- Third parties (e.g., regulators, judges, counsel, experts, external consultants)
- The firm's market position
- The firm's revenue, costs and profitability

Knowledge About the Law

This area is typically the focus of a law firm's knowledge management efforts—and it's a very important starting point. Knowledge about the law includes very explicit categories:

- ◆ Case law, commentary and interpretation
- ◆ Legislation and commentary
- ◆ Best practice (or model) documents
- ◆ Precedent (or form) documents

It should also include managing the tacit knowledge lawyers possess about the law. In managing knowledge about the law, don't ignore managing the knowledge your lawyers possess that has not been captured in best practice or precedent documents.

Knowledge About the Firm and Its
Practice Areas

As law firms grow, developing many practice areas and many offices, it becomes a challenge for staff to know about the information possessed by their firm. Law firms typically grow so that they can offer a better service to clients. The paradox for a growing law firm is that as it increases its size and ability to undertake broader ranging work, it often loses its ability to leverage this growth.

In a study of how leading law firms apply knowledge management principles to their practice,[3] 38% of firms did not consider knowledge about the firm and its practice areas as a catego-

---

[3] Curve Consulting, 2001/2 Global Law Firm Knowledge Management Survey Report.

ry of knowledge that needed to be managed. This was despite all the surveyed firms being multi-practice and multi-office firms, with an average of over 2000 staff, positioned to undertake global, multi-disciplinary work for their clients. In order to create global, multi-disciplinary teams, staff need knowledge about the firm and its practice areas. The following example illustrates the importance of managing this knowledge.

> The London based major projects group (described at the start of this Chapter) is asked to submit a tender to advise the Chinese Government on the construction of a power station project in China. Financing will come from U.S. and French based financial institutions. The power station will be constructed by an Australian company. To win this project, the major projects group must demonstrate its ability to advise the Chinese Government on all aspects of this project.
>
> The London partners must therefore know about the banking and finance practices in its New York and Paris offices, and the property practice in its Sydney office— before it can begin to prepare its bid for this project. Accessing knowledge about practice areas and offices is key to the major projects group preparing a bid for this work.

Knowledge About Clients

Understanding black letter law in a vacuum does not enable lawyers to provide their clients with commercially sound advice.

They must also know their clients. Through advising clients, lawyers acquire knowledge about their clients' business strategy and the markets in which their clients operate. Knowledge about clients may include explicit knowledge such as basic staff position and contact information, previous work performed for the client, fees generated through client work, and news relating to the client.

Lawyers also acquire significant tacit knowledge about a client which may not be easily stored in a system, but is critical knowledge that should be shared with others in the firm.

The following example illustrates why managing knowledge about clients is so important.

The major projects group wins the project to advise the Chinese Government, described in the earlier example. The project team is composed of lawyers from London, New York, Paris and Sydney. Each lawyer on the team will have direct contact with the client. Only the London major projects lawyers have experience in working with Chinese authorities. Managing this client relationship is particularly complicated, given the global spread of lawyers and the inexperience of those lawyers.

The major projects group places great emphasis on sharing knowledge about how best to deal with the Chinese Government. The group instigates regular telephone conference calls for the project team to discuss the progress of the project and share knowledge about the client.

As lawyers work with representatives of the Chinese Government, they post information about those individuals on the matter workspace shared internally by the project team. This ensures that lawyers know how best to work with the client and that all project team members have the same knowledge of this client.

Knowledge About the Commercial Market and Specific Industries

Knowledge about the commercial market and specific industries directly impacts how a law firm plans for future client needs. Law firms often overlook this important category of knowledge that is at the heart of the business of a law firm. Knowing about its clients and their industries also enables a law firm to be proactive in providing legal services to its clients. If a law firm has a clear understanding of market trends in a particular industry, it is able to explore how legal services may need to be adapted to meet industry developments. Recognizing these trends earlier than its competitors enables a law firm to lead its market.

A major law firm recognizes that significant changes are occurring in the banking industry around the world. It carefully monitors banking industry developments and examines predictions about further changes to the industry. Based on this analysis, the law firm closely examines how legal services must adapt to meet the changing needs of the banking industry. The firm uses this knowledge to make important changes to its services offerings—ahead of its competitors.

Knowledge About Staff Skills and Expertise

Capturing the skills and expertise of staff so that the firm can leverage its intellectual capital should be a priority in any knowledge management strategy. In the global study of leading law firms,[4] 25% of participants did not define staff skills and expertise as a category of knowledge that needed managing. Yet, the larger and more dispersed the firm, the less likely it is that the firm is leveraging its intellectual capital. A lawyer may not know of the firm's skills and expertise outside of his own office.

However, clients assume that staff in a law firm can build a cross-functional team or call upon experts within the firm when needed. Without the means of locating the skills and expertise of staff, a law firm is compromising its ability to do this.

In order to build the project team to advise the Chinese Government described earlier, the major projects partner must be confident that the firm has staff capable of undertaking this work.

....
4 *Id.*

The firm maintains a skills and expertise locator. This database captures the skills and expertise of staff, together with contact information. The skills and expertise locator enables this partner to locate colleagues throughout the firm who have expertise in, or have expressed an interest in, working on major projects involving cross-border financing.

Knowledge management not only enables this partner to find the right people to handle current work efficiently, it also supports the growth of this firm's major projects practice through identifying likely candidates to join this group.

Methodology and Processes

No matter how complex or specialized the matter, there is an element of repetition in how lawyers manage that matter. Lawyers use black letter law and documents—but they also know when to refer to that black letter law, and which documents to draft. There are basic steps that a lawyer applies to any process—from a basic conveyance to the most complex structured financing deal spanning three continents.

This category of knowledge focuses on understanding how an experienced lawyer manages a particular transaction. Knowledge management is about capturing that knowledge so that all can benefit from the experience.

A steep rise in the property market, combined with a consumer bank dropping its interest rates to the lowest in the market, has led to an unprecedented increase in mortgages. The bank seeks out external law firms to help manage the mortgage process. A small law firm which has previously managed a handful of mortgages for the bank seizes the opportunity to win a spot on the bank's panel of external law firms. A partner involved in the prior work develops a methodology based on his approach to the bank's work—and employs paralegals to perform the work based on his methodology. The firm wins a sizeable piece of the bank's mortgage work by leveraging the partner's knowledge.

Developing a methodology does not just apply to commodity work.

At a leading law firm with offices in three cities, the mergers and acquisitions partners are struggling with differing levels of quality among their staff, particularly in conducting due diligence. It appears that junior lawyers lack basic skills in how to manage a due diligence process. The differences in standard of work have caused the partners to lose confidence in delegating work to junior staff. Consequently, some of the partners see no alternative but to conduct the due diligence themselves.

Junior lawyers are frustrated because the partners give inconsistent or no instructions on how to conduct due diligence. Partners are frustrated because they are overworked.

The partners decide to develop a firm approach to conducting due diligence—providing lawyers with the basic framework for conducting this work.

The due diligence methodology provides a clear and consistent approach for junior lawyers to use—and partners notice a significant improvement in the quality of due diligence work. Their confidence is regained and the partners are now free to pursue other work.

Past Projects and Lessons Learned

Lawyers constantly draw on their prior experience to ask:

- What work have we done before?
- What did we learn from doing that work?

Their knowledge about prior work influences the work they will take on in the future, and the way they will perform that work. There is therefore a strong link between knowledge about past projects and the development of a methodology. There is also a link between knowledge about past projects and other core categories of knowledge, including best practice documents, the skills and expertise of staff and knowledge about clients.

Capturing knowledge about past projects may include:

♦ A description of the project

♦ Associated documents

♦ The skills and expertise of the project team

Knowing what the firm has done in the past enables it to know what it is capable of doing in the future. Through capturing knowledge about past projects, lawyers know which work they should be pursuing. Once they have the work, lawyers can draw upon their knowledge of past projects to know which documents to use, and who has the expertise to do the work.

Knowledge about past projects therefore supports both the business of law—using the knowledge to win new work, and the practice of law—using the knowledge to do the new work.

A medium size law firm has been very successful in representing parties applying for radio broadcasting licenses. The government authority responsible for issuing radio broadcasting licenses announces its intention to release two new licenses in the market. One of the firm's partners learns that a former client intends to apply for one of the licenses and is in the process of selecting a law firm to assist with the application.

Drawing upon the firm's database of past projects, the partner can quickly demonstrate to the client his firm's vast experience in applying for radio broadcasting licenses, based on the firm's prior application matters for other clients. The partner is also able to access information about the firm's prior work for this particular client, demonstrating the firm's understanding of this client's needs.

Confident that this firm is the best qualified to manage the application, the client retains this firm.

Once the firm has been retained, the partners responsible for managing this matter must pull together the team to work on the license application. By capturing knowledge about past license applications, the partners know which lawyers have the skills and expertise to work on this matter. They also know which documents were produced in past applications, and can use these past documents as the basis of the documents drafted for this client.

Knowledge About Third Parties

Lawyers work with many third parties and, over time, they acquire knowledge about those third parties. Third parties may include expert witnesses, consultants, accountants, other lawyers, or even judges. You may not be able to choose a judge, but knowing about the judge's approach may well influence how you approach your case.

A law firm often has to refer work to lawyers in other jurisdictions. When a lawyer needs to find a lawyer in Brazil, he sends an e-mail to the entire firm asking:

Does anyone know a lawyer in Brazil who can handle a patent application?

The lawyer receives the names of five lawyers in Brazil from across the firm. The lawyer contacts one of those lawyers, but does not store a record of the other four lawyers recommended by his colleagues. Two weeks later, another lawyer sends the same request via e-mail to the entire firm. This time, the lawyer receives no response. As a result, the lawyer has to spend many hours researching attorneys in Brazil before he can confidently refer the matter.

The firm decides to capture knowledge about the firm's contacts in other jurisdictions in a firm-wide database. Lawyers no longer send random e-mails. Rather, they refer to the firm's contacts database to locate lawyers in other jurisdictions.

Knowledge About the Firm's Market Position

A law firm must have a clear understanding of its competitors and market position in order to develop its business strategy. Managing this knowledge helps a firm to develop a business strategy that builds upon its market strengths and addresses its market weaknesses.

3

Knowledge About the Firm's Revenue, Costs and Profitability

A law firm knows which practice groups are the greatest revenue generators, and which are the most profitable. These are not necessarily the same groups. A firm also tracks the costs associated with operating the firm. Understanding where revenue comes from enables a firm to develop its strategy for increasing revenue. Understanding the costs associated with operating the firm helps the firm to formulate its strategy to reduce costs. Knowledge about a firm's profitability enables a firm to develop its strategy to grow profitability.

The Value of Knowledge

Because knowledge requires the application of human experience to information, knowledge is far more valuable than just information. There are also different levels of value attached to the categories of knowledge described above.

Once your firm has defined the scope of knowledge it should manage, based on the knowledge it uses, you should also apply a value to that knowledge. This value will determine how much effort your law firm puts into managing that knowledge.

Where the knowledge is readily available in the public domain, the law firm should pay little attention to managing that knowledge. On the other hand, where the knowledge is so unique to the law firm that it differentiates the firm in its market, the firm should focus heavily on managing this knowledge.

Consider the knowledge pyramid below:

- Precedent documents
- Client and matter information
- Staff skills and expertise
- Project methodologies
- Policies and procedures
- Easily accessible
- Searchable by categories and full text searchable
- Strictly maintained by the knowledge management organization

Highest Value Knowledge

- Best practice documents, e.g., transactional documents and research
- Regularly used information indexed by subject matter
- Easily accessible
- Searchable by categories and full text searchable
- Regularly maintained by the knowledge management organization

Highly Relevant Knowledge and Information

- Publicly available legal, industry and client information
- Full text searchable
- Limited maintenance by the knowledge management organization

General Information and Data

The Owners of Knowledge

When it comes to managing the knowledge you have defined, understanding who possesses that knowledge is a critical factor. Is the knowledge owned by one department in your firm, or do three departments currently maintain the same knowledge? The key questions to ask are:

- *Who possesses the knowledge?*
- *Who should manage this knowledge?*

Consider the following illustration.

A law firm wants to capture the skills and expertise of staff. On close examination, it identifies that three divisions in the firm manage some form of this knowledge. The human resources department captures knowledge about a lawyer's work experience before joining the firm. The marketing department captures knowledge about the lawyer's involvement in prior matters. Each practice group maintains information about its lawyers' skills and expertise on its intranet page.

Rather than continue to store this knowledge in three different places, the firm builds a skills and expertise locator, a database that combines the skills and expertise knowledge stored by the three groups. The human resources department, the marketing department and the practice groups will each use the same system to access information about the skills and expertise of lawyers. The firm decides that the practice groups should be responsible for maintaining information about the skills and expertise of their lawyers, with the human resources department and marketing department having limited responsibility for input of information.

The firm defines the following process: When a lawyer joins the firm, the human resources department creates a profile for the lawyer and adds the lawyer's résumé to the skills and expertise locator. The practice group knowledge manager works with the lawyer to keep the profile up to date. This means that at the end of each matter, lawyers must update their skills and expertise profiles. The marketing department directs the practice groups in how to capture information about prior matters by providing a project description template.

The skills and expertise locator is used by all practice groups and administrative areas, while maintenance is primarily the responsibility of each practice group.

Define the Scope of Knowledge Your Firm Should Manage

To define the scope of knowledge your firm should manage, follow these steps:

1. Define the broad categories of knowledge your staff use. Don't limit your definition to core explicit legal knowledge. Think about the knowledge you use in the practice of law and the business of law.

2. Consider whether the knowledge you have defined is currently explicit or tacit. If it is tacit, can it be made explicit? Or should it remain tacit?

3. Apply a value to the knowledge you have defined.

4. Determine who owns and should manage that knowledge.

Consider the following checklist to help you determine which knowledge you use and should manage:

KNOWLEDGE CATEGORY	TACIT OR EXPLICIT	VALUE (LOW, MEDIUM, HIGH)	OWNER OF THE KNOWLEDGE
The law ◆ Case law, commentary and interpretation ◆ Legislation and commentary ◆ Best practice (model) documents ◆ Precedent (form) documents)			
The firm and its practice areas			
Clients			
The commercial market and specific industries			
Staff skills and expertise			
Methodology and processes			
Past projects and lessons learned			
Third parties (e.g., regulators, judges, counsel, experts, external consultants)			
The firm's market position			
The firm's revenue, costs and profitability			

The following Chapter, "Defining the Scope of Knowledge Management," describes the many ways a law firm can manage its knowledge. There is a broad spectrum of systems and processes a law firm can employ to manage its knowledge—from the low cost and simple to implement—through to state of the art, firm-wide systems. While your firm should take a broad approach to the many types of knowledge your staff use—both in the practice and the business of law—managing knowledge comes at a price.

Paying that price should be almost entirely determined by the value that knowledge brings to your practice and your business.

Defining the Scope of Knowledge Management

Chapter Contents

Law firm A develops a knowledge management system which is essentially a repository of best practice research memoranda drafted by its lawyers. The firm carefully maintains the repository to ensure that only high quality content is included. Lawyers submit their work product. A team of senior partners reviews the work product and determines which research memoranda should be included in the repository. A dedicated team of information management specialists profiles the document by attaching metadata such as document description, author, date and key words to the document. The document profile will help staff to retrieve the document.

Law firm B invests heavily in an enterprise wide search engine. The search engine searches across all its systems, including the document management system, financial management system, client relationship management system, the firm's intranet and the internet. When staff search for knowledge, the search engine retrieves content across all underlying systems. The search engine ranks search results based on relevance.

> The firm does not build a team of knowledge managers to manage content. It does not develop a vetted repository of best practice documents. Rather, it relies on state of the art technology.

These two examples are typical of how many law firms approach knowledge management. While both approaches have some merit, they only represent a portion of what knowledge management should be in a law firm.

At law firm A, the focus is on ensuring that content is of a high quality—this is key. However, the firm's knowledge management system only contains a portion of knowledge used by staff—and represents only one means of managing knowledge. It does not contain knowledge about clients and industries. It does not provide a means of managing tacit knowledge. It does not enable people to find out about the skills and expertise of others at the firm. It does not contain methodologies associated with common matters. As a means of training and developing junior lawyers, it is not nearly as effective as a professional development program.

Law firm B's approach to knowledge management may take a broader view of the sources of knowledge that a lawyer uses, but there is little emphasis on the **management** of that knowledge. Technology may be good at capturing and disseminating knowledge—but how can it distinguish between knowledge and mere information?

Knowledge management involves understanding the difference between knowledge and information, and then applying a value to that knowledge. The most intelligent search engine on the market can still only guess the value of a piece of knowledge.

A technology-centric approach to knowledge management also ignores the large number of non-technology elements of knowledge management. Technology cannot create a culture that supports knowledge management, or an organization to facilitate knowledge management. At best, it can only manage a small part of the vast tacit knowledge floating around the firm.

Over time, as the content in the underlying systems grows, with no control over its quality, staff may face information overload—and simply end up with a "needle in a haystack" knowledge retrieval system.

Knowledge management—the leveraging of your firm's collective wisdom by creating systems and processes to identify, capture, disseminate and use the knowledge possessed by your law firm—sounds good in theory. The hard part is implementing this theory into the day-to-day operations of your legal practice and your legal business. It shouldn't be hard. There are many different ways a law firm can manage its knowledge—from simple, low cost initiatives to state of the art firm-wide systems.

There are *three key principles* you should follow in defining the scope of knowledge management at your firm.

First, you need to understand what knowledge you must manage before you can find the best way to manage that knowledge.

Second, you should not limit your thinking on the scope of initiatives that can help you manage that knowledge.

In Chapter 3, I defined "knowledge" and described the scope of knowledge used in the practice and business of law. In this Chapter, I define "knowledge management" and suggest that there are many ways to manage your knowledge. While knowledge management is often linked inextricably with technology, the best technology platform will only ever be one component that supports the identification, capture, dissemination and use of knowledge throughout your law firm. It may work well when you are managing explicit knowledge, but, as I described in Chapter 3, lawyers possess a great deal of tacit knowledge, which, by definition, cannot be captured in its entirety in a database.

Knowledge management is not just about making documents available via an intranet. It is about creating a learning environment in your firm—so that young lawyers develop into leading experts in their field. It is about sharing knowledge across practice groups—so that partners can cross-sell work to clients—and leverage the multi-disciplinary nature of your firm. It is about using your knowledge about clients and the market to take a strategic approach to your business.

The *third* key principle relates to the value of the knowledge you manage. Since any knowledge management initiative requires some form of investment, you should be clear on the value of the knowledge you plan to manage.

You should follow this simple rule—**base your investment in knowledge management on the value of the knowledge to your practice and your business.** The more valuable the knowledge, the greater the investment in knowledge management.

Defining Knowledge Management

In Chapter 3, I defined knowledge as the value added by people—context, experience and interpretation—to information. I also described how knowledge includes both explicit knowledge—formal and systematic knowledge, and tacit knowledge—knowledge that is highly personal, hard to formalize and therefore, difficult to communicate to others.[1]

....

[1] Nonaka,, "The Knowledge Creating Company," Harv. Bus. Rev. on Knowledge Mgmt. 27 (1998).

Knowledge management is the leveraging of your firm's collective wisdom by creating processes and systems to support and facilitate the identification, capture, dissemination and use of your firm's knowledge.

To understand this, let's break this definition into its components:

Leverage—there is a strong emphasis on getting the most out of your knowledge. This is all about using knowledge more than once, and building upon existing knowledge to create new knowledge, to achieve your firm's business objectives.

Collective wisdom—this is about getting a handle on what everyone in your firm knows. Not just lawyers—but all staff. Not just legal knowledge—but knowledge created and used in every aspect of your legal practice and business.

Systems and processes—knowledge management involves both technology and non-technology elements. Knowledge may well be captured in a database and disseminated via an intranet. However, sharing knowledge about how best to approach a regulatory authority may best be disseminated in a training program conducted by a senior partner to an audience of junior lawyers.

Support and facilitate—knowledge management is about creating an environment that encourages the leveraging of your firm's collective wisdom. Knowledge has a strong human element. Knowledge also evolves over time, as people acquire existing knowledge and adapt it to their own circumstances. Knowledge management systems and processes can, at best, support and facilitate the process of acquiring and developing knowledge. Creating a culture that expects knowledge sharing and an organization that facilitates the leveraging of knowledge are two important elements.

Identification—the first step in the process of managing knowledge is identifying the knowledge possessed by the people in your firm. In Chapter 3, I described the broad range of knowledge types that may exist in your firm. You must first identify the

knowledge you are trying to capture, in order to capture and disseminate that knowledge.

Capture—this word suggests an intention to gather the knowledge of your law firm—rather than an *ad hoc* catch-all of every piece of data or information floating around your firm. If this knowledge is explicit, it will probably be captured in one of your firm's information systems. If this knowledge is tacit, only part of it may be captured in a system, while the rest may only be captured in a conversation between the owner of the tacit knowledge and the seeker of that knowledge.

Dissemination—this step involves sharing knowledge with the people who seek the knowledge. Dissemination could occur through obtaining the results of a search of a database. Knowledge could also be disseminated in a structured forum, such as a training seminar. Tacit knowledge will probably best be disseminated in an informal exchange between the owner of the knowledge and the seeker of that knowledge.

Use—knowledge evolves over time. It is organic. Using knowledge usually leads to the creation of new knowledge, creating the cycle of knowledge management.

Your firm's knowledge—knowledge can be created both internally and externally. Once someone at your firm acquires knowledge—even if it was created externally—it forms part of your firm's knowledge. Knowledge shared is knowledge doubled.

A Word About "Create"

I have deliberately left the word "create" out of the defining steps of knowledge management—because this would narrow the definition of knowledge management. It suggests that knowledge management is only about managing knowledge created by your firm. As I suggest above, you should manage this knowledge—but you should also manage knowledge created elsewhere and used by your firm. Naturally, since knowledge evolves over time, and because of the significant human element, the use of knowledge will lead to the creation of knowledge.

One of the **outcomes** of knowledge management should be the creation of new knowledge. That new knowledge should then be identified, captured, disseminated and used by your firm.

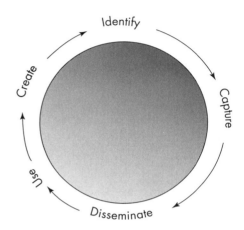

Knowledge Management Applied

The steps I outline above provide an overview of what knowledge management is about. Now let's apply these steps. There are some important factors to consider in applying knowledge management to your firm.

The method of knowledge management will depend on whether the knowledge you want to manage is tacit or explicit

If the knowledge is explicit, it can be easily identified, captured and disseminated. If the knowledge is tacit, by definition, it is hard to identify in its entirety and will therefore be difficult to capture and disseminate. You may need to look at ways to encourage shar-

ing of tacit knowledge, or opportunities to convert tacit knowledge into explicit knowledge.

The method of knowledge management will depend on the value of the knowledge you want to manage

In Chapter 3, I described the knowledge pyramid. Where knowledge is so unique to your firm that it differentiates your firm from its competitors, significant investment in knowledge management is not only justified—it is critical. For example, the firm may invest in developing methodologies and precedents relating to the area of practice in which the firm is the market leader. A team of information specialists may be dedicated to the management of that top-of-the-pyramid knowledge. The knowledge may be stored in a separate, carefully maintained system.

On the other hand, where information or data is readily available to the public, the firm should be careful in how much energy it spends on its management.

The method of knowledge management will depend on the speed at which the knowledge changes

Some lawyers practice in areas of law where changes are infrequent. The court rules of procedure don't change daily, so creating a precedent document explaining the rules or posting the rules on the firm intranet will suffice. Other lawyers are literally overwhelmed by the volume of changes to their area of practice, and may find it difficult to keep up. A tax lawyer may come across several tax rulings each week that significantly and immediately impact his clients. A precedent document is not helpful. In this case, a means of packaging current awareness material about tax rulings in an easily digestible format is probably the best method of knowledge management.

The method of knowledge management will depend on the sensitivity of the knowledge you want to manage

Since a step in the process of knowledge management is dissemination, you need to take care in deciding which knowledge can actually be disseminated—and to whom. Where knowledge is highly sensitive, few people should know about it. At best, others may be told of its existence and be referred to the holder of that knowledge.

The method of knowledge management will depend on whether the knowledge is relevant to all or to a few

In some respects, knowledge management is a balancing act. How do you give staff access to the knowledge they need without overwhelming them? The key is to provide knowledge management systems and processes that give staff the knowledge they need when they need it. In some instances, knowledge used by one practice group may have no relevance to any other group in the firm. Knowledge management initiatives may focus on building firm-wide knowledge management systems and processes, as well as practice group specific knowledge management tools.

Knowledge management is more than just a technology system

Indeed, technology is merely a facilitator. Databases are an effective means of capturing knowledge. Search engines enable identification and dissemination of knowledge. However, technology cannot do everything. It cannot apply a value to knowledge. It cannot capture tacit knowledge. It cannot replace professional development programs or mentoring in developing staff.

Knowledge management has a strong organizational element

Since knowledge is more than information and data, and involves a strong human element, creating a full text search engine over multiple repositories of unvetted content is not knowledge management. As I described earlier, there is a large **value** component of knowledge management. It therefore requires an organization to support and facilitate the steps of knowledge management. Chapter 5 discusses the knowledge management organization in detail.

Knowledge management has a strong cultural element

Knowledge management assumes that staff will readily share their knowledge and contribute to knowledge management initiatives. This is a big assumption in an environment that traditionally rewards hoarding of knowledge and does not reward creating more efficient ways to work. The time-based billing model leaves little room for investment in knowledge management. Chapter 6 discusses cultural aspects of knowledge management in detail.

Knowledge management can be large or small, simple or complex

It all depends on the knowledge you are managing and the objective of managing that knowledge.

Knowledge management is a phased process, evolving over several stages

To do knowledge management well, you need to begin at the beginning. There is simply no point to implementing an enterprise wide search engine if you don't use your document management system well. You should start with simple, high value, easy to deliver knowledge management initiatives—and build toward an all encompassing approach to knowledge management. Chapter 9 describes the implementation of knowledge management in detail.

The following example illustrates these last two points:

Twenty lawyers spread across five practice groups in a law firm are advising clients on new financial services reform legislation. Since the lawyers sit in different groups, they have little interaction with each other. The legislation however, will have a massive impact on the firm's client base—and of course, on the financial services industry. The firm acknowledges a need for the lawyers to work together in order to provide consistent and high quality advice to its clients.

As a first step, the firm creates a community of practice composed of the 20 lawyers. This group meets every other week during lunch to share knowledge about the new legislation and to discuss how it impacts their clients.

Material about the legislation becomes overwhelming, with daily news items about the legislation. While the regular meetings are valuable, the group realizes that it must find a means of sharing knowledge about the legislation on a daily basis. The group develops an intranet page where lawyers post current awareness items about the legislation, as well as advice provided to clients on the new legislation. The community of practice intranet page becomes an effective internal knowledge sharing tool.

Until now, lawyers in this group have simply used the community of practice as a means of keeping up to date on new developments, and applying that knowledge to specific client needs. After two months, the community of practice decides that it should market its services to the wider financial services industry. Having developed the means of capturing knowledge in this area, the lawyers are promoted as experts in this field and focus on winning new clients based on their newly acquired expertise.

Over time, the lawyers in this community of practice develop precedent documents and methodologies that can be applied to new matters.

The firm also recognizes an opportunity to develop an on-line service for financial services clients, building upon the internal knowledge management systems and processes developed by this group of lawyers.

Defining Knowledge Management Initiatives

In the earlier part of this Chapter, I discussed what knowledge management is. The scope of knowledge management at your firm will be determined by the scope of knowledge you need to manage. To define the scope of knowledge management at your firm, you should follow the steps outlined below.

Define the knowledge need

Since knowledge management is all about leveraging your knowledge to achieve your business objectives, your knowledge needs will be directly related to your business objectives. You should identify what knowledge you need in order to achieve your business objectives. For example, a transaction-centric practice whose business objective is to produce consistent, high quality documentation will need precedent documents. Chapter 3 described the many categories of knowledge a lawyer uses in practice and a law firm uses in business.

Is the knowledge tacit or explicit?

If knowledge is explicit, it should be easily identified, captured and disseminated. Sometimes, explicit knowledge is poorly managed. Consider this example:

> A practice group decides that it needs access to its best practice documents. The documents are currently stored in the firm's document management system, together with all firm work product. There is no means of distinguishing between best practice documents and all other work product. While the explicit knowledge exists, this firm must improve upon how this knowledge is managed.

If the knowledge is explicit, is it in a form that can be easily identified, captured and disseminated or does it need further work?

If the knowledge is tacit, can any of this knowledge be made explicit? If not, what is the best means of managing tacit knowledge that cannot be made explicit?

What is the value of the knowledge?

Since knowledge management requires some level of investment, you should be clear on how valuable is the knowledge you seek to manage. Value can be determined in several ways. Knowledge may be valuable if it is key to achieving your firm's business objectives. Knowledge is also valuable if it is not readily available and distinguishes your firm from its competitors.

The level of effort associated with managing knowledge should be directly related to its value.

Should knowledge management be a technology system or a program?

Deciding on what is the best means of managing knowledge will depend largely on whether the knowledge you seek to manage is tacit or explicit.

Where knowledge is explicit, you can develop technology systems to facilitate the capture, dissemination and use of that knowledge. If technology is the appropriate tool to manage knowledge, you should first look to leverage your current systems. It may become clear that your current technology infrastructure does not support your knowledge management objectives, thus creating a demand for new technology systems.

You may also find that, in some instances, a non-technology program is more effective in facilitating knowledge management at your firm. For example, a professional development program may be a more effective means of sharing knowledge between partners and junior lawyers.

Where knowledge is tacit, you should identify and develop the best means of sharing tacit knowledge. This will include addressing interaction:

- ◆ Between partners and other lawyers

- ◆ Within a practice group

- ◆ Between partners

- ◆ Between practice groups

- ◆ Between lawyers and support staff

- ◆ Between legal staff and administrative staff

You can develop programs to promote sharing of tacit knowledge throughout your firm, such as communities of practice and mentoring programs, and develop technology systems to facilitate sharing of tacit knowledge throughout your firm, such as developing a skills and expertise locator.

It may also be possible to make some tacit knowledge explicit. For example, a partner may be able to describe the steps associated with handling a particular matter. Typically, the only explicit knowledge that flows from a matter is the documentation, such as precedents and best practice documents. By developing a methodology, the partner articulates his tacit knowledge about the context in which to use those documents. He has therefore made explicit some of his tacit knowledge surrounding the conduct of a matter.

The Knowledge Analysis Model

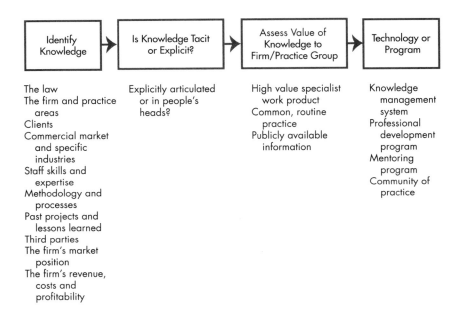

Identify Knowledge	Is Knowledge Tacit or Explicit?	Assess Value of Knowledge to Firm/Practice Group	Technology or Program
The law The firm and practice areas Clients Commercial market and specific industries Staff skills and expertise Methodology and processes Past projects and lessons learned Third parties The firm's market position The firm's revenue, costs and profitability	Explicitly articulated or in people's heads?	High value specialist work product Common, routine practice Publicly available information	Knowledge management system Professional development program Mentoring program Community of practice

Firm or Practice Group Knowledge Management?

The knowledge needs of staff in a law firm differ widely according to the type of law they practice. This means that the scope of knowledge management initiatives will vary widely across different practice groups. However, some knowledge management initiatives will apply across the entire firm—regardless of the practice group.

Law firms take one of two common approaches to defining the scope of knowledge management. Some firms begin by working with practice groups to define their knowledge needs and implement knowledge management at the practice group level. Over time, the firm identifies knowledge management initiatives that would be best implemented at the firm level. Other firms define the scope of knowledge management at the firm level, and then apply their approach to practice group knowledge management initiatives.

Each approach acknowledges that while knowledge needs will differ across practice groups, there are some fundamental knowledge management initiatives that will apply to all practice groups. The key is to take a flexible approach to knowledge management, allowing lawyers to define their knowledge needs and knowledge management initiatives that will meet those knowledge needs— while also taking an efficient approach to knowledge management, setting the direction for knowledge management at the firm level and providing an infrastructure to facilitate knowledge management among practice groups.

Your firm should be aiming for a consistent approach to knowledge management. You should have a clear understanding of the knowledge needs of every practice group, then develop a firm-wide definition of knowledge management. The next step should be to analyze existing practice group knowledge management initiatives in the context of firm-wide knowledge management initiatives and the needs of the practice group, as follows:

♦   identify the knowledge needs of each practice group

♦   identify gaps between the knowledge needs of each practice group and current knowledge management initiatives

♦   examine application of existing best practices across your firm

Because practice groups have different knowledge management needs, meeting their needs is fundamental to the success of knowledge management at your firm. Understanding that there will be similarities in the knowledge management needs of your practice groups and leveraging those similarities is also critical to the success of knowledge management at your firm.

Law Firm Knowledge Management—Some Illustrations

In a law firm, knowledge management includes initiatives to:

♦ capture and share explicit knowledge

♦ capture and share tacit knowledge, and

♦ address cultural and organizational barriers to the capture and sharing of knowledge.

The following pages describe the broad range of knowledge management initiatives in law firms. This is not an exhaustive list, but it will provide you with a starting point for your firm's knowledge management initiatives.

Managing Explicit Knowledge

The following are examples of specific knowledge management initiatives to support the identification, capture, dissemination and use of explicit knowledge:

Precedents

Known as precedents, forms or templates, these documents are generic, making no reference to a specific client or matter. They typically represent the most commonly used or the most valuable documents of a firm. Lawyers usually develop precedent documents by taking a best practice, matter specific document (or a series of these documents) and shaping it into the best starting point for a new document. A practice expert usually drafts the precedent document. Alternatively, a precedent drafting expert drafts the precedent, with extensive input from a practice expert.

Precedent documents may include several optional clauses, based on variances in the transaction, and may also include commentary on why particular language has been used.

Once a precedent document is drafted and published, lawyers would be expected to draft new transactional documents based on the precedent.

> The banking group of a law firm generates large, complex documents. At the heart of the banking practice, there are eight key documents used repeatedly in transactions, with variations based on the specific deal.
>
> The banking group has expanded rapidly in recent years, with lawyers in ten offices around the world. The practice must maintain a level of consistency across its offices. The partners of the banking group commit to creating a banking precedent development program, developing precedents based on the eight core documents used by its lawyers. Consequently, lawyers are able to produce the first draft of a document more efficiently, both by reducing the time it takes to create the first draft—and the ability to delegate drafting to more junior staff.
>
> Importantly, the partners of the banking group can also be confident that documentation produced by its group is of a uniformly high standard, regardless of the location of its lawyers.

Best practice document repositories

Best practice document repositories are databases of documents that have been identified by staff in a law firm as valuable work product. A document may be valuable because it is commonly used, rare and complex, or because it represents an example of excellent drafting.

Sometimes, documents in the best practice document repository may be turned into precedent documents, but not always. They may not lend themselves to more than one situation, or may not be used often enough to warrant the work involved in converting them into precedents.

The "best" best practice document repositories are ones which are carefully vetted to ensure that all content remains valuable content.

> The employment practice group of a law firm typically issues a letter of advice to its clients, which applies the principles of law to the client's specific fact situation. Since this group does not produce repetitive documents, precedent documents are not much use. However, similar fact patterns do arise, and there is great value in lawyers being able to access prior advice given to clients in similar situations. The group's extensive work in advising clients through letters of advice should be leveraged.
>
> The group develops a repository of its best practice letters of advice to clients. When a lawyer is presented with a new fact situation, he first searches the repository of best practice letters of advice to see whether the firm has ever advised on a similar fact situation or question of law.

Legal research tools and systems

Every law firm uses legal research tools and systems—either in hard copy or electronically. Lawyers may also need to keep abreast of daily developments in their area of practice. In some cases, the speed and volume of change can be simply overwhelming. Providing information in a form that is easily digestible is a key knowledge management initiative for any law firm.

> Lawyers in the tax practice of a law firm must stay abreast of the voluminous number of tax rulings that are released almost daily. Knowing about each tax ruling is critical to a lawyer advising his clients in an accurate and timely manner. The amount of information that a lawyer must digest is simply overwhelming. The best way for tax lawyers to address this issue is to rely on current awareness updates. The lawyers define the categories of knowledge they use and then implement a means of regularly searching each source of knowledge and delivering that knowledge in an easily digestible manner.
>
> The current awareness solution uses a combination of technology and human input to analyze the knowledge and present it in the most useful manner.

Managing Tacit Knowledge

Because tacit knowledge is by definition, hard to formalize, it may be misleading to talk about "managing" tacit knowledge. However, at a minimum, a law firm can implement initiatives that support and facilitate the sharing of tacit knowledge. Certainly, a law firm can convert some forms of tacit knowledge into explicit knowledge. The following are examples of specific knowledge management initiatives to support and facilitate the identification, capture, dissemination and use of tacit knowledge:

Processes and systems for sharing knowledge about the skills and expertise of staff

Clients assume that staff in a law firm can build a cross-functional team or call upon experts when needed. However, particularly in large and multi-disciplinary practices, the reality is that it is difficult to locate experts within the firm. One way to address this lack of knowledge sharing is to develop a database to capture the skills and expertise of its staff, together with contact information.

A law firm with six practice areas in ten offices markets itself as a global, multi-disciplinary firm, able to undertake complex, international transactions more efficiently than its competitors.

In reality, lawyers know little about their colleagues outside of their office and their practice group. Typically, projects are staffed on the basis of who knows who. There is little interaction between lawyers in different practice groups or offices.

The firm implements a skills and expertise locator, which contains information about:

- ♦ Staff name
- ♦ Staff contact details

- ◆ Expertise in the following:
  - – Area of law
  - – Type of transaction
  - – Clients
  - – Industries
  - – Country or region
- ◆ Skills in the following:
  - – Language
  - – Management
- ◆ Education
- ◆ Prior work experience

The skills and expertise locator does not attempt to capture tacit knowledge. Rather, it encourages lawyers to contact each other. It aims to connect people who hold the tacit knowledge with the people who seek the tacit knowledge. The system goes a long way toward facilitating sharing that knowledge.

Professional development programs and mentoring and coaching programs

One of the biggest challenges for a law firm is the development of its junior lawyers into market experts. The traditional ways to do this are:

- ◆ Professional development programs
- ◆ Mentoring and coaching programs

Both attempt to formalize the process of knowledge sharing between senior and junior lawyers. A typical professional development program will be a curriculum of topics that applies across the firm or to a specific practice group. Law firms provide rigorous training to their lawyers in the early years of practice—and continue to provide ongoing legal education during the course of a lawyer's career.

A mentoring and coaching program seeks to provide a framework for junior lawyers to develop close relationships with senior lawyers and learn about aspects of practice that may not be written in a manual or taught in a professional development program. These programs aim to encourage senior lawyers to develop a junior lawyer's tacit knowledge.

A national litigation group sees a wide variation in the approach their lawyers take, across several offices. This makes it difficult for partners in the group to confidently use staff from other offices. The partners of the group decide that the best way to create a group of lawyers who practice at a consistently high standard is to develop a comprehensive national professional development program for its lawyers.

As a result, partners see a marked improvement in the quality of work across all offices and begin to truly act as a national practice group, staffing projects with lawyers from different offices.

* * * *

A law firm loses 35% of its second year lawyers in a given year. Most of these lawyers move to other law firms. The firm learns that one of the significant drivers of this exodus is the lack of exposure junior lawyers have to senior lawyers. They perceive that another firm may offer a better learning and mentoring environment.

> Among many initiatives, the firm implements a coaching and mentoring program. Each junior lawyer is assigned a senior associate as a coach and a partner as a mentor. The senior associate and partner must make time to meet with the junior lawyer—and will be assessed on their performance in this area. The senior associate and partner receive training in how to play this role. The training improves their overall performance as staff managers. The program also provides junior lawyers with a forum to discuss their work—and to gain tacit knowledge from the firm's experts.

Communities of practice (or communities of interest)

A community of practice is a loose framework that draws together lawyers who work in different offices or practice groups, but share a common interest. It may be a common client or project. It may be an interest in new legislation or new industry developments. Lawyers in the community of practice see a value in sharing knowledge about that which draws them together. Over time, the community of practice may become a formal practice group—particularly where industry developments or changes to legislation create market demand for specialist legal services. On the other hand, the community of practice may cease to exist when it has served its purpose. For example, where the community of practice is based around a common project, it will end when the project ends.

The community of practice may share and manage their knowledge by using technology systems and non-technology processes. For example, the community of practice may share

knowledge by meeting regularly, or by building an intranet or database to capture and share knowledge.

Earlier in this Chapter, I described a group of lawyers spread across several practice groups who advise their clients on new financial services reform legislation. Since the lawyers sit in different groups, they have little interaction with each other. However, it is critical that these lawyers work together in order to provide consistent and high quality advice to the firm's clients.

The firm creates a community of practice composed of the 20 lawyers. This group meets every other week during lunch to share knowledge about the new legislation and to discuss how it impacts their clients.

Over time, as material about the legislation becomes overwhelming, the lawyers realize that regular meetings are not enough. The community of practice develops an intranet page to share knowledge about developments relating to the legislation. Lawyers post current awareness items, and letters of advice provided to clients on the new legislation. The community of practice intranet page becomes an effective internal knowledge sharing tool. It enables the firm to truly leverage the expertise acquired by its lawyers.

Methodologies based on common work processes

Developing a methodology involves identifying a lawyer's knowledge of the steps involved in a matter and capturing it in a form that can be used by others. Methodologies represent knowledge management at its best. A methodology identifies and captures an expert's tacit knowledge about how to manage a matter. This tacit knowledge becomes explicit knowledge, disseminated in the form of well-defined process steps, and is an excellent way of sharing knowledge between experts and seekers of that expertise.

A small law firm wants to win a position on the panel of outside law firms used by a bank to handle its mortgage work as described in Chapter 3. The law firm has three lawyers and one paralegal who have traditionally handled some matters for the bank in the past—including some mortgage work.

The lawyers realize that their firm could handle large amounts of the bank's mortgage work on a fixed fee basis if they could delegate this work to a team of paralegals.

To delegate this work, the lawyers must identify the steps involved in managing a mortgage matter, and develop documentation associated with every step of the process. The lawyers develop a methodology—articulating every process step and drafting the associated precedent documents.

The firm estimates what it will cost to have a paralegal manage a mortgage matter, requests a position on the bank's outside counsel panel, and wins a significant amount of work. The lawyers hire three extra paralegals and train them in the methodology. The lawyers spend a minimal amount of time supervising the paralegals, while the revenue of the law firm rises significantly.

Several practice groups of a large law firm conduct due diligence on behalf of their clients. Lawyers from the corporate, real estate and banking groups may conduct due diligence—though there is no common firm approach. This becomes a risk management issue for the firm—especially when lawyers from several practice groups are working for the same client.

The firm recognizes that each due diligence process will differ according to the type of transaction. However, there are some basic similarities in the approach all lawyers should take. Understanding the basic steps a lawyer should take in conducting due diligence is critical to the firm delivering a consistently high standard of work and eliminating inefficiencies caused by reinventing the wheel with every new due diligence.

Lawyers representing the practice groups involved in due diligence work form a working group to define the basic steps and documents used by all lawyers. The group drafts a methodology, setting out these basic steps, and attaches precedent documents associated with each step. Over time, the methodology is expanded to cover different types of transactions, though all are based on a common firm approach.

Know-how files

Know-how files are similar to methodologies, with some subtle differences. Developing a methodology involves identifying a common work process and mapping the steps involved in that process. Often, it also involves attaching relevant precedent and best practice documents to each process step.

Developing a know-how file usually begins with developing the precedent document or identifying the best practice document. There is an assumption that someone using a precedent or best practice document possesses a certain level of knowledge about the context in which to use these documents.

A know-how file adds context to a precedent or best practice document by describing the circumstances in which these documents should be used. Like a methodology, developing a know-how file involves capturing tacit knowledge about how and when these documents should be used. This knowledge is made explicit in the form of instructions on how and when to use these documents.

The litigation group of a law firm has a set of court forms and firm-developed precedent documents which are used by every lawyer in the group. The partners notice that junior lawyers often do not know which form or precedent to use. Partners either spend a great deal of time instructing junior lawyers on which document to use, or they simply find it easier to do the work themselves. Not delegating the work does not serve anyone well.

The partners realize that making forms and precedent documents available is not enough. Junior lawyers lack the knowledge about how to use these documents. Partners, on the other hand, naturally know when and how to use these documents—though their knowledge largely remains tacit—and is only ever shared in a training session or in a one-on-one conversation.

The partners annotate the court forms and precedent documents, describing how these documents should be used. As a result, junior lawyers can access a know-how file on a relevant type of case, and confidently access and use the appropriate document.

Partners see a significant improvement in the work of junior lawyers and experience a significant decrease in their workload. They now confidently delegate work to junior lawyers, while reducing considerably the time spent supervising their junior lawyers.

Debriefing

Lawyers accumulate a large amount of knowledge during the course of running a matter. When the matter ends, lawyers are usually excited to talk about their experience. This excitement is brief—typically ending when a lawyer moves on to the next matter. The purpose of debriefing is to capture as much of the knowledge acquired by staff working on a matter before it is forgotten. Debriefing is a classic example of how to capture tacit knowledge and make it explicit, or how to at least identify the owners of that tacit knowledge.

The debriefing process may involve several steps, and will vary across law firms. Typically, debriefing begins with the team leader providing a summary of the matter in an interview with knowledge management staff. This summary provides details relating to project management, client relationship, associated documentation, and lessons learned. The summary provides the framework for a team discussion on the matter.

The team is then brought together to discuss the elements of the matter in an open forum, where the team members are encouraged to speak freely about the matter. The purpose of the team meeting is to identify core pieces of knowledge that should be leveraged in future matters. The outcome of the debriefing session will be knowledge management staff working with the team members to capture and disseminate that knowledge. This may include:

- Adding matter documents to the best practice repository.

- Developing precedents based on matter documents.

- Developing a methodology based on the matter for future similar matters.

- Sharing knowledge about the client with colleagues who also work with this client.

- Capturing new skills and expertise acquired by staff during the course of the matter in the firm's skills and expertise locator.

- Adding a summary of the matter in the firm's matters/credentials database.

Knowledge management staff should facilitate the debriefing process to ensure that sessions achieve their purpose and staff speak freely about their experience.

A corporate practice group works on large-scale mergers and acquisitions, rapidly moving from one transaction to the next. The partners of the group know that similar issues arise in different transactions, but there is never time to pause and consider how best to address these issues. The only opportunity to share lessons learned during a transaction is the group's monthly meeting—yet there is little time to share any valuable insights acquired during a transaction with others.

Consequently, knowledge acquired during the course of a transaction tends to stay within the team working on that transaction.

The partners recognize that staff enjoy talking about a transaction until shortly after it has ended. Where the transaction has been particularly successful, it is indeed all the partners can talk about. The partners want to find a way to bottle that enthusiasm and capture all the knowledge floating around the office before it fades.

The corporate group introduces the debriefing process to capture that knowledge before it is lost forever. A knowledge manager interviews the transaction team leader to understand the basic elements of the transaction. Among a wide range of topics, the knowledge manager learns about how the transaction was managed, who was involved, what was learned about the client, what documents were created, and lessons learned. This interview enables the knowledge manager to identify the key issues emerging from this transaction, and create a framework for the group debriefing session.

The team working on the transaction attends a group debriefing session. Within the framework created by the knowledge manager, the group has an open and honest discussion about issues arising out of the transaction. It becomes clear that the partners could have managed the matter more efficiently. Documents could have been created more efficiently if a precedent existed. The client was particularly demanding about the style of documentation.

There are several outcomes from the debriefing session. Partners develop a project management methodology. The team develops a precedent based on the transactional documentation. Knowledge about the client's preferences is shared with colleagues who also work for this client.

When the team moves on to similar transactions, it has the tools available to manage the matter more efficiently. The client also recognizes a marked improvement in the quality of services provided by the law firm—and knows that this is a firm focused on meeting its client's needs.

Matters/credentials database

Lawyers are constantly asked to provide their qualifications to potential clients. Often, firms scramble to identify examples of prior matters they have handled which demonstrate their ability to undertake new work. Capturing knowledge about prior matters in a database eliminates the mad scramble approach. It also enables the firm to identify where its market strengths are, and where the firm should be concentrating its marketing efforts. This database also provides staff with a means of identifying who the experts are in the firm.

The insurance group of a firm wins its work by submitting tenders to undertake large-scale transactions. It is absolutely critical that the tender demonstrate the firm's ability to handle these transactions. The firm must therefore describe its prior projects.

Typically, the marketing department is called in to assist with a tender the day before it is due. Usually, what follows is a tense few hours in which marketing staff desperately try to collect relevant credentials to add to the tender document. This process occurs on a weekly basis.

The marketing department realizes that the same knowledge is used repeatedly—though often recreated. The firm implements a database of firm credentials, which stores knowledge about the major projects handled by the firm. The database contains a summary of the matter, parties and staff involved, documentation created, and any unique aspects of the matter.

While the database addresses the need to create tenders more efficiently, it has some by-products. The partners begin to analyze the type of work they won in the past, and decide to proactively market their services to potential clients, rather than react to a request for tender. The partners also realize that the best way to put a team together is to look at who worked on similar projects—and ensure that an expert's skills are leveraged in future matters.

Regular practice group meetings

One of the simplest, and most effective ways to share knowledge is the practice group meeting. Of course, this depends on the format and content of your firm's practice group meetings. If a meeting is heavy on "administrivia," you will probably not have a ready audience to participate. However, if your practice group meetings allow staff to share knowledge acquired about clients, matters and the legal and regulatory environment in which you operate, they can be very effective.

Reading and writing programs

Lawyers become leaders in their field when they acquire a unique depth of knowledge. A reading and writing program seeks to formalize the process of acquiring deeper knowledge of an area of law. On the reading side, lawyers nominate specific topics that they commit to focus on, and particular publications that they commit to reading. On the writing side, lawyers commit to writing a set number of articles for publication.

The knowledge acquired by each lawyer may be shared with others. Alternatively, the knowledge may remain with the specific lawyer—though others will know of the lawyer's expertise, and consult with that lawyer as appropriate.

Building a knowledge sharing office environment

Office design plays a role in knowledge management—by creating an environment conducive to knowledge sharing. There are many ways that the "water cooler" effect can be translated to practical and productive knowledge management initiatives. Here are some examples:

Partner open door policy. Partners are intimidating people at the best of times. A partner behind a closed door is close to totally unapproachable. Clearly, there are times when a door must be closed. The door should be closed then—and only then. Keeping the door open increases the opportunity for junior lawyers to approach partners and acquire valuable tacit knowledge.

Open plan office space. Again, it may not always be practical to draft documents in an open plan office space—but banks, accounting firms and management consulting companies have worked like this for years. An open office space promotes knowledge sharing and team collaboration. When serious document drafting or confidential conversations must take place, separate private space is available.

Office café. Some firms are already doing this. On each floor, an open plan coffee bar with stools and a table provides staff with a place to talk informally. This approach acknowledges that people will visit the kitchen at some stage of a day, and probably will chat to colleagues at the water cooler or in the corridor. The café space formalizes these traditional elements of office life—and seeks to encourage informal, tacit knowledge sharing.

Addressing Cultural and Organizational Barriers

Knowledge management is not just about specific initiatives to capture and share knowledge. It is also about creating a culture that is conducive to knowledge management—and building an organization of people who will support and facilitate knowledge management at your firm.

Knowledge management initiatives to build the right culture

To create a knowledge management culture, lawyers must take a long hard look at the traditional law firm culture and identify the barriers to knowledge management. There are many. Chapter 6 deals with this topic in depth, though it is worth mentioning two critical knowledge management initiatives that will address these cultural barriers.

Review the compensation system

Where a law firm bases its compensation levels purely on the number of billable hours, there is no room for knowledge management. There is no incentive to invest hours in initiatives that bring a longer term benefit to the firm. However, knowledge management requires significant investment by staff. Naturally, staff will have no incentive to make that investment if they are punished financially in the short term.

If your law firm is serious about knowledge management, you must review your compensation system to acknowledge staff investment in knowledge management.

Make knowledge management contribution a key element of career progression

Financial reward is one way a lawyer's contribution is acknowledged. The other significant way is through career progression. A key knowledge management initiative is to build contribution to knowledge management into your firm's career progression model.

There is no clearer signal to a lawyer that the firm is serious about knowledge management than making his compensation and career progression dependent on his contribution to the firm's knowledge management efforts.

Knowledge management initiatives to create the right knowledge management organization

Chapter 5 provides a detailed description of what your knowledge management organization should look like. Among the scope of knowledge management initiatives you will pursue, creating a knowledge management organization to coordinate and facilitate knowledge management is fundamental.

From Simple to Complex

In this Chapter, I have described many different knowledge management initiatives that may apply to some practice groups or firms more than others. My goal has been to demonstrate the vast range of knowledge management initiatives your firm should consider. Above all, you should not be constrained by whether the knowledge is tacit or explicit, and whether the capture and delivery mechanism involves technology or simply a human process.

To define the most appropriate knowledge management initiatives for your firm, simply follow the three key principles I described at the start of this Chapter:

1. Understand what knowledge you must manage before you identify the best way to manage that knowledge.

2. Don't limit your thinking on the scope of initiatives that can help you manage that knowledge.

3. Base your investment in knowledge management on the value of the knowledge to your practice and your business.

There is a fourth principle that you should also consider:

4. Begin with simple, discrete knowledge management initiatives, and over time, draw them together into more complex knowledge management tools and processes.

In Chapter 9, I describe this concept in more detail. For now, here is a simple illustration:

A medium size law firm with no firm-wide knowledge management program develops a knowledge management strategy aligned with its business objectives. The firm is literally starting from scratch. Until now, lawyers have relied on their own precedents and rarely shared them with others. Some practice groups have developed databases of interesting content over the years, but have not monitored the quality of content. There is no formal professional development program for lawyers. Rather, lawyers rely on external seminars or "on-the-job" training.

The firm really has its work cut out for it. Rather than building a single user interface into multiple systems and applications, the firm adopts a strategy to start with simple, high value knowledge management initiatives that will provide a solid foundation for more complex knowledge management. The firm estimates that it will take three years to achieve the desired knowledge management environment.

In the first 18 months, dedicating significant resources to knowledge management, the firm succeeds at building a precedent library, a best practice work product repository and a professional development program. The firm begins to see the benefits of knowledge management and there is a heightened level of enthusiasm among staff at the firm.

Despite this enthusiasm, some critical cultural barriers to knowledge management become evident. Some barriers are so deeply ingrained in the law firm culture that it may take years to overcome them. For example, lawyers feel that their compensation and career progression are strongly tied to their ability to amass a unique knowledge base, and the number of hours they bill. Many are therefore unwilling to share knowledge, since this will dilute their power base. Others are not willing to devote time to knowledge management, since this will negatively impact the number of hours they can bill.

In the second phase of the three year timeframe, the firm turns its attention to addressing those cultural barriers—and to tackling more sophisticated knowledge management initiatives.

With its precedent documents and repository of best practice work product, the firm has delivered important knowledge management tools. However, partners discover that both tools assume junior lawyers know what they are looking for. Of course, the lawyers who have attended the professional development program have learned about how to handle specific transactions and cases.

The firm recognizes that as discrete components, the precedent library, best practice work product repository and professional development program have limited value. By simply drawing all three together into a know-how file, lawyers can understand the context in which a precedent or best practice document should be used.

The firm focuses its second phase energies on developing know how files that provide lawyers with the steps involved in a number of core matters, and guide lawyers through the appropriate precedent and best practice documents they should use. By combining its core knowledge management tools, the firm leverages its explicit and tacit knowledge—and builds a powerful knowledge management environment, which directly supports its business objectives.

Define the Scope of Knowledge **Management** at Your Firm

To define the scope of knowledge management at your firm, follow these steps:

1. Have you identified the knowledge you need to achieve your business objectives?

2. Is the knowledge tacit or explicit?

3. Have you defined the value of that knowledge?

4. Is the appropriate knowledge management initiative a program or a technology system?

5. Is the knowledge management initiative a firm initiative or a practice group initiative?

6. Which of the following knowledge management initiatives help you achieve your business objectives:

   ♦ Precedents
   ♦ Best practice document repositories

- Legal research tools and systems
- Processes and systems for sharing knowledge about skills and expertise of staff
- Professional development programs
- Coaching and mentoring programs
- Communities of practice
- Methodologies based on common work processes
- Know how files
- Debriefing
- Matters/credentials database
- Regular practice group meetings
- Reading and writing programs
- Building a knowledge sharing environment
  - Partner open door policy
  - Open plan office space
  - Office café
- Building the right knowledge management culture
- Creating the right knowledge management organization

Developing the Knowledge Management Organization

A 200-lawyer firm adopts a knowledge management strategy that involves implementing knowledge management tools and processes in every practice group. A knowledge management committee, composed of the Director of Information Technology, the Head Librarian and representative partners from each practice group, developed the strategy. The implementation of the strategy is an ambitious project, involving some 40 to 50 initiatives across the various practice groups.

The firm has not appointed a Director of Knowledge Management, knowledge managers, professional support lawyers or information officers. Instead, the responsibility of implementing these initiatives lies with each practice group.

Within a practice group, partners assign knowledge management related tasks to staff. No credit is given to staff for their knowledge management efforts. Staff are expected to handle their knowledge management work in addition to a full client workload.

The only central coordination of this project is in the form of a bi-weekly meeting of the knowledge management committee. At that meeting, the committee members review the progress of all knowledge management initiatives and highlight any issues associated with the progression of those initiatives.

It becomes apparent that several practice groups are working on similar initiatives. Rather than combining their initiatives to produce a firm-wide solution, the groups pursue separate initiatives. In doing so, the groups compete for finite resources in the support functions, like Information Technology, Library and Precedents—and consequently, are delayed in the progress of their initiatives.

Over time, it seems that many practice groups cannot meet their initiative deadlines. Staff assigned to knowledge management tasks find it difficult to do both billable client work and knowledge management work. There is no real project management at the practice group level. As initiatives fall further behind schedule, the groups lose interest in knowledge management.

Despite its good intentions, the firm ultimately fails in its knowledge management efforts—through lack of direction, leadership and resources.

Knowledge management is hard work. While knowledge management is the responsibility of every person in your firm, it also requires a dedicated team of knowledge management staff to coordinate knowledge management related activities. In other words, you need staff dedicated to the tasks of identifying, capturing and disseminating knowledge in a form that others will use.

In this Chapter, I describe the many issues you need to consider in developing a knowledge management organization. These include who should lead the organization and the reporting relationship between the knowledge management organization and law firm management. I also look at which existing law firm functions should form part of the knowledge management organization—and which new roles should be created.

I consider the appropriate size of your firm's knowledge management organization and look at how best to position the knowledge management organization in your firm. This means establishing an appropriate management reporting structure to gain management's attention and building relationships with other functions in the firm to enable implementation of knowledge management across the firm.

In developing your knowledge management organization, you must pay careful attention to its size, composition and positioning. These three factors are critical to the success of knowledge management at your firm.

Size means the number of resources dedicated to implementing knowledge management initiatives. To implement your firm's knowledge management strategy, you will need sufficient dedicated resources to execute the implementation of specific initiatives.

Composition means the operational functions that form part of your knowledge management organization. Composition influences the scope of your knowledge management initiatives. The broader the composition of your knowledge management organization, the broader the scope of knowledge management is at your firm.

Knowledge managers, professional support lawyers, information officers and knowledge management system developers are pure knowledge management roles. Traditional law firm functions such as the library, precedents, professional development and intranet content should also become part of the knowledge management organization.

Positioning means (1) the reporting relationship between the knowledge management organization and management and (2) the relationship between the knowledge management organization and administrative functions and practice groups at the firm.

Knowledge management touches upon everything every person does at your firm. Since knowledge management is not a discrete function, the knowledge management organization cannot be viewed as an isolated administrative function. It must be able to implement initiatives across all functions and practice groups. It needs to establish strong relationships with key administrative functions to implement firm–wide knowledge management initiatives.

The knowledge management organization must have the attention of management and be able to influence the partnership to adopt the significant cultural change required to succeed at knowledge management.

Building a knowledge management organization means creating a new organization in your firm. Knowledge management is not an "easy out" for lawyers who decide they no longer want to practice law. You should appoint knowledge management resource persons with appropriate skills. To attract and retain the best knowledge management resources, you must build a career path and compensation track for knowledge management staff. I consider these issues later in this Chapter.

The Role of the Knowledge Management Organization

The knowledge management organization is responsible for:

- ♦ Determining knowledge management strategy

- ♦ Implementing knowledge management initiatives consistent with your firm's strategy

- ♦ Ensuring that knowledge management efforts align with your firm's business strategy

- ♦ Influencing management, partners and staff about the benefits of knowledge management

Should the Knowledge Management
Organization Be Decentralized or Centralized?

There are three common approaches to the knowledge management organization in law firms:

- ♦ Centralized

- ♦ Decentralized

- ♦ Hybrid

Centralized knowledge management organization

This means establishing a centralized knowledge management function that directs all knowledge management initiatives. This enables a law firm to take a consistent, cost efficient approach to knowledge management across the firm, eliminating duplication of development efforts in different practice groups and achieving economies of scale. However, it also assumes that practice groups will have the same knowledge management needs. Often, practice groups are forced to fit their knowledge management needs into a broad model, thus frustrating their own knowledge management objectives.

Decentralized knowledge management organization

In a decentralized knowledge management environment, practice groups or individual lawyers are able to pursue knowledge management initiatives without an overarching firm-wide strategy. In the short term, this provides lawyers maximum flexibility in designing knowledge management initiatives. However, knowledge management initiatives in these firms often suffer in the long term for the following reasons:

♦ Multiple, conflicting demands are placed on the firm's infrastructure to support widely varied knowledge management initiatives.

♦ The focus on practice group knowledge management needs, rather than firm-wide knowledge management needs, leads to duplication of development efforts and the loss of opportunity to leverage best practices across the firm.

Hybrid knowledge management organization

The best practice approach to knowledge management is a hybrid of the first two approaches. The firm sets the direction for knowledge management and provides an infrastructure to facilitate knowledge management among practice groups. Knowledge management methodologies are created at the firm level, which can then be applied directly to practice group knowledge management initiatives. Core knowledge management functions, such as precedents, library, legal research, and professional development, are managed at the firm level, and also provide assistance to practice groups in addressing practice group specific knowledge management needs. This approach enables practice groups to achieve their knowledge management objectives while benefiting from a firm-wide strategy—resulting in a cost efficient, flexible approach to knowledge management.

The Head of Knowledge Management

Your knowledge management organization should be led by a person who is responsible for:

- ♦ Knowledge management strategy
- ♦ Knowledge management operations
- ♦ Influencing change
- ♦ Managing knowledge management staff

Knowledge management strategy

The head of knowledge management must understand your firm's business objectives and develop a knowledge management strategy that aligns with your firm's business strategy.

In some cases, the firm may have developed its knowledge management strategy before appointing a head of knowledge management.

Once the strategy has been developed, the head of knowledge management must ensure that the firm's approach to knowledge management continually enables the firm to achieve its business objectives.

Knowledge management operations

The head of knowledge management is responsible for taking the knowledge management strategy and turning it into specific knowledge management initiatives that achieve the firm's knowledge management and business objectives. The head of knowledge management leads the development of firm-wide and practice group knowledge management initiatives to meet your firm's business objectives.

Influencing change

The head of knowledge management must build wide user support among lawyers and staff. He must continually advocate the objectives and benefits of knowledge management and the cultural change required to facilitate knowledge management at your firm.

He advises your firm's management on knowledge management, articulating knowledge management in business terms.

The head of knowledge management must ensure that knowledge management initiatives take a long term strategic view and add value to your firm.

Managing knowledge management staff

The head of knowledge management manages a large multi-disciplinary knowledge management organization across many locations and practice groups and must also engage resources from other areas of the business.

The following box illustrates how a law firm may define the specific tasks of its head of knowledge management. The firm also defines the professional experience, professional skills and personal skills required to perform this role. (In this illustration, the firm has already developed its knowledge management strategy and decided to appoint a head of knowledge management who has a legal background.)

HEAD OF KNOWLEDGE MANAGEMENT

Specific Tasks

- Chair all knowledge management related meetings.
- Meet regularly with knowledge management staff to direct the implementation and review progress of knowledge management projects.
- Meet with knowledge management partners and practice group heads to understand practice group business objectives and influence cultural change.
- Report regularly to the board on the progress of implementing practice group and firm-wide knowledge management initiatives.
- Develop and present the knowledge management budget to the board.
- Present pertinent knowledge management related proposals to the board.
- Define knowledge management initiatives aligned with the firm's knowledge management strategy and business objectives.
- Define and articulate priorities for implementing knowledge management initiatives.
- Review the success of knowledge management initiatives and demonstrate the return on investment to the board.
- Ensure that knowledge management initiatives reflect the policies of the firm.

♦ Be responsible for the overall management of the functions reporting into the knowledge management organization.

♦ Articulate the knowledge management needs of the firm to other functions, e.g., marketing, finance, IT, human resources and professional development.

♦ Articulate opportunities to leverage knowledge management with clients to the board and administrative functions.

Professional Experience

The head of knowledge management should be a lawyer with information and people management skills and experience who has a strong interest in implementing better ways for lawyers to work through knowledge management and has a track record in successfully implementing strategy. The head of knowledge management must:

♦ Understand the work processes and knowledge needs of a wide range of areas of legal practice.

♦ Possess an applied understanding of how to coordinate a knowledge management organization and implement change within the firm.

♦ Understand that the scope of knowledge management involves management of explicit and tacit knowledge, and management of commercial and legal knowledge.

- ◆ Possess an applied understanding of how information management, information technology and organizational processes can be used to capture a law firm's intellectual capital.
- ◆ Understand the cultural aspects of knowledge management to facilitate knowledge sharing, innovative thinking and creativity.
- ◆ Possess project management skills.

Professional Skills

The head of knowledge management must be able to:

- ◆ Build wide user support across the firm.
- ◆ Manage a large multi-disciplinary knowledge management organization across several offices, areas of the business and practice groups to implement firm-wide and practice group knowledge management projects.
- ◆ Coordinate and prioritize the implementation of many concurrent projects, including identifying appropriate resources, costs, benefits, critical success factors and timing.
- ◆ Understand the firm's business objectives and identify projects consistent with those business objectives and the firm's knowledge management strategy.
- ◆ Demonstrate the importance of knowledge management to the firm.

♦ Understand how the information technology platform and non-technology systems and processes can be used to capture the firm's intellectual capital.

Personal Skills

The head of knowledge management must be a logical thinker who can translate and implement the firm's business objectives and knowledge management strategy into specific initiatives. The head of knowledge management must possess an energetic personality, and team building, leadership and motivation skills. The head of knowledge management must be able to advocate the application and benefits of knowledge management to a broad range of users. Strong written and oral communication skills are essential. The candidate must have superior business analysis skills to understand the business needs of the group and translate those needs into knowledge management projects.

The head of knowledge management must have the ability to build relationships and work collaboratively with administrative areas to further knowledge management initiatives and to bring a knowledge management perspective to projects not owned by the knowledge management organization.

Who Should Lead Your Knowledge
Management Organization?

Many law firms struggle with the decision about who should lead the knowledge management organization. The threshold question is often whether the head of knowledge management should have a legal background. Another key question is whether your knowledge management organization should be led by a director or a partner of the firm.

Should it be a lawyer?

The background of the head of knowledge management reflects the culture of the law firm. Many law firms are adamant that a legal background is critical to a head of knowledge management's ability to influence cultural change. These firms argue that in a law firm, one must be a lawyer to influence other lawyers. If you should decide to appoint a head of knowledge management with a legal background, be careful not to ignore the importance of information management and people management skills required in this role.

Other law firms have made a deliberate decision not to appoint a lawyer, believing that knowledge management requires a strategic thinker, with commercial experience, who will drive a firm to think outside of the box. The head of knowledge management at these firms typically has a technology or management background.

The challenge for non-lawyers in this role is to learn about how lawyers work and to develop a strong trust relationship with the lawyers. Lawyers can be a tough and intimidating crowd. Where firms have appointed a non-lawyer to head their knowledge management organization, they often assign a partner to act as mentor to the head of knowledge management in the early stages of knowledge management at the firm.

Partner or director?

A natural extension of the decision to appoint a lawyer to head knowledge management is to consider whether he should be a partner. This decision is about giving knowledge management the greatest exposure within your firm to drive the cultural change necessary to succeed at knowledge management.

In a typical law firm, the partnership will more likely listen to another partner proposing significant cultural change over any other person. The partnership implicitly trusts that a partner understands the business, and knows that a partner has a vested interest in the firm's business affairs. The partnership will tend to believe that a partner, over any other, will lead the firm through knowledge management initiatives that are directly linked to the firm's business strategy.

On the other hand, a partner does not typically possess the specific knowledge management and general management skills and experience required to lead a knowledge management organization.

The role of the knowledge management partner may take different forms. The knowledge management partner may be directly involved in operational and strategic aspects of knowledge management. This would likely be a full time role.

Alternatively, the knowledge management partner may be a figurehead, working closely with a knowledge management director, focusing on influencing cultural change and having ultimate accountability for knowledge management at the firm. This would likely be a part time position.

In the example below, the firm sees the value of both a knowledge management partner and a knowledge management director.

The firm Knowledge Management Partner reports on knowledge management issues to the head of the firm. The partner will be ultimately responsible for the knowledge management organization led by the Director of Knowledge Management.

The partner will be responsible for building wide user support among lawyers and staff, and advising the board and the partnership on knowledge management initiatives, articulating knowledge management in business terms. The ideal candidate for this role is a partner who is a strategic thinker, understands how knowledge management can impact the firm's client service delivery, and can be a persuasive advocate of knowledge management to the partnership. In particular, the Knowledge Management Partner must be able to enlist wide support among the partnership for critical cultural changes.

We envisage that this role would require 30 to 50% of partner time.

The Director of Knowledge Management will manage a large multi-disciplinary knowledge management team, work closely with other areas of management to understand business objectives and implement initiatives, and understand how the information technology platform can be used to capture the firm's intellectual capital.

The Director of Knowledge Management should have a dual reporting line, reporting to the national Knowledge Management Partner, and to the position to whom all other directors report. The Director of Knowledge

> Management will be directly responsible for all knowledge management staff, including precedents, library, intranet content, professional support lawyers and information officers.

A dual director of knowledge management/ information technology (IT)?

Some firms may be inclined to create a dual director of knowledge management/IT, particularly at firms which take a technology-centric approach to knowledge management. This dual role provides its benefits and challenges. The main benefit of a dual role is that knowledge management technology solutions may be implemented more efficiently. However, the main challenge of this dual role is that when a firm faces major technology issues, knowledge management tends to take second priority. If attention on knowledge management is diverted to technology, it may hamper the firm's ability to progress knowledge management initiatives.

A strong focus on the technology elements of knowledge management also ignores the many non-technology aspects of knowledge management. These include tackling cultural impediments to knowledge management, such as the time-based billing model, the "knowledge is power" mindset and lack of interaction between practice groups. It also ignores the many knowledge management initiatives that do not involve technology. In Chapter 4, I described how many knowledge management initiatives may not involve technology at all, such as professional development programs, communities of practice and debriefing.

To Whom Does the Head of Knowledge
Management Report?

The reporting relationship of the head of knowledge management
tells a lot about how knowledge management is perceived at your
firm and the ability of your head of knowledge management to
make progress.

There are typically three reporting models for knowledge
management in law firms:

1. direct report to the CEO, managing partner or management committee
2. direct report to the executive director
3. direct report to the director of IT

Direct report to the CEO, managing partner or the management committee

This ensures that knowledge management is viewed as impacting all
aspects of the firm and directly linked to driving business objectives.
Under this reporting structure, the head of knowledge management
can influence cultural change, gain management support and ensure
that knowledge management is aligned with business objectives.

Direct report to the executive director

This may mean that knowledge management is viewed as an isolated administrative function, and that management may not fully
understand how knowledge management impacts all aspects of the
firm's business. This reporting structure compromises the ability of
the head of knowledge management to influence cultural change
or gain management support for long term investment in knowledge management.

Direct report to the director of IT

This reporting structure ensures that knowledge management is only viewed in technology terms—with little focus on non-technology aspects of knowledge management.

Composition of the Knowledge Management
Organization

While the head of knowledge management sets strategy, the successful execution of that strategy is largely dependent on the availability of adequate dedicated resources. It requires a significant level of human effort—both to create knowledge management systems and processes, and maintain those systems.

The composition of the knowledge management organization both reflects and influences the scope of knowledge management at your firm.

Law firms already have several functions that play a vital role in knowledge management and should fall within a newly formed knowledge management organization. These may include the library, precedents, legal research, intranet content and professional development.

There are also new knowledge management roles that have emerged in law firms in recent years. Firms with well-developed knowledge management organizations recognize that different skills are needed at various stages of knowledge management, and for different types of knowledge management initiatives. It is common for mature knowledge management organizations to have professional support lawyers, knowledge managers, information officers and knowledge management system developers, each playing a distinct role.

Since knowledge management is the responsibility of all staff in your firm, implementing knowledge management will also depend on resources available in other functions. While it may not be appropriate for all administrative functions to fall under the umbrella of the knowledge management organization, the organization must develop strong working relationships with those functions in order to execute your firm's knowledge management strategy. This is discussed later in this Chapter.

There are two key elements to consider in defining the composition of your knowledge management organization:

♦ which existing functions should now form part of the knowledge management organization?

♦ which new roles should be created?

Which existing functions should form part of the knowledge management organization?

Library

The library has traditionally been responsible for managing the collection and delivery of a large part of the explicit legal knowledge used by staff in a law firm. The library is responsible for collection, analysis, classification, packaging and delivery of knowledge to lawyers and staff. Library staff bring their superior information management skills to broader knowledge management initiatives.

Legal research/work product repository

Many law firms have separate legal research/work product repositories managed by a team of dedicated information management specialists. This function is responsible for collecting and publishing the best practice work product of a law firm. Staff are well versed in analyzing the value of work product, then categorizing and packaging work product in a form that makes it easy for staff to retrieve work product efficiently. These are core knowledge management skills.

Precedents

The precedents group is a dedicated team responsible for administering the firm's precedent document collection. The precedents group typically works with practice groups to develop and maintain precedents. Since precedents are a key knowledge management tool in law firms, this group should be a core knowledge management function.

Intranet content

The intranet is a chief knowledge delivery mechanism. Once the IT department has built your firm's intranet architecture, the management of intranet content is the responsibility of knowledge management staff.

Professional development

The training programs managed by your professional development team are some of the principal delivery mechanisms of tacit and explicit knowledge at your law firm. Indeed, training programs are a great example of how law firms can make the tacit knowledge of experienced lawyers explicit. The professional development function should ideally form part of your knowledge management organization.

Which new roles should be created?

Four knowledge management roles have emerged in law firms— the professional support lawyer, information officer, knowledge manager, and the knowledge management system developer.

Professional support lawyer

The primary role of the professional support lawyer is to focus on **content development.** Responsibilities include:

- ♦ Drafting precedents and other work product
- ♦ Developing and organizing training sessions
- ♦ Identifying and disseminating current awareness materials
- ♦ Developing content for the intranet and client publications.

At a law firm with no knowledge manager or information officer role, the professional support lawyer is also responsible for collection and dissemination of content.

Typically, professional support lawyers are retained at the practice group level.

Information officer

The information officer is typically responsible for **content delivery and research,** as follows:

- ♦ Information monitoring and dissemination of current awareness
- ♦ Indexing and data entry
- ♦ Conducting business and legal research
- ♦ Preparing and publishing intranet content.

The information officer is typically retained centrally and is often part of the library function.

Knowledge manager

There are two distinct definitions of the knowledge manager role evident in law firms. Some firms define the knowledge manager as a centralized management role, acting as deputy to the head of knowledge management and largely responsible for the day-to-day operational aspects of knowledge management. The range of responsibilities includes:

- Managing professional support lawyers
- Project managing implementation of practice group and firm-wide knowledge management initiatives
- Managing the library, precedents and other core knowledge management functions.

Other firms define the knowledge manager as a practice group specific knowledge management role, responsible for meeting the knowledge management needs of a practice group. In these firms, the knowledge manager is often responsible for elements of the professional support lawyer and information officer roles. Rather than creating content, the knowledge manager typically manages the creation of content by relying heavily on the contributions of lawyers and paralegals in the practice group. Responsibilities include:

- Identifying practice group knowledge needs
- Managing the implementation of a broad range of knowledge management initiatives in the practice group
- Coordinating resources to develop content
- Monitoring and distributing current awareness material.

In many law firms, the role of knowledge manager has also been created in administrative functions, such as human resources, finance, marketing and IT. The knowledge manager is responsible for the knowledge management needs of the administrative function, similar to the practice group knowledge manager.

Distinguishing among knowledge managers, professional support lawyers and information officers

The table below outlines the key differences among the roles of the knowledge manager, professional support lawyer and information officer. The table also illustrates how these differences apply to the development of precedents, a lawyer professional development program and the intranet.

KNOWLEDGE MANAGER	PROFESSIONAL SUPPORT LAWYER	INFORMATION OFFICER
Knowledge Management	Knowledge Creation	Knowledge Delivery
Defines knowledge management initiatives based on business needs of the group and coordinates the execution of knowledge management initiatives	Provides substantive content for knowledge management initiatives	Collects, packages and disseminates content
Develops and coordinates precedent drafting program	Drafts precedents	Publishes precedents
Develops lawyer professional development program	Drafts program materials	Publishes program materials and provides legal research links
Defines the purpose and content of the intranet page	Drafts intranet content	Maintains intranet content

Knowledge management system developer

The knowledge management system developer is responsible for
the technology elements of knowledge management at your firm.
The system developer works closely with the knowledge management organization and the IT department to:

♦ Design the knowledge management system (and
identify the components of the knowledge management system)

♦ Leverage existing technology tools

♦ Identify gaps and select new components of the
knowledge management system

♦ Implement the knowledge management system

The knowledge management system developer must understand the knowledge management requirements of lawyers and support staff, and how knowledge management technology solutions
can meet those requirements. The knowledge management system
developer is retained centrally, and typically has a dual reporting line
to the head of knowledge management and the director of IT.

★ ★ ★ ★

For each knowledge management role that you create at your
firm, you should draft a position description that outlines the role,
general responsibilities, specific tasks, professional experience, professional skills, personal skills and the reporting line. Where a
knowledge management position is created at the practice group
level, it is likely that the position description will differ across practice groups, since knowledge management needs differ across
practice groups. For example, a transaction-centric practice is
more likely to focus its knowledge management efforts on precedents. An advice-centric practice is more likely to focus its knowledge management efforts on best practice documents and current
awareness tools.

The box below is a sample position description for a knowledge manager at a firm with no professional support lawyers or information officers. It is a generic position description, applying to all areas of practice. At this firm, the knowledge manager is a practice group level role.

PRACTICE GROUP KNOWLEDGE MANAGER
POSITION DESCRIPTION

The Role

The practice group knowledge manager works within the firm-wide knowledge management organization and is responsible for:

- Developing knowledge management initiatives to meet the needs of his practice group within the framework of the firm knowledge management strategy
- Implementing firm-wide knowledge management initiatives in the practice group.

General responsibilities include:

- Assisting the practice group knowledge management partner in implementing knowledge management initiatives
- Identifying practice group knowledge needs
- Ensuring that practice group knowledge needs are being met
- Advocating the knowledge management needs of the practice group to the head of knowledge management

---

♦ Working closely with other members of the knowledge management organization to implement firm-wide knowledge management initiatives in a practice group, and share and leverage best practices

♦ Building wide user support among lawyers and staff.

Specific Tasks

♦ Attend all meetings of the practice group knowledge managers and related interest and focus groups.

♦ Meet regularly with the practice group knowledge management partner to review progress of knowledge management in the practice group.

♦ Report regularly to the head of knowledge management on the progress of implementing practice group and firm-wide knowledge management initiatives.

♦ Identify the knowledge management needs of the practice group in the context of meeting business objectives.

♦ Work with the head of knowledge management to identify initiatives that meet the knowledge management needs of the practice group.

♦ Define the business case for practice group knowledge management initiatives, including defining the business need, resources, timing, costs, critical success factors and criteria for measuring value.

♦ Implement practice group and firm-wide knowledge management initiatives in the practice group.

♦ Measure the value of knowledge management initiatives based on pre-defined criteria and demonstrate return on investment to the firm.

♦ Ensure that practice group knowledge management initiatives reflect the policies of the firm.

♦ Monitor external information sources and coordinate the collection, storage, retrieval and dissemination of legal, client and industry information to the practice and clients.

♦ Liaise with the library to ensure that print and electronic resources meet the research and current awareness needs of the practice group.

♦ Liaise with the legal research/work product repository group in the development of systems for the identification and collection of valuable work product.

♦ Liaise with the professional development group in the preparation and roll-out of professional development initiatives for the practice group.

- Liaise with the precedents group to manage practice group precedents — including review of existing precedents, modification to precedents, and identification and development of new precedents.
- Liaise with the intranet group in developing the practice group's intranet page and coordinating the identification, collection and publication of valuable content on the intranet.
- Liaise with the knowledge management system developer in developing the practice group elements of knowledge management technology tools.
- Collect and maintain information about the skills and expertise of all members of the practice group and assist the marketing group in collating and maintaining profiles and credentials for all lawyers in the practice group.
- Assist the marketing group in promoting knowledge management to clients in tenders and client presentations and collecting client information obtained by the practice group.
- Work with the head of knowledge management to identify opportunities to leverage knowledge management with clients in the form of client access to practice group initiatives and the development of client specific knowledge management products and services.

- ◆ Coordinate practice group continuing education meetings.
- ◆ Raise awareness among practice group staff about knowledge management.

Professional Experience

The knowledge manager should ideally be a lawyer with information management and business/work process analysis skills. The knowledge manager should have a strong interest in identifying better ways for lawyers to work through knowledge management. The knowledge manager should:

- ◆ Understand the work processes and knowledge needs of a wide range of aspects of legal practice.
- ◆ Understand that the scope of knowledge management involves management of explicit and tacit knowledge, and management of commercial and legal knowledge.
- ◆ Possess an applied understanding of how information management, information technology and organizational processes can be used to capture a law firm's intellectual capital.
- ◆ Understand the cultural aspects of knowledge management to facilitate knowledge sharing, innovative thinking and creativity.

While a background in law is necessary, it is not essential that the knowledge manager have extensive practice experience.

Professional Skills

The knowledge manager must be able to:

♦ Build wide user support among staff in his practice group.

♦ Work within a large multi-disciplinary knowledge management organization across several offices, areas of the business and practice groups to implement firm-wide knowledge management initiatives and to share best practices.

♦ Work closely with his knowledge management partner to understand the practice group's business objectives and to implement initiatives consistent with those business objectives and the firm's knowledge management strategy.

♦ Advocate the knowledge management needs of his practice group to the knowledge management organization and administrative functions.

♦ Understand how the information technology platform can be used to capture the firm's intellectual capital.

Personal Skills

To be an effective change agent, the knowledge manager must be a team player and possess an energetic personality, able to advocate the application and benefits of knowledge management to a broad range of users. Strong written and oral communication skills are essential. The candidate must be able to understand the business needs of the group and translate those needs into knowledge management initiatives. The candidate must be able to balance practice group and firm-wide priorities to further knowledge management initiatives. In order to engage staff at all levels, the candidate must have team building, leadership and motivation skills.

Reports

The knowledge manager will report directly to both the head of knowledge management and the practice group knowledge management partner.

Size of the Knowledge Management
Organization

A knowledge management organization needs sufficient dedicated resources to implement knowledge management initiatives. Where a knowledge management organization is small, firms tend to rely heavily on the input of practicing lawyers and paralegals. With the demands of client work, knowledge management tends to come second. Consequently, knowledge management initiatives often flounder.

While knowledge management is the responsibility of everyone at your firm, this does not mean that everyone brings the right skills to every step of the knowledge management process.

A lawyer will be the best person to create the raw material, but will not be the best person to package the content for future use.

The size of your knowledge management organization will largely depend on your firm's commitment to knowledge management. Among mature knowledge management organizations, the typical ratio is one knowledge management staff member to every 20 lawyers. A larger organization means less dependence on practicing lawyers and ensures that knowledge management receives the focus it needs.

Reporting Relationship Between Knowledge Management Staff and the Head of Knowledge Management

Earlier in this Chapter, I described how the best practice approach to knowledge management is one in which the firm sets the direction for knowledge management and provides an infrastructure to facilitate knowledge management among practice groups. This approach enables practice groups to achieve their knowledge management objectives while benefiting from a firm-wide strategy. To ensure a consistent firm-wide approach, knowledge management staff must work as a cohesive organization. There should be a direct reporting line between knowledge management staff and the head of knowledge management at your firm. Even where knowledge management staff are retained at the practice group level, it is key for the firm's consistent approach to knowledge management that all staff report to the same knowledge management head.

The Knowledge Management Organization in the Context of the Wider Firm

Knowledge management is central to the firm. To succeed, the knowledge management organization must engage the firm at all levels, including administrative functions.

The knowledge management organization must work closely with other administrative functions in a law firm for two key reasons:

♦ Functions outside of the knowledge management organization own critical knowledge that should be managed and leveraged across the firm.

♦ To implement initiatives across your firm, the knowledge management organization must be able to work closely with other functions.

The knowledge management organization must develop strong working relationships with key functions including IT, marketing, finance, human resources (and professional development if it does not form part of your knowledge management organization).

Relationship with information technology (IT)

While knowledge management is not purely information technology, your firm's technology platform plays a major role in supporting the capture and delivery of knowledge at your firm. Your knowledge management organization must have a close, formal working relationship with the IT function to ensure that you have the right technology tools, and that you use those tools appropriately to support knowledge management initiatives at your firm.

In particular, the knowledge management organization will work with IT to leverage the current technology platform, identify gaps and implement new knowledge management technology components. Ultimately, the knowledge management organization will work with IT to implement a knowledge management system that pulls together knowledge from different sources into a single user interface, as described in Chapter 7.

At many law firms, the IT department will also have knowledge management staff. The knowledge management system developer typically has a dual reporting line to the head of knowledge management and the director of IT.

Relationship with marketing

The marketing or business development function possesses critical knowledge about your firm's clients, your competitors and general industry developments. In preparing client proposals, it also gathers information about the skills and expertise of staff, and the firm's credentials. A strategic, business oriented law firm will see the value in sharing this knowledge beyond the marketing function.

Also, as your clients become more savvy about knowledge management, they will want to know about your firm's approach to knowledge management. The marketing function will increasingly play a role in promoting your approach to knowledge management to your clients.

Relationship with finance

The Finance department possesses critical elements of knowledge relating to the business of law. It is the chief source of knowledge relating to the firm's revenue, costs and profitability. It also stores critical information relating to the firm's clients, matters and practice groups in its systems. The firm can draw upon this information to develop its business strategy.

Relationship with human resources

A firm focusing on the capture of skills and expertise of staff will often find this information stored in the human resources information system. Also, the knowledge management organization must work closely with Human Resources to implement initiatives to support knowledge management, such as building knowledge management into compensation and performance evaluation criteria.

Relationship with professional development

Professional development is a critical element of knowledge management at law firms. Training initiatives are a principal knowledge delivery tool. Ideally, the professional development function should form part of the knowledge management organization. If it doesn't, then, at a minimum, a strong working relationship must develop between the knowledge management organization and professional development.

★ ★ ★ ★

Where the head of the knowledge management organization relies heavily on informal collaborative relationships with other functions, knowledge management initiatives may not have priority, and may not be implemented efficiently.

Where no direct reporting relationship exists, the head of the knowledge management organization should work with other functions in as formal an environment as possible. One effective means is by forming a committee, enabling different parts of the firm to exchange ideas and identify opportunities to implement knowledge management initiatives efficiently.

Embracing the involvement of all functions is crucial to the success of your knowledge management initiatives. Knowledge management is not the work of an isolated group. The firm that understands how knowledge management involves all aspects of its business and requires the input of all practice groups and administrative functions is the firm that will succeed at knowledge management.

The Knowledge Management Committee

To continually engage law firm staff in knowledge management, there should be a forum for representatives of practice groups and administrative areas to exchange ideas about knowledge management.

Creating a knowledge management committee can achieve the following:

♦ Eliminate the silo effect and duplication caused by many practice groups working in isolation

♦ Expedite knowledge management project implementation

♦ Identify opportunities to collaborate

♦ Ensure that knowledge management is consistently aligned with the firm's business objectives.

Composition

The typical knowledge management committee is composed of the head of knowledge management and staff representing a cross section of the firm. The committee should include partners representing the knowledge management needs of all practices and representatives of administrative functions, such as finance, marketing, professional development, human resources and IT.

Role

The purpose of the knowledge management committee should be to:

- ◆ Provide strategic direction
- ◆ Set policy
- ◆ Identify opportunities for practices and functions to collaborate on knowledge management initiatives
- ◆ Share best practices across the firm.

Separate from the Technology Committee

At some firms, the knowledge management committee operates as a sub-committee of the technology committee. This limits the knowledge management committee's ability to address the many non-technology aspects of knowledge management.

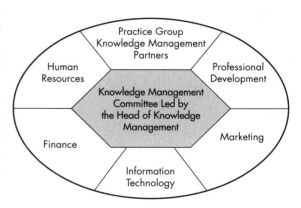

The Practice Group Knowledge
Management Partner

Many law firms have established the role of the practice group knowledge management partner. This partner is responsible for ensuring that the knowledge management needs of his practice group are met. This role is in addition to the partner's practice responsibilities.

Where the firm has a knowledge management committee, the practice group knowledge management partner is a member of that committee. Below is a sample role description for a practice group knowledge management partner.

PRACTICE GROUP KNOWLEDGE MANAGEMENT PARTNER
POSITION DESCRIPTION

The Role

The practice group knowledge management partner works within the knowledge management organization and is responsible for:

- ◆ Determining the knowledge management needs of his practice group within the framework of the firm's knowledge management strategy.
- ◆ Facilitating implementation of firm -wide and practice group knowledge management initiatives in the practice group.
- ◆ Liaising with the knowledge management organization to ensure that his practice group's knowledge management needs are addressed by the knowledge management organization.
- ◆ Directing a knowledge manager responsible for development of knowledge management initiatives within his practice group.

Specific Tasks

♦ Attend all meetings of the knowledge management committee.

♦ Meet regularly with the practice group knowledge manager to review progress of knowledge management in the practice group.

♦ Report regularly to the practice group head and the firm knowledge management partner on the progress of implementing practice group and firm-wide knowledge management initiatives in the practice group.

♦ Identify the knowledge management needs of the practice group in the context of meeting business objectives.

♦ Work with the practice group knowledge manager to identify initiatives that meet the knowledge management needs of the practice group.

♦ Review the business cases for practice group knowledge management initiatives, including defining the business need, resources, timing, costs, critical success factors and criteria for measuring value.

♦ Articulate the practice group's knowledge management needs to the firm knowledge management partner.

♦ Facilitate the implementation of practice group and firm-wide knowledge management initiatives in the practice group.

- Measure the value of knowledge management initiatives based on pre-defined criteria and demonstrate return on investment to the firm.
- Ensure that practice group knowledge management initiatives reflect the policies of the firm.
- Work with the knowledge management organization to identify opportunities to leverage knowledge management with clients.
- Raise awareness among practice group staff about knowledge management.

Personal Skills

To be an effective change agent, the practice group knowledge management partner should be a partner who is well respected by his practice group. The partner must possess an energetic personality, able to advocate the application and benefits of knowledge management to a broad range of users. He must understand the business needs of the group and communicate those needs to the knowledge manager and other members of the knowledge management organization. The practice group knowledge management partner must be able to balance practice group and firm-wide priorities to progress knowledge management initiatives. The partner must have a firm-wide perspective and understand that it is critical to share best practices across different practice groups.

Reports

The practice group knowledge management partner advises both the practice group head and the firm knowledge management partner on the progress of knowledge management in the practice group.

Time

The time commitment of a practice group knowledge management partner will vary depending on the stage of his practice group's knowledge management initiatives, but should be in the range of five to eight hours per week.

Career Path and Compensation Model for Knowledge Management Staff

Building a knowledge management organization requires significant investment by your law firm. Once you have recruited dedicated knowledge management staff, you need to develop and retain those people so that your firm benefits from that investment in the short and long term.

Professional support lawyers are often drawn from the ranks of practicing lawyers in a firm. In the past, making the switch from practice to knowledge management was regarded as a softer option, requiring fewer hours and less pressure. It was not uncommon for professional support lawyer compensation to be lower than that of a practicing lawyer. The reasons for this included perceived better quality of life such as part time hours and job flexibility. However, many firms offering a lower salary to professional support lawyers experienced difficulty in attracting high quality candidates to the professional support lawyer role. This suggests that better quality of life may not be enough for a lawyer to accept a reduction in salary.

There was also little focus on building a career path for professional support lawyers and other knowledge management staff.

With the development of knowledge management organizations at law firms, this is changing. Knowledge management is no longer viewed as a soft option for practicing lawyers. While practicing lawyers will continue to make the switch to knowledge management, they will have to acquire new skills to perform their new roles.

If your firm is going to invest in building a knowledge management organization, you should look for ways to develop your knowledge management staff and create an environment that rewards (and does not punish) the choice to pursue a career in knowledge management. The way you compensate knowledge management staff reflects the value you place on knowledge management at your firm.

Over time, as your knowledge management organization matures, and your knowledge management staff build on their expertise in this area, you will need to create a career path for your knowledge management staff. Like your lawyers, if you do not offer a career path, your knowledge management staff will leave—and take their valuable know-how with them.

Develop Your Knowledge Management
Organization

To develop your knowledge management organization, follow these steps:

1. Have you appointed a head of knowledge management:
   Director?
   Partner?
   Director and partner?

2. Does the head of knowledge management report directly to senior management?

3. In creating your knowledge management organization:
   (a) which existing functions form part of the knowledge management organization?
   Library
   Legal research
   Precedents
   Intranet
   Professional development
   (b) which new roles have been created?
   Knowledge manager
   Professional support lawyer
   Information officer
   Knowledge management system developer

4. Have you developed strong working relationships between the knowledge management organization and other key functions?
   Human resources
   Marketing/business development
   Information technology
   Finance
   Professional development

5. Have you formed a knowledge management committee?

6. Have you appointed practice group knowledge management partners?

7. Have you developed a career path for knowledge management staff?

Creating a Knowledge Management Culture

Chapter Contents

The Director of Information Technology and Head Librarian of a law firm form a knowledge management committee and develop the firm's knowledge management strategy. The committee presents the strategy to management, who pay scant attention to it. Believing strongly in the benefits knowledge management will bring to the firm, the knowledge management committee decides to pursue initiatives by finding a few enthusiastic partners to sponsor the initiatives at the firm. Management has little involvement. The knowledge management committee hopes that by working with a few partners, it will develop knowledge management "champions" who will infuse the rest of the firm with their enthusiasm.

The knowledge management committee has difficulty finding its champions. The firm's business model is based on the billable hour. The partners fear that knowledge management could actually decrease the firm's revenues, since lawyers will spend less time on their work, and therefore bill less for their work. The partners simply cannot see how knowledge management will help increase revenue or profitability.

Further, since partner and lawyer compensation is closely tied to the number of hours billed, there is little room for lawyers to invest non-billable time in developing content for knowledge management initiatives.

Since management is not involved in implementing knowledge management, it has not provided the committee with additional funding. This means that no dedicated resources can be hired. Instead, the committee must rely on existing staff finding time in addition to their current workload to implement knowledge management at the firm. Progress is slow, since staff can only work on knowledge management in their spare time. Progress is limited, since staff do not have all the necessary knowledge management skills.

Despite these barriers, the knowledge management committee decides to institute knowledge management initiatives with a few partners. These initiatives are practice group specific and the committee works closely with a partner and staff in the practice groups. Since partners receive no billing relief, they must either fit in their knowledge management commitments around their full workload, or sacrifice some of their billable hours to invest in knowledge management. This could affect their compensation, though the partners hope management will acknowledge their contribution to the firm in this area.

Initially, it is easy to find enthusiastic lawyers to work on their practice group knowledge management initiatives. However, these lawyers soon discover that their compensation and career progression are closely tied to the number of their billable hours. With no recognition or reward for their efforts, lawyers resent having to contribute any substantive time to knowledge management.

Nevertheless, the committee quickly identifies similar knowledge management needs across a number of practice groups, and recommends firm-wide initiatives that involve lawyers sharing knowledge across practice groups. In theory, the initiatives should help the firm to leverage its knowledge across all practice groups. However, the committee finds little interest among the practice groups for these firm-wide initiatives, and in some cases, encounters strong resistance from the groups.

On closer examination, the committee learns that partner compensation is based on a combination of their individual and practice group performance. Partners receive no financial incentive for referring work to colleagues in other practice groups. Indeed, some practice groups overlap in their practices, and may compete with each other in the market.

Despite the best efforts of the knowledge management committee, and the enthusiasm of some partners, knowledge management never gets off the ground. Most practice groups never understand why knowledge management is critical to the firm. Management remains uninvolved and never embraces knowledge management as a key business driver, which will help the firm achieve its business objectives.

The firm culture provides no incentive to work more efficiently, and to pursue knowledge management efforts that promote efficiency. The few enthusiastic partners who were meant to be the knowledge management champions lose interest over time. They are not rewarded or acknowledged for their knowledge management efforts. They receive no billing relief or credit for their efforts. Indeed, some are actually penalized for their efforts in the form of lower compensation when their billable hours drop.

The firm fails to acknowledge the value of working more efficiently. Its revenue model, compensation system and career progression model all support inefficient work practices. There is no incentive for staff to reduce the time spent on work, or to look for opportunities to work with other practice groups.

Management's lack of vision means that the firm misses out on opportunities to increase revenue, decrease costs, increase profitability and achieve many of its other business objectives.

Knowledge management is about finding more efficient ways to work in order to increase revenue, decrease costs and ultimately increase the profitability of your firm. However, the traditional time-based billing model of a law firm encourages lawyers to work inefficiently. The longer it takes to do work, the greater the revenue will be for your firm.

Law firms have managed to be highly profitable under this business model in the past. There is, however, one major drawback of this business model. Revenue only grows if the number of fee-earning people in your firm grows. In other words, the ratio of revenue:staff never changes.

Knowledge management is about seeking ways to change that ratio, so that your fee-earning staff generate greater revenues, reduce costs and ultimately generate greater profits for your firm. To achieve this, law firms must first commit to alternative billing systems.

Knowledge management also requires significant investment and a long term strategy. The traditional law firm business model is a short term business model, requiring little investment. Committing to finding more efficient ways to work and investing in knowledge management is counter-intuitive to the traditional law firm business model.

There are many other cultural barriers to knowledge management. Some of these cultural barriers are broader than knowledge management and go to the heart of how a law firm operates. These cultural barriers do not just hamper knowledge management. They limit your law firm's ability to achieve its business objectives.

The current law firm culture tends to penalize contribution to knowledge management by not acknowledging time spent on knowledge management in staff performance and compensation reviews. Your firm must first focus on rewarding contribution to knowledge management. Over time, you should work toward a culture where contribution is simply a given. When you reach this point, you will know you have succeeded at creating the right culture for knowledge management—and for the growth of your law firm.

The target knowledge management culture is one in which staff are expected to share knowledge and contribute to knowledge management initiatives at your firm. Ultimately, there should be no need to reward your staff for contributing to knowledge management. Instead, it should be viewed as a negative if staff do not contribute to knowledge management. While this is your goal, law firms have a long way to go in achieving this culture.

There are three parts to this Chapter. In the first part, I describe the cultural barriers to knowledge management in law firms. I also describe why the law firm culture is conducive to knowledge management and why it is worth pursuing knowledge management at your firm. In the second part, I describe the knowledge management culture you should seek to achieve. In the third part of this Chapter, I present a number of ways to address cultural barriers to knowledge management. The goal is to develop a culture in which knowledge management is not just rewarded, but expected, and where there are no internal barriers to the growth in your firm's profitability.

The Time-Based Billing Model

The time-based billing model is probably the single greatest barrier to knowledge management for two reasons:

1. Billing by the hour is an incentive to work as inefficiently as possible, while knowledge management is all about working more efficiently. If law firms continue to bill by the hour, there is simply no incentive to reduce the time spent on specific tasks.

2. Since billing time is the only way staff can generate revenue, there is no incentive to invest in non-billable activities.

Under the time-based billing model, it makes no sense to spend non-billable time on knowledge management when the end result is an ability to perform work in a shorter time frame, thus generating lower revenues.

However, there are some fundamental flaws with the time-based billing model:

1. **It assumes that clients will continue to pay for inefficient work practices.** I suggested in Chapter 1 that as law departments become increasingly sophisticated in their management of outside counsel, they will become less tolerant of paying for inefficient work practices. In other words, clients will increasingly demand higher value work at a lower cost.

2. **It means that your firm's revenue will always be limited by the number of fee-earning staff you employ.** As you continue to add to your firm's infrastructure, you will never increase the ratio of revenue:staff.

3. **It leaves no room for investment in the future growth of the firm.** The time-based billing model is essentially a short-term and short-sighted business model. Staff are focused on reacting to their current client needs. There is little focus on the future growth of the firm, such as developing new client relationships or developing innovative services to meet the future needs of clients. The danger is that while your firm focuses solely on its current client work, your competitors may be taking a longer-term strategic approach and developing proactive and innovative legal services to meet changing client needs.

4. **It creates an unsatisfying work environment for your staff.** Under this model, staff are rewarded on the basis of quantity, rather than the quality of their work. They are literally rewarded for working as inefficiently as possible. However, a law firm is a learning environment, filled with highly intelligent people who need to be constantly engaged in the pursuit of more knowledge in order to remain motivated. Which lawyer wants to be handling the same matters for twenty years? Which lawyer wants to work around the clock on a task that could easily be handled by a more junior staff member in half the time?

5. **It does not leverage your law firm's senior staff.** This point is connected to the two points above. Under the sliding scale of a law firm's hourly rates, your senior partners generate significantly more revenue per hour than your junior staff. This is an incentive for senior lawyers to bill as many hours as possible, rather than delegating work and focusing on building your client base. Your partners would probably be delegating more work and doing more client relationship building (and generate more revenue for your firm) if there were less emphasis on the number of hours each partner billed.

Shifting to a value-based billing model

What if you could charge for work on the basis of its value to your client? Value-based billing is not about reducing the revenue generated by your firm, and it is certainly not about reducing your firm's profitability. It is about agreeing with your client on a appropriate fee for a given piece of work and then working as efficiently as possible to increase your revenue:staff ratio. The following example illustrates this.

A real estate group in a medium size law firm drafts and negotiates leases for a major property client of the firm. Last year, the firm handled 80 leases for the client. The firm charges by the hour and the cost of drafting and negotiating each lease ranged between $5,000 and $7,500. The client wants more certainty in its external legal costs and requests that the firm fix its cost per lease at $5,000. The client estimates that it will send 200 leases per year to the firm under a fixed fee arrangement.

The partners agree to this arrangement, realizing that the firm's revenue will grow by between $400,000 and $600,000 with the increased number of leases sent to their firm. Their first incentive is to ensure that they work efficiently enough to spend no more than $5,000 of their time on each lease. The second incentive is to reduce that amount of time even further, in order to increase their profit margin on each lease.

Through the development of precedents and methodologies, the partners are able to delegate work to more junior lawyers. This requires an investment of $75,000 in partner time to develop the precedents and methodologies.

At the end of the first year, the firm has handled 200 leases at $5,000 each, generating revenue of $1,000,000. The partners analyze the cost per lease based on the time spent drafting and negotiating each lease. They realize that the cost has dropped to $3,000. If the firm billed based on the time spent on each lease, it would have billed $600,000. For an initial investment of $75,000, the firm has billed $400,000 more under a fixed fee arrangement, than under a time-based billing model.

There is an additional revenue benefit flowing from the introduction of a more efficient lease process. With the reduction in partner time spent on each lease, partners have more time to focus on additional client opportunities.

Moving away from the time-based billing model is not just the domain of the commoditized legal practice. Any practice, no matter how unique, has some degree of repetition. A mergers and acquisition practice group that acted for five major clients in a given year can analyze the cost of each matter and the similarities between the matters—and estimate the cost of handling a matter in the future.

Clients want to understand the cost of the transaction as early as possible—and this includes knowing what the legal costs associated with the transaction will be. Consider the following example:

The mergers and acquisitions group of a firm agrees to handle the legal work relating to the potential acquisition of a company for its client for a fee of $100,000. The client is willing to pay this fee since if the deal succeeds, it predicts its market value will soar.

The partners agreed to this fee based on an analysis of the cost of handling five similar transactions in the past year. While the partners are confident that their analysis is accurate, they know that they must carefully manage this matter and not blow out the budget.

Through careful project management, use of knowledge management tools such as precedent documents and methodologies, and more efficient use of staff, the group stays well within budget. The client successfully acquires the company and as predicted, its market value soars. The client is delighted with the result and particularly with the work of the law firm.

At the end of the matter, the partners analyze the real cost of handling this transaction. If the firm had billed the client by the hour, the cost of the matter would have been $65,000. Since the client agreed that the value of this work was $100,000, the difference of $35,000 is pure profit for the firm.

Shifting to a value-based model frees the firm to find more efficient ways to work, and therefore increase profitability based on level of efficiency.

Other Major Cultural Barriers

There are other cultural barriers to knowledge management in addition to the time-based billing model.

Partner compensation models that reward the individual, not the firm

The partner compensation model of a law firm strongly influences the culture of a firm. There are two prevalent partner compensation models in law firms—*the revenue-based compensation model and the lock-step compensation model.*

In a *revenue-based compensation model,* a partner's compensation is almost solely determined by the amount of revenue generated by the partner. This model is designed to encourage partners to be entrepreneurs and grow their businesses. Under this model, the partners are almost solely focused on growing the profits of their own practices, rather than growing the profits of the entire firm. Practice groups tend to operate as separate business units which just happen to share the cost of a common infrastructure.

Since partner compensation is based on the revenue generated (and under a time-based billing model, by the number of hours billed), there is simply no incentive to invest in non-billable activities, and certainly not in finding more efficient ways to work.

There is also no incentive to share work with others, since there is usually no reward for referring work to colleagues. This is particularly incongruous to a multi-disciplinary law firm, which markets itself to clients as a provider of services across a range of practice areas. Why would a corporate lawyer refer work to a tax lawyer if the corporate lawyer receives no financial benefit from that referral? Yet, doesn't a client expect that its corporate lawyer would refer work to the tax lawyer if that lawyer could better handle the matter?

The revenue-based compensation model may breed entrepreneurs, but why be part of a larger firm if you're not going to use it to your advantage? Law firms carry tremendous overheads. Lawyers should be seeking ways to gain the maximum benefit from paying for those overheads. Focusing on the profitability of the individual rather than the firm usually means that partners do not derive the rewards that come from working in a massive infrastructure.

Under a *lock-step compensation model,* the profits of the firm are pooled and then distributed based on seniority and overall contribution to the firm. Revenue generated directly by a partner is just one criterion in assessing overall contribution. Other criteria may include contributing to knowledge management or business development at the firm. Under this model, partners are forced to think as a firm, not just as individuals. If a lock-step compensation model operates well, it should create an incentive for partners to seek out ways to grow the firm, and to leverage the massive infrastructure that the partners must pay for.

Limited interaction between practice groups

In a large, multi-disciplinary practice, it is not unusual to find very little interaction between practice groups. This is especially true in law firms with a revenue-based compensation model, where partners are only focused on growing their own practices. When lawyers do not see the value of sharing knowledge outside of their practice group, they are limiting the firm's growth opportunities. It is very difficult to implement firm-wide knowledge management initiatives. In this environment, lawyers are simply not interested in exploring opportunities outside of their practice group.

Overlap in areas of practice between lawyers in different practice groups

This is often the result of the limited interaction between practice groups. When different practice groups are handling similar matters, they may be competing with each other in the market. This means that the groups are even more unwilling to share their knowledge. There may also be risk management implications for the firm if different practice groups take different approaches to the same piece of work.

Knowledge is power

There is a high degree of competitiveness among individuals and practice groups at many law firms. Lawyers perceive that to become partners, they must amass a unique knowledge base. To keep this knowledge unique, they must not share it with others. In a "knowledge is power" culture, lawyers think knowledge management means losing one's unique knowledge base, and therefore, one's power base. Of course, this defeats the purpose of building a large, multi-disciplinary law firm in which lawyers leverage the skills of others to deliver the best solution to their clients. Knowledge management assumes a willingness to share knowledge.

"Our work is unique and is of no value to others"

This is a variation on "knowledge is power." Lawyers believe that each piece of work is so uniquely crafted for each client, that it could not possibly have any future application to other clients or circumstances. This is a fallacy. All legal work involves a certain degree of repetition, no matter how unique. Once lawyers realize this, they will look for opportunities to find more efficient ways to handle the repetitive elements of their work.

There are also lessons learned from each piece of work that could have a broader application to the practice group and the firm. When lawyers understand this, they will begin to share lessons learned with their group and the firm.

Fear of peer judgment

Lawyers confidently draft work product for clients, but are often reticent about sharing their work product with their peers. They fear that their peers will judge their work as inferior. This fear factor may hamper a lawyer's willingness to share work product with others in the firm.

A decentralized culture

Where a firm with multiple offices has a decentralized culture, it is difficult to implement a firm-wide approach to knowledge management. Consequently, knowledge management initiatives tend to succeed in small pockets of the firm—but the firm never gains the full benefit knowledge management can bring to the firm.

Differences in regional cultures

Like a decentralized culture, different regional cultures challenge a firm's ability to implement firm-wide initiatives. Without a consistent approach to knowledge management, firms usually experience inconsistent levels of knowledge management across different offices. This makes it difficult to move lawyers across different offices. From a risk management perspective, it may also mean inconsistencies in the quality of work sent to clients.

Global law firms should pay careful attention to understanding how each office works, how it interacts with its clients, and what its business objectives are. In particular, the firm's approach to knowledge management must meet the needs of different cultures while achieving the firm's overall business and knowledge management objectives.

Limited training and mentoring of junior lawyers

Some law firms recruit young lawyers, pay them large salaries, and do nothing to develop their skills. Without training junior lawyers, firms often do not derive the return on their recruiting investment. When law firms do not offer adequate training and mentoring of junior lawyers, the following usually occurs:

1. The quality of legal work produced by poorly trained lawyers is low.

2. Partners do not feel confident delegating work to junior staff and thus carry the burden of doing the work themselves.

3. Lawyers realize they are not developing their skills, grow dissatisfied and leave the firm.

4. The firm loses its lawyers before they become profitable, and does not derive the return on their initial investment.

Lack of senior management support

If senior management does not understand the value of knowledge management, it will not support knowledge management—nor will the rest of your firm. Senior management must be engaged in knowledge management—not just understand it, but invest in it and constantly reinforce the message that knowledge management is key to how you work at your firm.

Knowledge management is perceived as the work of an isolated group

In some firms, management has appointed a Director of Knowledge Management and rebranded the library as "Knowledge Management" or created a knowledge management function within the IT department. There is no expectation for staff across the practice groups and administrative functions to get involved in knowledge management. Without the contribution of all staff to knowledge management, your firm will fail in its knowledge management efforts.

Knowledge management is perceived as an IT initiative

If knowledge management is synonymous with IT, staff think that this is about developing databases. At these firms, it is a challenge to make lawyers understand that this is more than IT. Although the IT department can build some of the tools to capture and disseminate knowledge, without the involvement of staff to develop content and implement non-technology knowledge management processes, knowledge management will have a very limited scope, impact and life span.

Staff are not rewarded or acknowledged for their knowledge management efforts

This issue is directly related to the time-based billing model. Since lawyers are expected to bill as many hours as possible, there is simply no room for knowledge management. If there is no acknowledgement in lawyer performance assessment or compensation review, lawyers get the message very quickly that this work is not valued.

Knowledge management is perceived as a soft option

This is often a barrier faced by lawyers who decide to pursue a career in knowledge management as an alternative to the traditional practice of law. There are two illustrations of this cultural mindset. The first is the law firm that pays its lawyers working in knowledge management less than practicing lawyers. The second is the law firm that recruits lawyers with no appropriate knowledge management skills into knowledge management roles. These two illustrations send a message that knowledge management is not valued at the firm.

Practice groups that believe their knowledge needs are unique and will not benefit from a firm-wide approach to knowledge management

This is often prevalent in law firms where some practice groups have developed knowledge management initiatives before the firm focuses on knowledge management. Since these groups have invested in knowledge management, they feel a strong sense of ownership. Because they have had complete freedom in developing their knowledge management solutions to meet their knowledge needs, they may be less willing to adopt a firm-wide approach to knowledge management. They are likely to argue that their knowledge needs are unique, and that they will not benefit from an overall knowledge management strategy.

Indeed, the firm should look carefully at the work of these practice groups—and ensure that any firm-wide approach to knowledge management gives appropriate recognition to these practice group knowledge management initiatives. The firm must also ensure that in allowing practice groups to address their knowledge management needs, they use firm-wide best practice processes and systems where appropriate.

These cultural barriers to knowledge management limit the growth and profitability of your law firm. Overcoming them is fundamental to your firm's future success.

Why the Law Firm Culture Is Conducive to Knowledge Management

Given the number of cultural barriers to knowledge management in law firms, you may be wondering whether it is really worth tackling knowledge management at your firm. Apart from the obvious benefits knowledge management brings to your firm, there are elements of the law firm culture that are actually conducive to knowledge management, as follows:

- The legal services market is a knowledge-based market.
- A law firm is a learning organization.
- The law is constantly evolving, requiring lawyers to stay abreast of frequent changes to laws and regulations.

The legal services market is a knowledge-based market

Lawyers sell their knowledge. This is their only product. Knowledge management is about leveraging that product so that the firm can derive as much value from that product as possible.

A law firm is a learning organization

Lawyers are intelligent, academically minded people who crave the acquisition of new skills and expertise throughout their careers. Leading law firms encourage their lawyers to learn new skills to become the market leading experts in their practice area. These firms invest significantly in lawyer training and mentoring programs. In some respects, a law firm is an extension of law school.

Knowledge management relies on the willingness of staff to acquire knowledge, and leverage that knowledge across an organization.

The law is constantly evolving

It is a constant challenge for lawyers to keep up with the frequent changes to laws and regulations in their practice area. In some practices, the changes can be simply overwhelming. Lawyers must find a way to acquire knowledge about changes to the law in order to maintain their practices.

Knowledge management enables lawyers to manage the process of acquiring the barrage of new knowledge they face every day of their practicing lives.

The Target Knowledge Management Culture

Ultimately, there should be no need for your firm to reward its people for their knowledge management efforts. Instead, their contribution to knowledge management should be expected.

You should aim to create a culture in which lawyers:

- ♦ Share their knowledge with others in their practice group and across the firm.

- ♦ Look for opportunities to refer work to others and to collaborate on projects.

- ♦ Seek out skills and expertise from others in the firm.

- Think like a firm, not like a practice group.

- Are proactive and strategic, not reactive.

- Seek out ways to work more efficiently.

- Think of your law firm as a business, and seek out ways to use their knowledge to grow that business.

- Value investment in the future.

- Continually raise the bar of legal excellence at your firm.

- Commit to creating a more dynamic learning environment.

Given the number of cultural barriers to knowledge management prevalent in law firms today, it will take several years for most law firms to achieve the target knowledge management culture.

Addressing Cultural Barriers

Identifying cultural barriers is the first step

In order to address cultural barriers to knowledge management, you must first identify what those barriers are. This sounds so obvious, yet many law firms do not take the time during the knowledge management planning stage to consider the scope of cultural barriers the firm faces. These firms know that there are some cultural barriers, though they do not have a clear understanding of the breadth and depth of those barriers. Consequently, firms are placed in a reactive position, left to address cultural barriers as they appear. Typically, the cultural barrier is clouded in high emotion, and addressing the barrier seems insurmountable. Staff affected by this barrier may feel frustrated, disenchanted and in the end, defeated.

By being clear at the outset on the range of cultural barriers to knowledge management, you can plan how best to tackle them. Understanding the breadth and scope of those barriers will also impact your knowledge management strategy. The more complex the barrier, the longer it will take to address. For example, revamping the partner compensation model is usually a huge undertaking and may take some time. On the other hand, building knowledge management into partner and practice group business plans should be quite straightforward.

There may be other circumstances that affect the firm's priority in addressing certain cultural barriers. For example, if a firm is undergoing a major organizational review involving the reshuffling of practice groups, you may not be able to address cultural barriers involving practice group interaction until that review is completed.

The key is to understand the environment in which you operate. This means understanding the cultural barriers to knowledge management, and the order in which those barriers can be addressed.

Management must be in front of, and behind cultural change

One of the cultural barriers described earlier in this Chapter is the lack of senior management support. This is the first barrier the firm must address.

Without management support and commitment, the knowledge management organization will simply be left to work around these cultural barriers. Nevertheless, management's failure to adequately address cultural barriers will ultimately limit the effectiveness of a firm's knowledge management efforts. There are three elements of management's involvement in overcoming the cultural barriers to knowledge management.

Management must tell the firm that knowledge management is a business imperative. The role of your knowledge management organization is to present a case to management on how knowledge management can help drive the achievement of your firm's business objectives. Unless management understands that knowledge management is about achieving the firm's business objectives, you will not have its full attention.

Once management understands that knowledge management is a key business driver, it must relay that message to the rest of the firm.

Management must make knowledge management a top priority and make a substantial financial investment in knowledge management. This means creating a knowledge management budget (separate from the library or IT budget). It also means funding dedicated knowledge management resources and giving billing credit to fee earners working on knowledge management initiatives.

Management must adopt specific initiatives to overcome cultural barriers. Some cultural barriers will be complex and so deep-rooted that it takes several years and strong commitment to overcome them. Others will be relatively straightforward.

The best way to overcome cultural barriers is to take the following approach:

1. The firm identifies the cultural barrier.

2. Management sends a clear message about the cultural behavior it expects.

3. Management supports its message through the adoption of specific initiatives to overcome the cultural barrier and reach the target culture.

Put simply, the methodology is to identify the barrier, send a message about the target culture, and support the message with substantive actions to remove the barrier and achieve the target culture.

BARRIER ⟹ MESSAGE ⟹ ACTION

Many of these substantive actions involve building knowledge management into the firm's business processes. This means building knowledge management into your firm's:

♦ Compensation system

♦ Budgeting system

♦ Billing system

♦ Career progression model

♦ Business plans

♦ Management reporting

Compensation system. In a firm where staff compensation is based solely on the number of hours billed, there is no room for non-billable, investment time spent on knowledge management. To acknowledge that knowledge management is an important contribution to your firm, staff must be rewarded not only for the number of hours they bill, but for the contribution they make to their practice group and your firm through their knowledge management efforts. Making knowledge management a criterion in the assessment of staff compensation is crucial.

Budgeting system. Knowledge management requires significant investment to be successful. Your firm's budgeting system should allow for investment in knowledge management. Ideally, your firm should establish a separate knowledge management budget. Investment in knowledge management should also be reflected in partner, practice group and administrative function budgets.

Billing system. Your firm should address whether it encourages practice groups to work with each other. The true value of working in a multi-disciplinary law firm is the opportunities it creates for lawyers to collaborate on multi-disciplinary matters. From a risk management perspective, partners should refer work to colleagues who possess more appropriate expertise in a particular area. Partners should be rewarded for this, receiving billing credit for referring work to others.

Career progression. When fee-earning staff perceive that their career progression is solely based on the number of hours they bill, non-billable activities will always take second place. If your firm believes that knowledge management is key to its future success and states that it places high value on the contribution of staff to knowledge management, it must acknowledge the contribution of staff as a criterion in career progression.

Business plans. Your knowledge management strategy should reflect your firm's business strategy. In turn, your firm's business plans—whether they be practice group, partner or administrative function business plans—should acknowledge how knowledge management will help achieve your firm's business objectives.

Management reporting. Partners, practice groups and administrative functions should be held accountable for their knowledge management efforts. Knowledge management related activities should be highlighted to management through your firm's reporting mechanisms.

Illustrating How to Address Cultural Barriers

The following table illustrates the application of the barrier/message/action methodology for addressing cultural barriers to knowledge management. Just as the earlier list of cultural barriers is not an exhaustive list, this table does not provide all the answers for how to overcome cultural barriers to knowledge management at your firm. My purpose is simply to demonstrate how straightforward the process should be if your firm is really committed to knowledge management.

BARRIER	MESSAGE	ACTION
The time-based billing model.	The firm is committed to adopting alternatives to the time-based billing model.	Conduct market research on what other billing models clients want. Estimate the average cost of conducting core matters. Adopt alternative billing models, e.g., premium billing or flat fee arrangements, where appropriate.
Partner compensation models that reward focus on the individual, not the firm.	The firm is committed to building a knowledge-sharing environment and leveraging the multi-disciplinary nature of our firm.	Make knowledge sharing within and across practice groups an important factor in the measurement of partner compensation. Reward partners for referring work to others. Provide billing relief for partners to pursue specific knowledge management initiatives that add value to your firm. (Treat knowledge management initiatives as though they are client matters.)
Knowledge is power.	Our firm believes sharing knowledge is more powerful.	Acknowledge contribution to knowledge management in the partner and lawyer compensation systems. Acknowledge contribution to knowledge management in the lawyer career progression model.

BARRIER	MESSAGE	ACTION
"Our work is unique and is of no value to others."	We can all learn from every matter handled by our firm, no matter how unique.	Conduct process mapping: ♦ Identify specific repetitive work processes that could be handled more efficiently. ♦ Map the process steps. ♦ Identify knowledge associated with each process step. ♦ Articulate the process and design a system to enable more efficient work processes and delivery of service to clients. Conduct post-matter debriefing sessions to identify knowledge acquired during a matter that could have broader application to the way the firm conducts future matters. Capture a summary of completed matters in the knowledge management system.
Fear of peer judgment.	We should leverage our client work product by sharing it with others.	Acknowledge contribution of work product to the firm's knowledge management system in the compensation system and career progression model.

BARRIER	MESSAGE	ACTION
A decentralized culture/differences in regional cultures.	We take a firm-wide approach to knowledge management, which acknowledges the needs of different cultures and achieves our firm's business and knowledge management objectives.	Understand the knowledge needs of each practice group across all offices and develop a firm-wide knowledge management strategy that meets the needs of all practice groups and offices. Include knowledge management as a criterion in the compensation system and career progression model in all practice groups and regions. Introduce knowledge management as a topic in partner, practice group and regional reports. Develop a core set of knowledge management requirements for all practice groups and regions.
Limited interaction between practice groups.	We act as one firm and leverage the multi-disciplinary nature of our practice.	Amend the compensation system and billing system to reward sharing work between practice groups. Invest in knowledge management initiatives that promote knowledge sharing across practice groups, e.g., coordinate the drafting of national precedents that are relevant to multiple practice groups.

BARRIER	MESSAGE	ACTION
Overlap in areas of practice between lawyers in different practice groups.	We act as one firm and leverage the multi-disciplinary nature of our practice.	Amend the compensation system and billing system to reward sharing work between practice groups. Identify knowledge management opportunities involving multiple practice groups and provide funding for the development of cross-practice group knowledge management initiatives. Share best practice knowledge management systems and methodologies between practice groups.
Limited training and mentoring of lawyers.	We are committed to creating market leading lawyers.	Enhance systems and programs to train partners and lawyers in areas of practice. Develop a mentoring program for lawyers. Acknowledge contribution to training and developing others in the compensation system and career progression model. Give partners and lawyers fee relief for time spent on developing and delivering training programs.

BARRIER	MESSAGE	ACTION
Knowledge management is perceived as the work of an isolated group.	Knowledge management is the responsibility of everyone.	Build knowledge management into the compensation system, career progression model, budgeting system, business plans and reporting system.
Staff are not rewarded or acknowledged for their knowledge management efforts.	Staff are expected to contribute to knowledge management.	Build knowledge management into the compensation system, career progression model, budgeting system, business plans and reporting system.
Knowledge management is perceived as an IT initiative.	Knowledge management is key to our business. It involves technology and non-technology systems and processes to leverage our knowledge.	Adopt a wide scope of knowledge management. Raise staff awareness about the scope of knowledge management. Provide funding for non-technology and technology knowledge management initiatives. Develop a knowledge management organization, separate from the IT department.
Knowledge management is perceived as a soft option.	We are committed to developing the leading knowledge management organization.	Recruit staff with appropriate knowledge management skills. Compensate knowledge management staff equivalent to, or higher than, the market rate. Compensate professional support lawyers equivalent to practicing lawyers. Develop a career path for knowledge management staff.

BARRIER	MESSAGE	ACTION
Practice groups that believe their knowledge needs are unique and will not benefit from a firm wide approach to knowledge management.	Our firm takes a strategic firm wide approach to knowledge management, acknowledging that the differing needs of our practice groups can best be met under the umbrella of a firm-wide knowledge management strategy.	Develop a firm wide knowledge management strategy. Examine practice group approaches to knowledge management and identify and leverage best practices. Define a core set of knowledge management requirements that all practice groups and regions must meet.

Knowledge Management Must Reflect the Culture of the Firm

My focus in this Chapter has been on identifying and addressing the fundamental cultural barriers that will hinder the best intentioned knowledge management efforts from succeeding. While it is critical that you identify and address these barriers, you should not ignore the fundamental culture of your law firm. There will clearly be elements of your firm's culture that make it a successful firm.

Making cultural change is not about dumbing down your culture—or compromising how you do things. It is about understanding what your cultural strengths and weaknesses are—and addressing those weaknesses.

Where a strength of your firm is its emphasis on encouraging individual thinking, you should encourage that individuality. While the firm will expect lawyers to contribute to practice group and firm-wide knowledge management initiatives, it will also encourage informal knowledge sharing networks.

Where a strength of your firm is its emphasis on practice group needs, allow practice groups to determine their knowledge needs under the umbrella of a firm-wide approach to knowledge management.

If your firm is a global law firm with a decentralized culture, respect the regional differences in your culture, and reflect these differences in your approach to knowledge management.

In essence, you should maintain those elements of your culture that are your firm's strengths, while encouraging cultural change that addresses your firm's weaknesses and supports the growth of your firm.

Create Your Firm's Knowledge Management Culture

To create your knowledge management culture, follow these steps:

1. Have you identified the potential cultural barriers to knowledge management at your firm?

2. Have you identified the elements of your culture that are conducive to knowledge management at your firm?

3. Do you have management commitment to knowledge management?

   ♦ Does management understand the value of knowledge management?

♦ Has management provided significant funding for knowledge management?

♦ Does management tell the firm that knowledge management is a key business driver?

4. Have you identified the target knowledge management culture?

5. Is management sending a clear message to your firm about its commitment to cultural change?

6. Is your firm backing up management's message with substantive actions to address cultural barriers?

   ♦ Have you built knowledge management into your:
     - Compensation system?
     - Budgeting system?
     - Billing system?
     - Career progression?
     - Business plans?
     - Management reporting?

7. Does your approach to knowledge management reflect the culture of your firm?

Knowledge Management Technology

A law firm has implemented a number of technology systems and applications that store important information and knowledge of the firm. These systems and applications have not been integrated and sit as separate components of the firm's technology platform.

There are three systems that store the firm's work product. The first is a document management system to manage the process of drafting documents and to store the firm's work product. The firm also has a firm-wide repository of vetted best practice documents which resides in a separate database with a different user interface to the document management system. Finally, the firm's precedent documents reside in yet another database with a different interface to the document management system and best practice document repository.

The firm has a financial management system to store the firm's financial and timekeeping information, including time recorded, time billed, revenues recovered, and expenses incurred. It has a human resources information system that stores information relating to staff. It also has a client relationship management system that stores information relating to the firm's clients.

The firm's legal research technology systems include a library catalog system and subscriptions to on-line research services.

Staff rely heavily on the firm's e-mail system. The firm also has a website, an intranet and extranets. Finally, it has the capability to develop customized databases.

These systems and applications are not integrated. When staff want to retrieve knowledge, they must first know which system contains the knowledge, and then search that system to retrieve that knowledge. Since systems and applications sit separately, there is a lot of duplication of stored content. Also, since systems and applications were developed separately, the firm has no standard taxonomy applied to content in the various systems, making it difficult to retrieve all the knowledge relating to any particular topic.

The six practice groups of the firm have each developed their own database to store knowledge relevant to their practice area. Each group also has a site on the firm's intranet to present additional knowledge that is not available in its database.

The practice group databases have given the groups the flexibility to build knowledge management solutions specific to their knowledge needs. Some practice groups developed their databases in reaction to a perceived need rather than based on a strategic analysis of the group's business need or an understanding of the group's work processes.

Staff find it difficult to retrieve relevant high quality content. Content is not categorized according to a firm taxonomy and the databases do not have full text search capability.

Practice groups have not developed a process for maintaining the databases. Instead, they rely on staff to contribute content. Over time, some of the practice groups have lost enthusiasm for maintaining their databases. These groups are left with databases containing outdated content of questionable quality. Not surprisingly, these groups simply don't use their databases.

There is little coordination between practice groups in the design and implementation of their databases. Most of the databases have similar functionality and the lack of coordination has led to duplicative development efforts. Typically, the practice groups tell the IT department that they want a specific technology solution, rather than defining a business need and letting the IT department define the best technology solution. The IT department is placed in a reactive position, responding to ill-defined practice group requests. This means that development is slow. Because the IT department responds separately to the needs of each practice group, the resources of the IT department are pulled in several directions. The IT department therefore cannot provide the best service to the practice groups.

It becomes clear that much of the content in the practice group databases could be better managed in the firm's best practice document repository. A dedicated team maintains this repository, ensuring that content is of the highest quality. Once the team approves content, it profiles each document, categorizing it according to a taxonomy developed by the team. This repository also has a powerful search engine. Staff can retrieve accurate content quickly through a combination of the full text search capability and the categorization of content.

The evolution of the practice group intranet sites is similarly a story of lack of coordination across the groups, lack of resources to build and maintain content and lack of strategy regarding the use of the intranet as a knowledge-sharing tool. There is no firm-wide intranet strategy to provide practice groups with guidelines about the format and content of intranet sites. Despite initial efforts of the firm to develop the intranet as the principal portal into its knowledge, there is great variation across the practice groups in their use of the intranet. This wide variation renders the intranet largely ineffective as a firm-wide knowledge sharing tool.

The above example illustrates some of the issues facing law firms today in their use of technology to support and facilitate knowledge management. The legal technology market provides an array of technology solutions for every aspect of the practice and business of law. Your law firm must decide which, of the vast range of available technology systems and applications, will support and facilitate your knowledge management efforts.

For many law firms, knowledge management is synonymous with technology. However, while technology plays a critical role in the capture and dissemination of knowledge, it is not the sum total of your knowledge management efforts. Some knowledge management initiatives will not involve technology at all. If this is the first Chapter in this book you are reading, I encourage you to read the preceding Chapters, in particular Chapters 3, 4, 5 and 6.

Because technology changes so rapidly, this Chapter does not attempt to provide a comprehensive review of the knowledge management systems and applications available in the market. Rather, I will focus on the issues associated with using technology to support and facilitate knowledge management at your firm. Throughout this Chapter, I make reference to some of the common law firm systems and applications, though this is not intended to limit the scope of systems and applications you should consider as you build your knowledge management system.

Keys to the Knowledge Management System

In using technology to support and facilitate knowledge management at your firm, you should consider some key principles relating to:

- The scope of your knowledge management system

- The knowledge management system's technology platform

- Capturing knowledge in your knowledge management system

- Disseminating knowledge via your knowledge management system

The knowledge management system

1. Be clear on the scope of knowledge you plan to manage before you implement a knowledge management system.

2. Define the components of your knowledge management system based on the scope of knowledge you wish to manage and your knowledge management and business objectives.

The knowledge management system's technology platform

3. Leverage the technology systems and applications you already have.

4. Apply business rigor to implementing knowledge management technology.

5. Select technology systems and applications that integrate with others.

6. Select systems and applications that are easy to use.

Capturing knowledge

7. Store each piece of knowledge only once in your systems and applications.

8. Apply standards to the capture of knowledge. (Be aware of the "garbage in, garbage out" syndrome.)

9. As you capture knowledge, categorize knowledge according to a firm taxonomy. (Do not just rely on full text searching to retrieve this knowledge.)

10. Attach an appropriate level of security to knowledge.

Disseminating knowledge

11. Users should be able to find what they are looking for, quickly and accurately, regardless of time or location.

12. The technology source should be invisible to the user.

13. Knowledge should be presented in multiple views, based on the needs of the user.

14. The knowledge management system should support and facilitate sharing knowledge across practice groups and offices.

15. The knowledge management system should allow sharing knowledge with clients.

16. As you build your knowledge management system, ask these questions:

```
┌─────────────────────────────────┐
│   What is the scope of our       │
│ knowledge management system?     │
└─────────────────────────────────┘

┌─────────────────────────────────┐
│  What technology do we need to   │
│      build this system?          │
└─────────────────────────────────┘

┌─────────────────────────────────┐
│     How will we capture          │
│       knowledge in the           │
│ knowledge management system?     │
└─────────────────────────────────┘

┌─────────────────────────────────┐
│  How will we disseminate         │
│   knowledge through the          │
│ knowledge management system?     │
└─────────────────────────────────┘
```

Consider each of these principles below.

Define the Scope of Knowledge

Your decision to implement a particular knowledge management technology solution should depend on the type of knowledge you wish to manage. In Chapter 3, I described the many categories of knowledge a law firm possesses. You should be clear on the scope of knowledge you plan to manage and then determine the value of that knowledge to your firm. Understanding the scope of knowledge and its value will help you evaluate the most appropriate technology system or application to store knowledge.

Define the Components of Your Knowledge Management System

Your knowledge is likely stored in multiple systems and applications. Ultimately, users should be able to access knowledge from a single user interface, described later in this Chapter. Initially, once you have defined the scope of knowledge you plan to manage, you should be clear on the technology sources of that knowledge. In defining your knowledge management system, you must also consider your knowledge management and business objectives. If your objective is to share knowledge across the firm, you need to think about how to do this.

You need to ask how will you use technology to:

- Share knowledge across your firm?
- Share knowledge with your clients?
- Enable easy capture of knowledge?
- Enable quick, accurate access to knowledge?

Leverage What You Have

Most law firms have the basic components of a knowledge management system. Once you have defined the scope of knowledge you plan to manage, you should look at the technology systems you already have and assess whether you use these systems as well as you could. In other words, have you leveraged what you already have?

You should only look at implementing new systems if your current technology systems cannot meet your knowledge needs.

> Our law firm reviews how the firm currently uses technology—both the use of firm-wide systems and practice group applications—to meet those knowledge needs. It examines the functionality of each system and application and the human processes surrounding the use of each system and application. It assesses how well each of its systems meets the knowledge needs of the firm, identifies the gaps, and decides either to leverage what it already has, or acquire new technology components that fill the gaps.

The table below illustrates the firm's analysis:

SCOPE OF KNOWLEDGE	TECHNOLOGY SOLUTION
The law	
♦ Case law, commentary and interpretation	On-line services
♦ Legislation and commentary	On-line services
♦ Best practice (or model) documents	Databases

SCOPE OF KNOWLEDGE	TECHNOLOGY SOLUTION
♦ Precedent (or form) documents	Document management system
The firm and its practice areas	Website, Intranet
Clients	Client relationship management system
The commercial market and specific industries	Database or new application
Staff skills and expertise	Database or new application
Methodology and processes	Database or new application
Past projects and lessons learned	Database or new application
Third parties (e.g., regulators, judges, counsel, experts, external consultants)	Database or new application
The firm's market position	Database or new application
The firm's revenue, costs and profitability	Financial management system

The firm assesses that some categories of knowledge are well managed by the firm's existing technology systems. In some instances, however, the systems are not well used. For example, the document management system could be better used to store precedent documents and to identify best practice documents. There is no need to replace the document management system.

Rather, the firm focuses on how to improve the use of the document management system.

The firm also realizes that there are some categories of knowledge that are not well managed. The firm has two options. It can develop its own database or it can purchase a new application. Where the firm marks categories of knowledge as requiring a "database or new application," it develops a requirements definition for each of those categories. The requirements definition describes what the firm requires from a technology solution to manage that category of knowledge. For each category of knowledge not currently managed, the firm reviews applications against a requirements definition. In some cases, the firm selects a new application. In other cases, it concludes that the firm can build a database internally to meet the defined requirements.

The firm therefore takes a two-pronged approach to its knowledge management technology platform:

1. It leverages its current technology platform

2. It examines whether to build or buy new technology systems to fill the gaps.

Apply Business Rigor to Implementing Knowledge Management Technology

Since the components of your knowledge management system will require significant investment, you should be very clear on the business need, as well as the knowledge need, for each new knowledge management technology initiative. Defining a clear business need and demonstrating how the technology will meet that business need ensures that knowledge management technology initiatives are closely tied to the business needs and knowledge needs of your firm. Chapter 9 discusses this in more detail.

As our firm reviews the practice group databases, it is clear that the knowledge and business needs of the practice groups could be better met by having each group define its business and knowledge needs and leaving it to the knowledge management organization and the IT department to determine how best to meet those needs. Thus, rather than tell the IT department that it needs a specific technology solution, each practice group now defines its business and knowledge needs and presents them to the knowledge management organization.

The knowledge management organization then determines whether a technology solution is appropriate to meet the knowledge and business need of the practice group. In some cases, the appropriate knowledge management solution may not involve technology at all.

If the knowledge management organization concludes that a technology solution is appropriate, it considers whether the knowledge and business need can be met through the use of an existing system or application. At this stage, it engages the IT department in reviewing the available technology solutions. This involves examining firm-wide systems and applications, and considering existing practice group technology solutions.

> If no technology solution exists, the knowledge management organization and the IT department work with the practice group to develop a technology solution to meet their knowledge and business need.

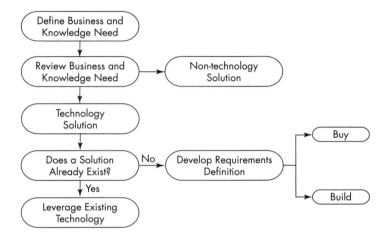

Make Sure Your Systems Integrate

You should select technology systems and applications that integrate with all other systems you use. This is critical if you want to leverage the knowledge stored in several discrete systems. Knowledge stored in integrated systems is much more powerful than knowledge stored in separate systems, as illustrated below.

One of the gaps for our law firm is the ability to manage knowledge relating to past projects. When the firm defines its requirements for managing knowledge about past projects, it defines the following categories:

- Name of project
- Name of client
- Value of project to the firm (amount billed to the client)
- Project team
- Client information
- Project description
- Key documents
- Lessons learned
- Acquired skills and expertise

The firm identifies that most of this knowledge is already captured in the firm's systems.

FIELD NAME	KNOWLEDGE SOURCE
Name of project	Financial management system
Name of client	Financial management system
Value of project to the firm (amount billed to the client)	Financial management system
Project team	Financial management system
Client information	Client relationship management system
Project description	
Key documents	Document management system

FIELD NAME	KNOWLEDGE SOURCE
Lessons learned	
Acquired skills and expertise	Skills and expertise locator

As this table illustrates, the firm already stores an enormous amount of information about its past projects. However, finding that information would require a lawyer to search across four discrete systems. By integrating these four systems, the combination of all the information relating to past projects becomes valuable knowledge.

The firm realizes that in building its project database, it can draw upon the information stored in the other four systems and simply build two additional fields—the project description and lessons learned.

Your Knowledge Management System
Should Be Easy to Use

Your knowledge management system should be easy for staff to use. This means it should be easy for staff to create, disseminate and capture knowledge. It should also be easy for staff to access knowledge.

Store Content Only Once

Since a knowledge management system will typically draw upon data, information and knowledge stored in many disparate systems and applications, it is likely that there will be a high degree of duplication of content in those systems and applications. Duplicative content leads to many inefficiencies. First, there are the duplicative maintenance efforts required every time content is updated. Second, there is a danger that over time, content will not always be updated in every system, creating inconsistencies across systems and applications. Third, when users know that there are inconsistencies in content across systems, they lose confidence in the accuracy of content.

You should minimize the duplication of content in these systems and applications. This means first understanding where content is stored, and then reducing the storage of content to only one location, accessible to other systems.

The following diagrams illustrate the importance of managing the number of locations in which the same content may be stored.

In this first diagram, the client "Curve Consulting LLC" is stored in four systems of the law firm. Since each system stands apart from other systems, the client name must be entered separately into each of the four systems. The client's name is described differently in each of the systems. If someone at the firm searches for every reference to Curve Consulting LLC, it will only find content stored in the financial management system. It will not be able to find content relating to this client in the projects database, client relationship management system or document management system. The variations in client name therefore hamper the firm's ability to draw together all knowledge relating to this client.

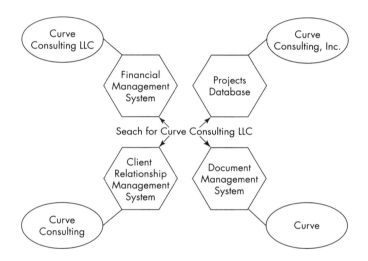

In the second diagram, the firm has ascertained that the first system entry of a client name is when the client name is entered in the firm's financial management system, at the start of the client relationship. In other words, the client name originates in the firm's financial management system. The firm realizes that it can integrate its financial management system with its document management system, client relationship management system and projects database. Rather than rely on staff to enter the client name in a consistent format in every system, the client name is only entered once, at the beginning of the client relationship. From that point, the client name is fed from the financial management system into all other systems where the client name appears.

Consequently, when staff search for all content relating to Curve Consulting LLC, they can be confident that their search results return content stored in all the firm's systems and applications.

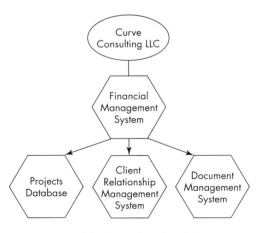

Seach for Curve Consulting LLC

As the firm conducts its review of its current technology platform, it realizes that content may reside in several different places. It conducts a data mapping exercise to ascertain where content is duplicated and then embarks on a project to ensure that content is stored in only one place, and accessible to other systems.

Apply Standards to the Capture
of Content (Or Avoiding "Garbage In/ Garbage Out")

Knowledge management technology is only a tool to capture and disseminate content. It cannot guarantee the quality of the content. To ensure a high quality of content, you need staff to develop work processes surrounding the identification and capture of knowledge.

As you make decisions regarding the use of technology to manage your knowledge, you should consider:

How do you capture content?

You should develop a consistent approach to the capture of content. You also need to make it as easy as possible for staff to capture content.

How do you determine the value of content?

You need to determine the value of particular content. This will impact the level of effort you apply to managing content in your knowledge management system.

How do you categorize content?

The way you categorize content will determine your ability to retrieve that content in the future. Categorizing content based on a firm taxonomy is critical to retrieval and must take place at the content capture stage. I discuss the need for a taxonomy in further detail below.

Who is responsible for capturing content?

You should assign responsibility for capturing content. Otherwise, no one might take responsibility. You may want to build processes for lawyers to identify knowledge that should be shared, with minimal lawyer effort. You should also have knowledge management staff responsible for capturing content.

Who is responsible for maintaining content?

Building a knowledge management system is just the beginning. For the system to succeed, you must develop work processes surrounding the maintenance of content. At the start of this Chapter, the practice groups lost interest in their databases when they realized that content was outdated and of little value. The content of a knowledge management system must be continually reviewed for its value.

Is content already stored somewhere else?

It is possible that content stored in one component of your knowledge management system may be stored elsewhere. Before you build any new application, you should make sure that the content is not already captured in another component of your knowledge management system.

Our law firm has a repository of best practice work product that is carefully maintained by a dedicated knowledge management team. Lawyers submit work product to the knowledge management team through the document management system for possible inclusion in the repository. The team reviews the quality of content and assesses its value to the firm. If the team ascertains that the work product is valuable enough for inclusion in the repository, it profiles the work product and publishes it in the repository. At regular intervals, the knowledge management team reviews the currency of content in the repository and asks the submitting lawyer to comment on the continuing relevance of the work product.

Categorize Knowledge According to a
Firm Taxonomy

Knowledge management is all about leveraging the knowledge of your firm by accessing knowledge stored in multiple locations. The key assumption is that knowledge will be described consistently across all your systems and applications. This is a very dangerous assumption. Since the components of your knowledge management system were developed as discrete systems, by different people, it is more likely that there are wide variations in how a piece of knowledge is described.

This is not just about integrating disparate systems. Practice groups and offices will also likely have very different approaches to how they describe a piece of knowledge. This very simple example below illustrates this issue.

The corporate group refers to a "deed" as an "agreement" in its work product repository. The real estate group describes a "deed" as a "deed" in its work product repository. A real estate lawyer wants to find all deeds drafted by the firm for a particular client. Knowing that the corporate group has acted for this client, the real estate lawyer searches in the corporate group's work product repository. When the real estate lawyer searches for a "deed" in the corporate group's work product repository, he cannot retrieve any documents. He does not know that the search term he should have used was "agreement" and his search is futile.

To retrieve knowledge stored in all components of your knowledge management system, there must be a common language applied to the description of that knowledge. A taxonomy is a set of categories used to classify the knowledge stored in your knowledge management system. When people use different categories to classify the same piece of knowledge, it becomes extremely difficult to share that knowledge.

Since the purpose of capturing knowledge is to disseminate that knowledge, it is critical that your firm applies a common language to the description of knowledge in your knowledge management system. The common language should apply across all practice groups and offices.

Developing a taxonomy is a complex and time intensive initiative. You face the challenge of developing a taxonomy that:

♦ can be applied to content in all systems and applications

♦ meets the needs of all practice groups and offices.

You should therefore develop a taxonomy with several layers. There must be a firm layer that enables staff to search for knowledge across different systems and applications, regardless of practice group or location. You also need to give staff the opportunity to drill down to taxonomy levels that meet the specific needs of a practice group or office.

In other words, you must strike a balance between the differing needs of practice groups and offices and the objective of sharing knowledge across all practice groups and offices. The key is to ensure that knowledge can be accessed across your firm and not become lost because it was stored under another name.

> Our firm decides to implement a powerful search engine that sits across all its systems and applications, allowing staff to retrieve content stored in all systems. Understanding that this full text search engine may return a lot of information which is irrelevant to the user, it also develops a system to categorize knowledge based on a firm taxonomy. Since terminology differs across existing systems, practice groups and administrative areas of the firm, the firm undertakes a taxonomy initiative to develop a common firm-wide language that applies to its systems and applications.

Attach an Appropriate Level of Security to Knowledge

Knowledge management is all about sharing knowledge across your firm. However, there are circumstances in which knowledge should not be freely shared. To fulfill your duty of confidentiality to your clients, some content should only be made available to a limited number of staff working with the client. Similarly, there should be different levels of access to your firm's financial information. The information that partners and the heads of administrative functions see is completely different to that information shared with the wider firm.

Your knowledge management system should enable different levels of security to be attached to content stored in the system. Your system should enable access to be defined by an individual or group. Examples of groups include practice group, client team, project team, administrative function, partners, lawyers, paralegals, and secretaries.

Your system should also allow different levels of access to be attached to content. For example, staff may be able to edit a document—or they may only have "read only" access, where they can read the document, but not edit it. They may be able to see that a document exists but not be able to access it. They may not even see that a document exists, if the document is highly sensitive.

While managing access to content is key, you should be careful not to create a "silo" environment, where staff can only access knowledge created within their practice group or administrative area. There is a fine line between managing security and creating a silo environment. The key is to make as much content available to everyone, while still protecting the firm's duty of confidentiality to its clients, and protecting sensitive information. One way to do this is to review levels of security attached to content over time. Content may become less sensitive over time or it could be made less sensitive by removing sensitive components, such as client references. Security attached to that content should be relaxed, so that the wider firm can benefit from the content.

Our firm identifies that staff need to be able to manage access to content in the firm's knowledge management system. The practice groups are particularly concerned about how to protect client confidentiality. They want the ability to limit access to specific documents stored in the document management system to staff directly working on a client matter. Practice groups want the flexibility to determine not only who accesses each document, but the type of access granted. Typically, the practice group can see that a document exists, but only the client team can read and edit the document.

When a matter has ended, practice groups review matter related documents and identify any best practice documents that would benefit the wider firm. The practice group removes all client references from these documents, and security on those documents is modified to give access to the wider firm.

The finance group is also concerned with managing access to content in the financial management system. While it would like to share access to the financial management system with partners, it knows that content in the system is highly sensitive and access to content must be carefully managed. The finance group creates different departments within the firm, and grants a range of access levels to the different groups. For example, while partners can see the firm's work in progress reports, junior lawyers can only see their individual time reports.

Provide Easy Access to Knowledge

Accessing knowledge easily has several elements. Staff should be able to find what they are looking for:

- ♦ Quickly
- ♦ Accurately
- ♦ Regardless of time
- ♦ Regardless of location

As you decide where to store knowledge, you should consider carefully how your staff will retrieve that knowledge. Will they access knowledge from a remote location? Will they need access to knowledge at all hours of the day? Will they be able to accurately pinpoint the knowledge they are searching for?

> Our firm implements a powerful enterprise wide search engine, available through the firm's web-based knowledge management system. Staff are able to securely access the knowledge management system from anywhere and at any time, and search the system based on a combination of full text searching and browsing by defined categories.

Make the Technology Source Invisible
to the User

A lawyer shouldn't need to know that working documents are stored in the document management system, financial information relating to a client is in the financial management system and client contact information is in the client relationship management system. The technology source should be invisible to the user.

> Our firm implements a portal that sits above all the systems and applications of the firm. The portal is the interface to the firm's knowledge management system. Staff access knowledge from this interface without needing to know where the knowledge is stored.

Present Knowledge in Multiple Views

The knowledge needs of your staff differ widely across roles, practice groups, administrative areas and offices. Staff will access different types of knowledge based on their roles or their area of interest. A partner can access practice group financial data while a junior lawyer will probably only be able to see his billable hours. A corporate lawyer will want access to corporate precedents, while a tax lawyer will want access to the latest tax rulings. As you develop your knowledge management system interface, you need to consider how best to present knowledge based on the needs of staff. Since knowledge needs differ widely, you need a flexible system that supports the presentation of knowledge in multiple views. For example, lawyers may want to access knowledge clustered according to a client, matter, industry or area of law. Ideally, your knowledge management system should allow users to control to some degree, what knowledge is presented to them.

Our firm's first version knowledge management system has a single user interface that everyone in the firm uses to access the following views of knowledge:

- Firm—presenting knowledge relating to the firm
- Region—presenting knowledge relating to a specific region
- Practice group/administrative area—presenting knowledge relating to a specific practice group or administrative area

Our firm's second version of its knowledge management system user interface adds more views of knowledge, with the system administrator determining each user's interface based on his staff profile. In the second version, the following views are added:

- Area of law—knowledge relating to a particular area of law
- Industry—knowledge relating to a specific industry
- Client—knowledge relating to a specific client
- Matter or project—knowledge relating to a particular matter or project

In the third version of its knowledge management system, the user is able to personalize his interface by determining which views of knowledge he sees in his knowledge management system interface.

From his user interface, a mergers and acquisitions lawyer working in the telecommunications industry can access knowledge relating to the telecommunications industry, legal developments in mergers and acquisitions, his five major clients and his two current matters. He sets his user interface into the knowledge management system to display the following views:

- ♦ "Our firm"
- ♦ "Our region"—North America
- ♦ "Our practice group"—Corporate mergers and acquisitions
- ♦ "My area of law"—mergers and acquisitions
- ♦ "My industries"—telecommunications
- ♦ "My clients"—top five clients
- ♦ "My matters"—two current matters

Facilitate Knowledge Sharing Across Practice Groups and Offices

Your knowledge management system should be consistent with your knowledge management strategy of leveraging the knowledge of the firm to support the firm's business objectives. The power of knowledge management in a law firm is truly realized when lawyers share knowledge not just within their practice groups, but across all practice groups. A lawyer in the banking practice should be easily able to search for material relating to the corporate practice.

Similarly, the value of knowledge management in a multi-office firm is only realized when staff can access the knowledge of all offices.

To be able to share knowledge across practice groups and offices, you need:

A standard technology platform across all offices

The only way your firm can really capture, share and leverage its knowledge across all offices is to have a standard technology platform. This will allow your firm to act as one, allowing staff to share knowledge regardless of location.

Content and format standards

You should implement a consistent look and feel in the presentation of knowledge from different practice groups. You should also introduce a common standard in the quality of content stored in the systems and applications that form your knowledge management system. For example, if you have a firm intranet, you should develop an intranet format template for practice groups to use as they develop their intranet sites. You should also develop a set of guidelines for intranet content. Achieving consistency in format and content across practice groups enables staff to confidently search the knowledge of other practice groups.

A firm taxonomy

You should develop a common language across the practice groups to describe content in your knowledge management system. Developing a firm-wide taxonomy, which is applied to the knowledge of all practice groups, will allow staff to confidently search across the practice groups for valuable knowledge.

> The six practice groups of our law firm have taken different approaches to the content and format of their knowledge management tools. This makes it almost impossible for one practice group to access the knowledge of another practice group. Recognizing the limitations of having practice groups define the content and format of their knowledge management tools, the firm develops guidelines for the format and content of practice group knowledge management tools.
>
> The firm also knows that staff will still find it difficult to locate the valuable knowledge of others because there are wide variations in the terminology used across the practice groups to describe knowledge. The firm embarks on an initiative to develop a firm-wide taxonomy, based on the different taxonomies of the practice groups, which allows staff to identify valuable knowledge created by other practice groups and offices.

Facilitate Knowledge Sharing with Your Clients

Your firm should be building a knowledge management system that could allow sharing knowledge with your clients. As you develop best-in-class knowledge management tools internally, you may want to consider making these tools available to your clients. Chapter 11 discusses the possibilities of sharing knowledge with your clients.

> As our firm develops its knowledge management system, it identifies a number of instances where it could make knowledge available to its clients. By developing a secure means of sharing knowledge, the firm offers clients access to their billing information and their final work product (including letters of advice and transactional documents).

The Evolution of the Knowledge Management System

The single repository approach

The original knowledge management system found in law firms is typically a single repository of high value knowledge. The repository is stringently reviewed to ensure content is of the highest quality. Typically these single repository knowledge management systems focus on maintaining the firm's internal work product.

Maintaining these repositories is a manually intensive process. Staff identify valuable work product typically stored in other technology systems (such as a document management system) and submit work product for entry in the firm's knowledge repository. Knowledge management staff then determine whether the submitted work product is valuable for re-use. Knowledge management staff enter a summary profile of valuable work product into the secure repository that includes a description of the work product, including relevant categories from the firm's taxonomy. The work product may also be stored in the secure repository or remain in its native system, with links from the summary profile.

While the vetted system approach ensures a high level of quality of content, there are some issues associated with this approach.

These repositories tend to be narrow in the scope of knowledge they contain. Traditionally used to store best practice work product, they are not designed to manage knowledge relating to the firm and its practice areas, clients, finances, skills and expertise, past projects or knowledge about third parties.

The multiple systems and applications approach

In recent years, a second approach to designing the knowledge management system has emerged in law firms, based on an understanding that knowledge may reside in several systems and applications. These firms focus on finding the best way to locate knowledge across multiple systems rather than developing a single-repository knowledge management system. Knowledge is then typically delivered to staff via a single user interface into multiple systems and applications.

While this system approach assumes a broader scope of knowledge to be managed, firms may not be paying enough attention to assigning value to the content in its systems. Instead, too much emphasis is placed on technology tools such as intelligent search engines to automate the process of retrieving content. Quality may have been traded for quantity.

Combining the two approaches

The knowledge management system should combine quantity and quality. As knowledge management systems evolve into the single user interface to retrieve knowledge stored in multiple systems and applications, consider taking the best from the single repository approach. You should first understand that there is a wide range in the value of content in your systems. You should then focus on assigning value to content, as discussed in Chapter 4, and then design your knowledge management system to reflect the range in the value of that content. Where knowledge is highly valuable, you should have qualified staff carefully manage this knowledge to maintain its high quality. Where content falls into the lower tier of the knowledge pyramid, an intelligent search engine may be enough to retrieve knowledge.

The following diagram demonstrates how your knowledge management system may give users a single interface into the many categories of knowledge they want to access. Under this model, users do not need to know in which system or application the content is stored. They simply retrieve content through their single user interface. In developing a single user interface, you ideally want to give staff the ability to determine what their interface looks like (as described earlier in this Chapter under "Present knowledge in multiple views").

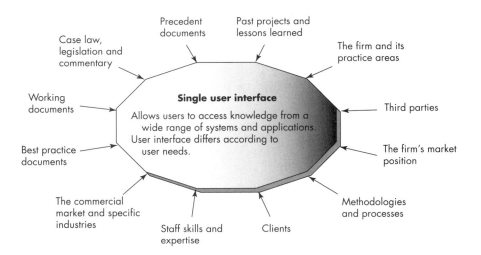

From a knowledge retrieval system to a knowledge management system

Law firm efforts to develop a broader knowledge management system described above tend to focus on building a system to capture and disseminate knowledge. To create new knowledge or to re-use knowledge retrieved from the knowledge management system, staff still must access a separate application, such as a word processing application or a database. In other words, the "use" and "create" steps of knowledge management, as described in Chapter 4, tend to fall outside the scope of law firm knowledge management systems.

The next step in the evolution of the law firm knowledge management system will be a system that allows users to perform all the steps of knowledge management in the knowledge management system—identification, capture, dissemination and use of your firm's knowledge.

Create Your Knowledge Management System

As you create your knowledge management system, consider the following:

1. Have you defined the scope of knowledge you want to manage?

2. Have your reviewed your current technology platform to see if it meets your knowledge needs?

3. Are you leveraging your current technology platform?

4. Have you committed to implementing knowledge management technology?

5. Do your technology systems integrate with each other?

6. Have you selected systems and applications that are easy to use?

7. Have you applied standards to the capture of knowledge?

8. Have you developed a firm taxonomy?

9. Have you attached appropriate security to the content?

10. Can staff find what they are looking for?

11. Is the technology source invisible to the user?

12. Can you draw knowledge from multiple systems?

13. Is knowledge presented in multiple ways to suit the needs of the user?

14. Does your knowledge management system support and facilitate knowledge sharing across practice groups and offices?

15. Does your knowledge management system support and facilitate knowledge sharing with your clients?

16. Do you have processes in place to manage the content in your knowledge management system?

17. Have you considered the other elements of knowledge management, namely scope, culture and organization?

PART

How to Approach
Knowledge
Management

The Knowledge
Management Strategy

A few partners in a 100 lawyer firm are interested in applying knowledge management principles to their practices. The partners do not know of each other's interest in knowledge management, and do not share their best practices.

Instead, each partner separately instructs the IT department to develop a knowledge management solution. The IT department responds to each partner's request by developing the solution as defined by the partner. There is no examination of whether the requested solution is appropriate. The partner does not define a business need. No one challenges the appropriateness of the partner's request.

There is also no examination of whether another practice group has already tackled this issue and developed an appropriate solution.

Since the IT department is reacting to each partner request, this finite resource is pulled in several directions, often developing several similar solutions for different practice groups at one time.

The practice group knowledge management initiatives tend to be basic and unsophisticated. Several have been expensive to develop, since the lawyers are often unclear about the purpose and scope of the knowledge management initiative.

While there are areas of high activity in knowledge management, the firm has no minimum knowledge management standard so it faces a risk management issue. Some practice groups have excellent precedents and professional development programs. For the other practice groups that do not have these, no one is managing the quality of their work product across all offices of the firm.

Not surprisingly, knowledge management at this firm tends to be reactive, duplicative and limited. This is inefficient knowledge management.

What Is the Knowledge Management Strategy?

The knowledge management strategy is the blueprint for the development of knowledge management processes and tools at your firm. It describes the firm's knowledge management philosophy, vision and objectives. It also highlights the firm's current approach to knowledge management. The strategy typically outlines short term, mid term and long term goals, and contains specific recommendations to move the firm from its current approach to knowledge management, to the achievement of its knowledge management objectives.

In particular, the strategy addresses:

- Defining the **scope** of knowledge and knowledge management at your firm

- Creating a knowledge management **organization**

- Developing a **culture** that supports knowledge management at your firm

- Building a **technology** platform to facilitate the identification, capture, dissemination and use of knowledge at your firm.

Since knowledge management needs will differ by practice group, the strategy should reflect this. While the strategy should provide a firm-wide framework for knowledge management, it must also be flexible enough to enable practice groups to develop knowledge management processes and tools that meet their needs.

Why Your Firm Needs a Knowledge Management Strategy

There are four main reasons why your firm needs a knowledge management strategy.

A strategy engages all staff and galvanizes firm support for knowledge management

The process of developing the strategy should involve engaging everyone at the firm. First, you should conduct interviews and focus sessions with staff to identify how they work, and how they use knowledge to do their work. Second, you should consult with representatives of all practice groups and administrative functions on the key issues and opportunities. This methodology ensures that knowledge management meets the needs of the entire firm. It also gives your staff ownership in the process. These two factors will be critical during the implementation of knowledge management initiatives.

A strategy presents a clear picture of the breadth and complexity of knowledge management

A strategy clarifies the breadth and complexity of the issues that need to be addressed. It enables a firm to prioritize knowledge management initiatives based on value and complexity. Knowledge management requires significant investment and ongoing commitment from management and staff. Your firm therefore needs a clear picture of what it is investing in, and committing to.

A strategy gets the firm to speak a common language

The process of drafting and adopting a knowledge management strategy gives your staff a frame of reference and articulated goals for the firm's approach to knowledge management.

A strategy helps knowledge management implementation stay on track

The strategy should be a living document, which sees your law firm through the implementation of knowledge management in the short, mid and long term. Every time a knowledge management initiative is identified, you should test whether that initiative aligns with your firm's knowledge management strategy. This process will help you to remain focused on pursuing knowledge management initiatives that meet your firm's knowledge management objectives and business objectives.

Elements of the Knowledge Management Strategy

Your firm's knowledge management strategy is essentially about how your firm plans to invest in working smarter. The strategy should be more than a strategy for delivering content via technology tools. It should cover all the issues described in the preceding Chapters.

Place the knowledge management strategy in the context of your firm's business

The strategy should articulate the firm's approach to knowledge management in the context of your firm's current position and its business objectives. In doing this, it should lay out the key challenges your firm faces, and describe how knowledge management will help the firm address those challenges. Consider:

- ◆ What are your business objectives?
- ◆ What are the current challenges facing your business?
- ◆ How can knowledge management help you address those challenges and achieve your business objectives?

Articulate the objectives and benefits of knowledge management at your firm

You should define your knowledge management objectives as succinctly as possible and describe the benefits knowledge management can bring to your firm. Consider:

- ◆ What are your knowledge management objectives?
- ◆ What are the benefits of knowledge management?

♦ What is the cost of not implementing knowledge management?

Describe your firm's philosophy and approach to knowledge management

Your approach to knowledge management should reflect the culture of your firm. In the strategy, you should articulate your approach to, and your philosophy regarding, knowledge management. Consider:

♦ Will knowledge management be centralized, decentralized, or a hybrid of the two?

♦ What are the key strengths of your firm's culture, and how can knowledge management operate most effectively in the context of your culture?

Where relevant, describe knowledge management in the context of e-business

♦ If your firm offers e-business solutions, how will knowledge management support and facilitate them?

Consider knowledge management in the context of your clients

♦ How will knowledge management support business development?

♦ How will your firm promote knowledge management to its clients?

♦ Will your firm give its clients access to its knowledge management initiatives?

Describe critical success factors affecting knowledge management at your firm

For many law firms, knowledge management requires a leap of faith. It involves significant investment, the development of a new knowledge management organization, the introduction of new technology tools and substantial cultural change. As you draft your knowledge management strategy, consider:

- ♦ What are the key cultural, organizational and technological factors that may affect the success of knowledge management at your firm?

Identify the investment required to implement knowledge management at your firm

You should be clear on the significant investment required to succeed at knowledge management. It may be difficult to give accurate costs associated with knowledge management at the strategy stage, but you should at least include a high level cost estimate. Consider:

- ♦ What is the cost of creating a knowledge management organization?
- ♦ What is the cost of implementing or developing technology tools and non-technology initiatives?
- ♦ What is the cost of having partners, lawyers and administrative staff dedicate time to knowledge management?

Identify hard and soft measures of the value of knowledge management

Hard measures mean measuring knowledge management in financial and usage terms. Soft measures mean measuring the value of knowledge management based on anecdotes.

♦ How will you measure, and demonstrate the value of knowledge management initiatives at your firm?

Define the timeline for implementing the strategy

The best knowledge management programs take several years to implement. Specific knowledge management initiatives should be implemented based on their value and complexity. The best approach is to begin with high value, easy to implement "quick wins" that demonstrate the value of knowledge management early on and help build firm support for the more complex knowledge management initiatives. Consider how long you will need to achieve your firm's knowledge management vision.

♦ What do you plan to achieve in the short term? How long is the short term period?

♦ What do you plan to achieve in the mid term? How long is the mid term period?

♦ What do you plan to achieve in the long term? How long is the long term period?

Your strategy should address each of these elements. You should:

♦ Describe why each element is a critical component of knowledge management.

♦ Define your firm's current approach to each element.

♦ Describe your objectives relating to each element.

♦ Articulate specific high level recommendations relating to each element to achieve your objectives.

In Chapters 3 through 7, I described the key elements of knowledge management a law firm must consider:

♦ Scope

♦ Organization

◆ Culture

◆ Technology

Scope

There are two parts to defining scope—the scope of knowledge you will manage and the scope of knowledge management at your firm.

Scope of knowledge

Your strategy should define the **scope of knowledge** your firm intends to manage. In Chapter 3, I described how lawyers use many categories of knowledge—**legal** and **non-legal, explicit** and **tacit**—both for the **practice of law** and the **business of law**.

You need to be clear on the scope of knowledge to be managed before you can define the scope of knowledge management at your firm. You should address the following:

◆ Is your firm's focus on managing legal knowledge or on all knowledge used at the firm?

◆ Which of the following categories of legal knowledge (knowledge relating to the practice of law) will your firm manage?

   – Case law, commentary and interpretation

   – Legislation and commentary

   – Best practice (or model) documents

   – Precedent (or form) documents

◆ Which of the following categories of non-legal knowledge (knowledge relating to the business of law) will your firm manage?

- The firm and its practice areas

- Clients

- The commercial market and specific industries

- Staff skills and expertise

- Methodology and processes

- Past projects and lessons learned

- Third parties (e.g., regulators, judges, counsel, experts, external consultants)

- The firm's market position

- The firm's revenue, costs and profitability

♦ Will the firm manage only explicit knowledge, or examine ways to address tacit knowledge?

♦ What value do you attach to each category of knowledge?

♦ Who owns the knowledge you plan to manage, and who should manage that knowledge?

The checklist in Chapter 3 should help you define the scope of knowledge at your firm.

Scope of knowledge management

In Chapter 4, I defined "knowledge management" as the leveraging of your firm's collective wisdom by creating systems and processes to identify, capture, disseminate and use the knowledge possessed by your law firm. The **scope of knowledge management** will affect the level of investment your firm makes in knowledge management. There are many different ways a law firm can manage its knowledge—from simple, low cost initiatives to firm-wide, state of the art systems. In your strategy, you should define the scope of knowledge management at your firm.

I suggested four key principles you should follow in defining the scope of knowledge management at your firm.

1. You need to understand what knowledge you must manage before you can find the best way to manage that knowledge.

2. You should not limit your thinking on the scope of initiatives that can help you manage that knowledge.

3. In deciding how best to manage your knowledge, you must place a value on that knowledge. You should base your investment in knowledge management on the value of the knowledge to your practice and your business. The more valuable the knowledge, the greater the investment in knowledge management.

4. You should begin with simple, discrete knowledge management initiatives, and over time, draw together the discrete initiatives into more complex knowledge management tools and processes.

As you draft your knowledge management strategy, you should address the following:

♦ Will knowledge management initiatives be purely technology driven, or will the firm implement technology and non-technology systems and processes to manage knowledge?

♦ How will the value of your knowledge determine the level of investment in knowledge management initiatives?

♦ Will knowledge management be a firm initiative, a practice group initiative or a combination?

Organization

In Chapter 5, I described the role of a dedicated knowledge management organization in a law firm. While knowledge management is the responsibility of all staff at your firm, many knowledge management related tasks require specialist skills and a significant time commitment. Neither is readily available among lawyers, paralegals and secretaries. To successfully implement your knowledge management strategy, you need staff dedicated to the tasks of identifying, capturing and disseminating knowledge throughout your firm.

You should consider three critical factors:

♦ Composition

♦ Size

♦ Positioning

Composition

As you draft your strategy, consider:

♦ What is the role of the knowledge management organization?

♦ Should the knowledge management organization be centralized or decentralized?

♦ Who will lead knowledge management at your firm?

  – Should it be a director or a partner?

  – Should it be someone with a legal background?

♦ What will be the role and responsibilities of your head of knowledge management?

♦ Which existing functions will form part of the knowledge management organization?

  – Library

274

- Legal research
- Precedents
- Intranet
- Professional development

♦ Which new knowledge management roles should be created?

- Knowledge manager
- Professional support lawyer
- Information officer
- Knowledge management system developer

♦ What skills are required for knowledge management roles?

♦ What will be the reporting relationship between knowledge management staff and the head of knowledge management?

♦ What is the career path for knowledge management staff?

♦ Will there be a knowledge management committee? What will be its role?

♦ Will there be practice group knowledge management partners?

Size

♦ How many knowledge management staff will there be?

Positioning

♦ Who will the head of knowledge management report to?

◆ What is the relationship between the knowledge management organization and administrative functions?

– Human resources

– Marketing/business development

– Information technology

– Finance

– Professional development

◆ What is the relationship between the knowledge management organization and the practice groups?

Culture

The only product of a law firm is its knowledge. Law firms are filled with great minds eager to develop their knowledge base — so a law firm is essentially a learning organization. Constant changes to the law mean that lawyers continually struggle with how best to keep up with those changes. Thus, a law firm should have the right culture for knowledge management.

However, as I described in Chapter 6, this is not always the case. Despite the obvious benefits knowledge management brings to an organization, especially one whose revenue is based on its knowledge, there are potentially many cultural barriers to knowledge management that your firm may need to address.

On the other hand, there may be aspects of your culture that make your firm successful. It is important that your knowledge management strategy reflects your culture—particularly, the strengths of your culture. The key is to find the balance between:

◆ Adapting knowledge management principles to fit your firm's culture; and

♦ Adapting your firm's culture to progress knowledge management.

The balance should be based on understanding the strengths and weaknesses of your culture.

You should consider the following:

♦ What are the strengths of your culture?

♦ What are the cultural barriers to knowledge management you need to address? For example:

- Will the time-based billing system discourage lawyers from contributing to knowledge management?

- Does the partner compensation model encourage knowledge sharing across your firm?

- Is there limited interaction between practice groups?

- Is there overlap in areas of practice between lawyers in different practice groups?

- Do lawyers perceive that knowledge is power?

- Do lawyers think that their knowledge is unique and of no value to others?

- Do lawyers fear judgment by their peers?

- Does your firm have a decentralized culture?

- Are there differences in regional cultures within your firm?

- Does your firm adequately train and mentor its junior lawyers?

- Do you have senior management support?

- Is knowledge management perceived as the work of an isolated group?

- Is knowledge management perceived as an IT initiative?

- Are staff rewarded or acknowledged for their knowledge management efforts?

- Is knowledge management perceived as a soft option?

- Do practice groups believe that their knowledge needs are unique and would not benefit from a firm-wide approach to knowledge management?

♦ What elements of your firm's culture are conducive to knowledge management?

♦ What is your firm's target knowledge management culture?

♦ Do you have management commitment to knowledge management?

♦ What specific actions will you take to address cultural barriers?

♦ Do you need to build knowledge management into your firm's:

- Compensation system?

- Budgeting system?

- Billing system?

- Career progression model?

- Business plans?

- Management reporting?

Technology

Building a technology infrastructure to support the capture and dissemination of knowledge is fundamental to knowledge management. In Chapter 7, I described the technology elements of knowledge management. As you develop your strategy, your should consider:

- ♦ What will your knowledge management system look like?
  - Will the firm develop a single user interface into multiple applications?
  - Will the firm focus on developing a firm-wide, heavily vetted, work product repository?
  - Will the firm develop a combination of these two approaches?
- ♦ What technology tools do you have?
  - Does the firm have the fundamental components of its knowledge management technology platform?
  - Is each tool already leveraged, or are there opportunities to improve use of the existing tools?
- ♦ What tools do you need?
  - Are there clear gaps in your firm's technology platform?
- ♦ What approach will you take to selecting and implementing technology solutions?
- ♦ What approach will you take to capturing knowledge?
- ♦ What approach will you take to disseminating knowledge?

★ ★ ★ ★

If you cover these questions, you should have a fairly comprehensive knowledge management strategy.

How to Develop Your Knowledge
Management Strategy

Knowledge management affects everyone at your firm, and everything they do. For the strategy to succeed, it needs to be developed and adopted by the entire firm. While it is unrealistic (and impractical) for everyone at your firm to be involved in the drafting process, there are steps you can take to engage all staff in the strategy development process.

Engage the firm

Form a knowledge management team

This should be a small group, responsible for the day-to-day project work associated with drafting the knowledge management strategy. This team will conduct fact-finding to understand the work processes and knowledge needs of the firm, identify issues and opportunities relating to knowledge management, draft the strategy, and present it to management.

Ideally, you will already have a head of knowledge management who can direct the team. In Chapter 5, I described how drafting your firm's knowledge management strategy is one of the key roles of the knowledge management head. However, if you have not yet appointed a head of knowledge management, the team should be composed of senior people who understand your firm's business, have a good understanding of knowledge management and are well respected in the firm. The composition of your team will depend on the politics of your firm. You should consider including the IT director, head librarian and the head of professional development in your team. Ideally, the managing partner, or at least a well respected partner should be part of your team.

The knowledge management team should report directly to your firm's management.

Form a knowledge management committee

The knowledge management committee should represent the interests of all practice groups and administrative functions. Ideally, the members of the knowledge management committee should be senior people at your firm, such as practice group and administrative heads.

The committee is a consultative body that meets at key points of the strategy development project. The purpose of the committee is to ensure that the strategy accurately reflects the needs of your firm.

A powerful by-product of forming a committee is that it galvanizes support for knowledge management and encourages cooperation across practice groups and administrative functions. The concept of a firm-wide initiative requiring the cooperation of all practice groups and administrative functions is sometimes foreign to a law firm. The knowledge management committee helps build that cooperation at the earliest stages of knowledge management at your firm, well before the firm makes any significant investment in knowledge management.

Project planning

Your knowledge management team should define the project objectives, timeline and tasks relating to the development of the knowledge management strategy. Since understanding the needs of the firm is so critical, the team should consider how best to find out what those needs are.

The team should decide whether it should gather this information through interviews, focus sessions or surveys. Interviews and focus sessions are preferable to surveys—you can engage people in open discussion about knowledge management and how it applies to their work.

At this stage, the team should also meet with the knowledge management committee to explain the project objectives and project steps. As an outcome of that meeting, the team should work with the knowledge management committee to identify and schedule interviews and focus session candidates.

Understand your firm's knowledge needs

You must understand how lawyers and staff work, and how they use knowledge to do their work. By identifying the current work processes and knowledge needs of your lawyers and administrative functions, you will identify key issues to be addressed in pursuing knowledge management at your firm. The following is a recommended approach:

Conduct interviews or focus sessions with key management to identify and understand the strategic business issues and cultural issues facing your firm. You should interview managing partners, the executive director, the heads of human resources, professional development, finance, marketing and IT, and administrative heads of your offices. These interviews and focus sessions will help to frame the knowledge management strategy in light of your firm's business objectives, and enable you to understand the issues to be addressed in creating a knowledge sharing culture.

Review the firm's business strategy and other key firm management documents. Since the knowledge management strategy must align with your firm's business strategy, you should be familiar with the firm's business strategy, and any associated documents.

Conduct focus sessions with lawyers to understand their current work processes and knowledge needs. The purpose of these focus sessions is not to ask lawyers to define knowledge management initiatives. These focus sessions are designed to have lawyers tell you what they do, and how they use knowledge to do it.

Given that work processes and knowledge needs differ according to practice groups, you should conduct focus sessions based on practice groups.

If your firm has multiple offices, you should not let geography place limitations on conducting practice group-centric focus sessions. You should conduct national or global focus sessions via videoconference.

Practice group-centric focus sessions involving staff from all offices have many positive outcomes. Lawyers are able to share ideas with their colleagues in other offices about better ways to work. Also, lawyers in one office may identify a knowledge need that has been addressed in another office. Most importantly, these focus sessions help to galvanize a practice group's thoughts on knowledge management, which ultimately benefits the firm.

If you have a practice group scattered across multiple offices, make sure that there are representatives from each office in the focus session.

The focus sessions should be composed of a cross section of lawyers, who can talk about the knowledge needs of partners, senior lawyers and junior lawyers. When forming your focus group invitation list, it is important that the focus session attendees can speak intelligently about the business objectives of their practice, so that you understand what knowledge the group needs to meet its business objectives.

Conduct focus sessions with administrative staff to understand their perspective on law firm work processes and knowledge needs. You should conduct separate focus sessions with administrative staff to gain their perspective on lawyer work processes and knowledge needs, as well as their own work processes and knowledge needs.

Conduct interviews with key clients to understand their requirements for delivery of legal services. The knowledge management strategy must be closely aligned with the business objectives of the firm. Understanding client needs is therefore critical to the development of the knowledge management strategy.

You should interview a small number of key clients as part of this process. Interviewing clients not only informs you about what clients expect, it also presents your firm as client focused and proactive. You should probably include your head of marketing or a client relationship partner in these interviews.

Develop the strategy

Analyze results and identify the key findings

During the process of conducting interviews and focus sessions, you should be hearing some common themes. These are the key findings you want to address in your knowledge management strategy.

Identify knowledge management best practices

In analyzing how the firm currently uses knowledge to operate, your knowledge management team should look at industry best practices. The team should then consider the key issues facing your firm in the context of knowledge management best practices.

Draft a findings report

Your knowledge management team should report the results of the interviews and focus sessions to your knowledge management committee.

Since the focus sessions are practice group-centric, the findings report may also present a snapshot of how each practice group works and uses knowledge to do its work. For example, the summary of practice groups may cover the following topics:

♦ Description of work processes

♦ Current knowledge management tools and processes

♦ Knowledge management best practices

♦ Knowledge management opportunities

The process of drafting a findings report makes the team focus on the issues to be addressed in the knowledge management strategy, as well as identifying existing best practices within your firm that could be leveraged across the firm.

Draft the strategy

You should develop the knowledge management strategy by applying knowledge management best practices to the key findings from the interviews and focus sessions. In your strategy, you will draft recommendations to move your firm from its current practice to best practice. The elements of the knowledge management strategy, discussed earlier in this Chapter, should provide a guide for the format and content of your strategy.

Get Management to Adopt Your Knowledge Management Strategy

Your knowledge management team can draft a well thought out knowledge management strategy that contains all the elements I described in this Chapter—but without management's adoption of the strategy, it will gather dust.

In order for your knowledge management strategy to be effective, management must adopt it. Management support moves knowledge management from theory to action.

You must present your knowledge management strategy to management in terms that will make them sit up, pay attention, and provide support and investment. To do this, you need to articulate how your knowledge management strategy will help the firm to achieve its business objectives.

Develop Your Firm's Knowledge Management Strategy

To develop your firm's knowledge management strategy, follow these steps:

1. Form a knowledge management team.

2. Form a knowledge committee, representing all practice groups and administrative functions.

3. Define the project objectives, timeline and tasks relating to the development of the knowledge management strategy.

4. Conduct interviews, focus sessions or surveys to gather information.

5. Explain the project objectives and project steps to the knowledge management committee.

6. Invite representatives from all practice groups and administrative functions to interviews and focus sessions.

7. Interview key management staff.

8. Conduct focus sessions with lawyers and administrative staff in all practice groups.

9. Interview key clients.

10. Analyze the results and produce a key findings report.

11. Seek the feedback of the knowledge management committee on the key findings.

12. Draft a knowledge management strategy that:

   ♦ Places the knowledge management strategy in the context of your firm's business strategy.

   ♦ Articulates the objectives and benefits of knowledge management at your firm.

   ♦ Describes your firm's philosophy and approach to knowledge management.

   ♦ Describes knowledge management in the context of e-business.

   ♦ Considers knowledge management in the context of your clients.

   ♦ Describes critical success factors affecting knowledge management at your firm.

   ♦ Identifies the investment required to implement knowledge management at your firm.

   ♦ Identifies hard and soft measures of the value of knowledge management.

♦ Defines the timeline for implementing the strategy.

♦ Describes the key elements of knowledge management at your firm:
- Scope
- Organization
- Culture
- Technology

Implementing Knowledge Management

Chapter Contents

A law firm adopts a knowledge management strategy, engaging the firm in its development and gaining management support. In the absence of a knowledge management organization, the knowledge management team must now turn the high-level strategy recommendations into specific initiatives.

The strategy contains over 40 recommendations, covering all elements of knowledge management—scope, culture, organization and technology. The team soon realizes that it will take a number of phases of implementation before it can achieve all its knowledge management objectives.

The team begins asking each practice group to define knowledge management initiatives that will deliver high value to the practice group.

The project team also identifies firm-wide knowledge management initiatives to implement the strategy recommendations. It soon discovers that many of those firm-wide initiatives require the involvement of other administrative functions in the firm. For example, to develop a skills and expertise locator, it needs to work closely with the human resources department and marketing department (traditionally the owners of information about staff skills and expertise).

The knowledge management team also needs management to modify some of the firm's systems and processes that create cultural barriers to knowledge management. For example, the team needs management to commit to building knowledge management into the firm's compensation system, budgeting system, career progression model and reporting structure.

The team therefore must work closely with three areas—practice groups, administrative functions and management. It drafts a project plan of all the knowledge management initiatives to be implemented at the practice group level and at the firm level—and then begins to work on implementing those initiatives.

The team faces challenges working with each of the three areas.

The practice groups do not draft business cases for their nominated initiatives, so it is often difficult to see how a knowledge management initiative meets a business need. The practice groups also do not develop project plans for their initiatives, so they tend to underestimate the time, resources and cost involved in implementing their nominated initiatives.

Over time, it becomes clear that the practice groups have not thought through the value of, or the investment necessary to, implement their knowledge management initiatives.

As the team begins to work on the implementation of firm-wide initiatives, it experiences difficulty in engaging administrative functions. To implement a skills and expertise locator, the team must rely heavily on the human resources department and the marketing department. However, both departments have other major initiatives they must advance, and they cannot commit substantial resources to knowledge management at this stage.

The team has a hard time gaining the attention of management. Since management is working on a merger with another law firm, it cannot focus on knowledge management and the fundamental changes it must make to the firm's systems and processes at this time. Management also holds off on hiring knowledge management staff and investing in some of the technology tools critical to knowledge management.

Implementation of the strategy is much slower and more limited than originally anticipated. The firm never truly commits to adopting knowledge management into its work practices, systems and processes. Ultimately, the firm fails to achieve its knowledge management objectives.

A law firm can develop a well thought out knowledge management strategy that reflects the culture of the firm and aligns with the firm's business strategy—but the strategy will have no effect if it is poorly implemented.

This Chapter deals with this all-important step—turning your knowledge management strategy into specific initiatives that will achieve your knowledge management and business objectives.

There are two key variables you must consider in prioritizing the implementation of knowledge management: the value and complexity of the initiative.

Once you have prioritized your initiatives, you can plan to implement those initiatives in three main phases—the short term, mid term and long term.

As you implement initiatives, you will need to address how to:

♦ Gain sufficient funding for initiatives

♦ Communicate the progress of knowledge management to the firm

♦ Involve management in knowledge management implementation

♦ Develop collaborative relationships between the knowledge management organization and the firm

♦ Measure and demonstrate value of initiatives.

This Chapter explores these major elements of implementation:

♦ Turning your knowledge management strategy into specific initiatives

♦ Prioritizing implementation based on the value and complexity of specific initiatives

♦ Defining the phases of implementation

♦ Implementing knowledge management initiatives.

Who Will Lead Implementation?

One of the first strategy recommendations you should implement is selecting a head of knowledge management, if your firm does not already have one. The head of knowledge management is responsible for implementing your knowledge management strategy. Chapter 5 describes the role of the head of knowledge management in detail.

You also need partners responsible for knowledge management in each practice group to spearhead the identification and implementation of knowledge management initiatives in their groups. Your firm should appoint practice group knowledge management partners as soon as the strategy has been adopted. Ideally, each group would also have dedicated knowledge management staff working closely with this partner.

The knowledge management committee, described in Chapter 5, should also be formed early in the implementation phase. Like the knowledge management partners, it will play a pivotal role in the implementation of the firm's knowledge management strategy.

Turn Your Knowledge Management Strategy into Specific Initiatives

The knowledge management strategy typically contains high-level recommendations about how the firm can achieve its knowledge management objectives. The challenge is to turn those strategy recommendations into specific initiatives that meet the objectives of the recommendations. Each initiative should be a well defined project, with a series of tasks that meet tangible goals and ultimately achieve the objectives stated in the strategy recommendations. Consider the following illustration:

STRATEGY RECOMMENDATION	SPECIFIC INITIATIVES
"Develop programs to promote sharing of tacit knowledge throughout the firm."	Develop a skills and expertise locator. Develop a mentoring program. Conduct debriefing sessions at the conclusion of matters. Implement a partner open door policy.

Each of the initiatives listed in the right column is a discrete project with a clear objective. Each can be drilled down to the task level. Once you have determined specific initiatives that meet the strategy recommendation, you need to determine the order in which you will implement each initiative.

Define the Value and Complexity of
Each Initiative

For each specific initiative, you should develop a high-level project plan and a business case. These two documents enable you to define the value and complexity of initiatives.

The project plan—defining the complexity of the initiative

The project plan will give you a clear picture of the **complexity** of implementation, i.e., the level of effort involved in implementing the initiative.

The project plan should define the tasks involved in implementing the initiative and estimate the:

- ◆ Time
- ◆ Resources
- ◆ Cost

associated with the initiative.

The project plan should also include critical success factors affecting the initiative, since these contribute to the complexity of implementation. Critical success factors are factors that will impact the success of your initiative. Beyond ensuring that the project has adequate resources and funding and an appropriate time frame, you must identify other critical success factors that may impact the success of an initiative. Management support and firm-wide acceptance of the initiative are examples of critical success factors.

Consider the example of how a firm plans for the development of a skills and expertise locator. The firm begins by defining the project tasks:

PROJECT TASKS

The high level tasks associated with developing a skills and expertise locator are:

- ◆ Define the requirements.
- ◆ Determine who currently owns and maintains this information.
- ◆ Define the information fields.
- ◆ Select an appropriate technology platform.
- ◆ Build or buy a new system, or enhance an existing system.
- ◆ Convert data from existing sources.
- ◆ Collect additional data.
- ◆ Input additional data.

PROJECT TASKS
◆ Design a process for maintaining information. ◆ Train staff. ◆ Roll out the skills and expertise locator.

The next step is to define the time, cost and resources involved in progressing the tasks defined above. Time will largely be determined by the availability of resources and the level of investment in the project.

The firm determines its project time frame by identifying the resources needed to complete each task, and confirming the availability of those resources. The firm identifies the following resources will be needed:

- One knowledge manager full time for six months
- One human resources staff member for five days
- One marketing staff member for five days
- One IT developer, half time for six months

The firm also estimates the cost of implementing a skills and expertise locator. In its estimate, it includes the cost of buying a new system and retaining additional resources to implement this project on time. It estimates an investment of $100,000.

Based on its knowledge of available resources and estimated cost, the firm estimates it will take six months to implement a skills and expertise locator, as the following project plan illustrates.

ID	Task Name	Duration
1	Define the requirements for a skills and expertise locator	15 days
2	Determine who currently owns and maintains skills and expertise information	15 days
3	Define the information fields in a skills and expertise locator	15 days
4	Select an appropriate technology platform for the skills and expertise locator	30 days
5	Implement a skills and expertise locator (build or buy a new system, or enhance an existing system)	20 days
6	Convert data from existing sources to the skills and expertise locator	10 days
7	Collect additional data	20 days
8	Input additional data into the skills and expertise locator	20 days
9	Design a process for maintaining skills and expertise information	20 days
10	Train staff in how to use the skills and expertise locator	15 days
11	Roll out the skills and expertise locator	1 day

Timeline columns: 4th Quarter (Oct, Nov, Dec) | 1st Quarter (Jan, Feb, Mar) | 2nd Quarter (Apr, May, Jun) | 3rd Quarter (Jul, Aug, Sep) | 4th Quarter (Oct, Nov, Dec) | 1st Quarter (Jan, Feb, Mar) | 2nd Quarter (Apr, May, Jun)

> The timing of the project will also be affected by critical success factors at the firm. For example, if the IT department is in the midst of implementing a firm-wide document management system, it may have to delay implementing a skills and expertise locator. Even with the appropriate resources and money, the firm must still make sure that the timing of the skills and expertise locator implementation fits into the firm's overall business priorities.

The business case—defining the value of the initiative

Drafting a business case will give you a clear picture of the **value** of the initiative. Value is based on the relationship between the initiative and the achievement of your firm's knowledge management and business objectives.

The business case should cover:

- ♦ Business need

- ♦ Current situation

- ♦ Benefits

associated with each initiative. It should also identify criteria for measuring the value of the initiative.

Business cases typically include the level of investment and resources required to implement an initiative, since value is determined by the return on investment. The business case also includes the critical success factors and timeframe. The business case should draw upon the project plan for this information.

Consider using a form like this one:

Proposed Initiative—short description of desired solution, e.g., repository of market intelligence	
Business Need	**Current Situation**
Describe the business need driving the development.	Describe current methods of meeting the business need.
Project Benefits/Value	**Project Investment**
Describe quantitative and qualitative benefits of this project.	Describe resources needed to pursue the project, including lawyers, support staff, technology staff and administrative areas, and define other project costs, such as external resources and technology.
Critical Success Factors	**Project Timeline**
Define the factors that will affect the success of this initiative.	Define the time it will take to implement this initiative.
Criteria for Measuring Value	
Articulate the measurement of value.	

Below is an illustration of how the firm implementing its skills and expertise locator may define its business case:

Proposed initiative
Implement a skills and expertise locator.
Business need
As a large, multi-disciplinary law firm, we must be able to identify and leverage the skills and expertise of our firm members to anticipate and meet the needs of our clients as efficiently and profitably as possible.

Current Situation

No systematic approach exists to identify the skills and expertise of our staff.

Typically, staff may gain knowledge about the skills and expertise of colleagues through informal means based on their location or the matters they work on. Their interaction with colleagues outside of their practice group, office, or floor is limited.

This particularly limits their ability to leverage our firm's skills and expertise in:

- ◆ Forming the most competent multi-disciplinary teams
- ◆ Developing the skills and expertise of less experienced staff
- ◆ Producing best quality work quickly and cost-effectively.

Consequently, we may be compromising our ability to:

- ◆ Respond to client needs
- ◆ Ensure that the right expert is involved in a client matter
- ◆ Pursue new areas of expertise.

Benefits

A skills and expertise locator would enable our staff to identify the appropriate skills and expertise in the firm and promote knowledge sharing within the firm, as follows:

- ◆ The manager of a client matter can efficiently locate appropriate skills and expertise within the firm to create an expert team, regardless of office or practice group.

♦ Less experienced lawyers can locate and consult with a subject matter expert, ensuring that clients receive accurate advice (thus supporting the firm's risk management policy).

♦ Resources can be more efficiently allocated by ensuring that the appropriate staff are involved in work.

♦ Partners can explore the creation of new practice groups, communities of interest, services and products.

Investment $100,000

♦ Software, hardware and training costs for a new system

♦ One knowledge manager full time for six months

♦ One human resources staff member for five days

♦ One marketing staff member for five days

♦ One IT developer half time for six months

Critical success factors

♦ Staff contribute skills and expertise information.

♦ Staff maintain skills and expertise information.

♦ The firm understands the value of the skills and expertise locator.

♦ Management supports implementation of the skills and expertise locator.

♦ Document management system implementation has been completed.

♦ Human resources, marketing and IT can dedicate resources.

Project timeline

6 months

Criteria for measuring value

♦ Usage of the skills and expertise locator

♦ Number of e-mails sent, searching for skills and expertise of staff

♦ Evidence of how:

   – Partners create expert teams

   – Lawyers locate and consult subject matter experts

   – Resources are allocated

   – New practice groups, communities of interest, services and products are created

---

Introducing this business rigor to your knowledge management initiatives at the start of your knowledge management implementation ensures that knowledge management is consistent with your firm's business objectives.

Prioritize Implementation of Initiatives

There are two key variables you must consider in prioritizing the implementation of knowledge management:

♦ The value the initiative brings to the firm's knowledge management and business objectives, and

♦ The complexity of implementation.

Consider the following graph:

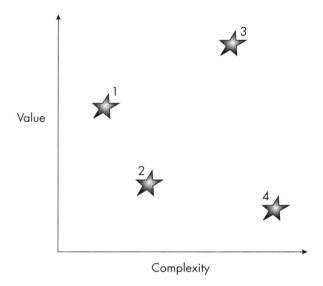

In this graph, the law firm has identified four types of initiatives.

Type 1 knowledge management initiatives bring high value to the firm and are easy to implement.

Type 2 knowledge management initiatives bring value (though less than Type 1 initiatives) to the firm and are easy to implement.

Type 3 knowledge management initiatives bring high value to the firm but involve a complex implementation.

Type 4 knowledge management initiatives bring less value to the firm than Type 3 initiatives and involve complex implementation.

Now consider how a firm may want to tackle the implementation of these initiatives.

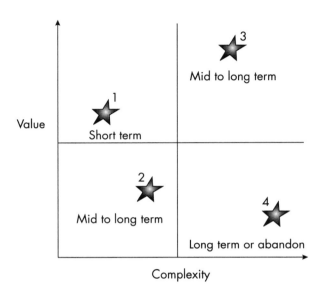

The graph demonstrates that firms should prioritize the implementation of knowledge management initiatives based on their value and complexity.

Once you have prioritized your initiatives, you can plan to implement those initiatives in three main phases—the short term, mid term and long term.

Take a Phased Approach to Implementation

Successful knowledge management programs take several years to implement. You should plan the implementation of your strategy in three main phases:

◆   Short term

♦ Mid term

♦ Long term

Each phase typically lasts for 12 to 18 months, which means that it will probably take three to five years to implement your knowledge management strategy.

During the **short term** phase, your goal is to build a strong foundation for knowledge management at the firm, through:

1. implementing simple initiatives that will form the basis of more sophisticated initiatives; and

2. raising awareness among your staff about the benefits of knowledge management.

You should first focus on "quick wins" that are simple to implement and will deliver high value to the firm. Ideally, these "quick wins" demonstrate how obvious the benefits of knowledge management are to the firm.

During the **mid term** phase, you can begin to implement more complex knowledge management initiatives, building upon the work achieved during the short term. These initiatives are also high value, but may not have been possible without the implementation of the simple initiatives. Also, more complex initiatives usually require greater understanding and acceptance of knowledge management in your firm. This understanding and acceptance typically comes from the experience people gained during the short term phase.

The **long term** phase is the period in which you develop sophisticated knowledge management systems and programs that achieve the firm's knowledge management vision as stated in the strategy. This phase usually involves a process of drawing together the discrete knowledge management initiatives implemented in the short term and mid term, and creating firm-wide knowledge management systems and programs.

	SHORT TERM	**MID TERM**	**LONG TERM**
Scope	Focus on explicit knowledge: ◆ Develop a firm wide best practice document repository. ◆ Develop a firm-wide precedent drafting program. ◆ Refine the firm-wide professional development program. ◆ Develop a firm intranet.	Focus on tacit knowledge: ◆ Develop a skills and expertise locator. ◆ Introduce debriefing. ◆ Develop methodologies for common work processes.	Develop know-how files based on methodologies, best practice documents, precedents and professional development programs. Develop knowledge management products for clients.
Organization	Appoint a head of knowledge management. Create a knowledge management committee. Appoint knowledge management partners.	Build the knowledge management organization by recruiting dedicated knowledge management staff.	Develop a career path for knowledge management staff.
Culture	Raise awareness in the firm about the value of knowledge management.	Build knowledge management into the firm's business processes (business plans, compensation system, career progression model).	Introduce alternatives to the time-based billing model.
Technology	Leverage existing tools.	Identify gaps in the existing technology platform and implement new technology tools.	Implement a knowledge management system, which pulls together all knowledge in a single user interface, with multiple views based on user needs.

Even at the strategy stage, you should have a high level idea of the appropriate phase in which to tackle specific recommendations. For example, if there are significant cultural barriers to knowledge management which management must address, it is unlikely that all those barriers would be addressed in the short term. The complexities associated with introducing fundamental cultural change may need to wait for the mid term or long term.

On the other hand, a strategy recommendation to define the scope of knowledge the firm plans to manage is a fairly straightforward and critical early step in implementing knowledge management at the firm. It is a simple, high value step that should occur in the short term. The chart above illustrates how a firm may begin with relatively simple initiatives in the short term, moving to more complex initiatives in the mid and long term.

As you begin to plan the implementation of specific knowledge management initiatives, consider whether each initiative should be implemented in the short term, mid term or long term, based on its value and complexity.

Take a Parallel Approach to Implementation

As you turn recommendations into specific initiatives, you will find that there are some initiatives that should be implemented at the practice group level, and others that should be implemented at the firm level.

In Chapter 5, I described three approaches to implementing knowledge management in a law firm:

- ◆ Centralized
- ◆ Decentralized
- ◆ Hybrid

I suggested that the hybrid approach is the best practice approach to knowledge management. Under this approach, the firm sets the direction for knowledge management and provides an infrastructure to facilitate knowledge management among practice groups. The knowledge management strategy and methodologies are created at the firm level, which can then be applied to practice group specific initiatives. Initiatives that apply to the firm are managed at the firm level.

This approach acknowledges that different practice groups have different knowledge needs, yet knowledge management initiatives can be implemented more efficiently within the framework of a firm-wide strategy.

Setting the direction for practice groups at the firm level also ensures that the firm takes a consistent approach to knowledge management, with all practice groups working to achieve the firm's knowledge management and business objectives.

Also, practice groups may identify knowledge management initiatives that have wider application across the firm, and should therefore become firm-wide initiatives, managed by the knowledge management organization.

All of this suggests that firms should follow a parallel track in the implementation of knowledge management initiatives. There will be:

♦ Firm-wide initiatives

♦ Practice group initiatives

Firm-Wide Initiatives

Firm-wide initiatives are those knowledge management initiatives that affect everyone in the firm. Naturally, the head of the firm's knowledge management organization should manage the implementation of those initiatives. Addressing the foundation issues of defining the firm's scope of knowledge and knowledge management, creating a knowledge management organization, addressing cultural barriers to knowledge management and developing a technology platform to support knowledge management are best managed as firm-wide initiatives. To implement firm-wide initiatives, you should follow the steps outlined at the start of this Chapter, namely:

- ◆ Turn your knowledge management strategy into specific firm-wide initiatives

- ◆ Prioritize implementation based on the value and complexity of specific initiatives.

- ◆ Define the phases of implementation.

- ◆ Implement the initiatives.

Practice Group Initiatives

Practice group initiatives are those initiatives that directly address the knowledge management and business needs of a practice group. Since a practice group understands its knowledge management and business needs better than others, it is appropriate for practice groups to determine its knowledge management initiatives—under the guidance of the knowledge management organization.

Identify knowledge management initiatives

When you conducted focus sessions during the strategy stage to find out how practice groups gather and use knowledge to do their work, you identified opportunities for knowledge management in the practice groups—though only at a high level. As you move from strategy to implementation, you need to revisit the practice groups and ask them to define specific knowledge management initiatives based on their value and complexity.

Ideally, each practice group will have a knowledge management partner or other staff member who is responsible for implementing knowledge management in its group.

A good starting exercise is to ask each practice group to identify three "quick wins"—those knowledge management initiatives that are simple to implement and of high value to the practice group. To help each practice group identify its short term initiatives, you should work with practice groups to develop business cases and project plans (described earlier in this Chapter) to guide them through the process of understanding the value and complexity of their initiatives.

This process forces practice groups into a discipline of pursuing knowledge management initiatives that directly meet a business objective.

Knowledge management initiatives will differ between practice groups. For a transaction based practice, such as banking or corporate, it is likely that these initiatives will have a documentation focus. These groups will probably concentrate on developing precedents and identifying best practice documents. For an advice based practice, such as tax or employment law, there will likely be an emphasis on managing the volume and speed of developments in the law, and access to prior letters of advice. A litigation practice may focus on developing manuals or training programs on managing a case. Consider the following illustration:

The corporate group of a law firm identifies that it would gain tremendous value from developing a core set of precedent documents. These documents would be approved by the firm-wide corporate group and form the basis of every new document produced by the corporate group. The knowledge management organization works with the corporate group to develop its business case for the development of precedent documents.

The corporate group defines its proposed initiative as:

- ◆ Develop precedent documents for the ten core documents used by the corporate group.

It defines its business needs as:

- ◆ Our clients expect consistency and high quality in our documents, across all our offices.
- ◆ There is a high risk of giving bad advice, associated with inconsistent language in our documents.
- ◆ Our partners need to leverage their expertise and find ways to delegate work to junior staff.

The corporate group describes the current situation as follows:

- ◆ Lawyers use different forms of documents, resulting in inconsistent work product across the practice.
- ◆ Our group has no way of managing our risk exposure due to bad language in documents produced by our lawyers.

- Clients complain that they receive inconsistent documents from our firm, damaging our client relationships.
- Partners have difficulty delegating work to junior lawyers and must spend more time than necessary on drafting and reviewing documents.
- Our group must write off a large amount of time associated with inefficient drafting processes.

The group articulates the following benefits:

- Enables partners to delegate drafting to junior lawyers, freeing partners to focus on high-value work and generate greater revenue
- Increases consistency in documentation
- Reduces drafting time, resulting in lower write-offs
- Improves the quality of work product, resulting in lower risk exposure.

While there are solid business reasons for developing precedents, the corporate group should also be clear on what it will cost the group to develop the precedents. Arguably, the business needs defined above are so critical that developing the precedents is really a business imperative. However, knowing how much it will cost to address this business need is important.

The corporate group develops a project plan, outlining the tasks associated with developing its ten precedent documents, and analyzes the related costs, resources and timeline. As it defines the resources needed to develop the precedents, it realizes that a significant investment in partner time is required. The corporate group sees two options:

1. Dedicate a partner to work full time on the development of the precedents. Estimated project time is 6 months.

2. Partners contribute to the development of the precedent documents in addition to their practice commitments. Estimated project time is 12 to 18 months.

The corporate group concludes that the business need for the precedents is so strong that it must complete the project in the next 6 months. It estimates the following investment:

♦   One full time partner for 6 months
♦   Lawyer time to contribute sample work product
♦   Professional support lawyer (25% of his total time) to assist the partner in drafting and to manage the project
♦   Precedents administrator (10% of his total time) to help administer development of documents.

The group defines the following critical success factors:

♦   Corporate lawyers provide best practice documents as a starting point for precedent development.
♦   Corporate partners agree on precedent document language and format.

- The precedent drafting partner is able to leave his client work for 6 months.
- The professional support lawyer is able to dedicate adequate time to assisting the partner.
- The precedents team has available resources to assist the corporate group.

Even at this early stage, the group should define its criteria for measuring value:

- Usage of precedents
- Level of consistency in documentation
- Level of quality of documentation
- Amount of write-off time
- Delegation of work by partners to junior staff
- Avoidance of risk
- Ease of drafting

The corporate group drafts the following business case and presents it at its monthly practice group meeting.

Proposed initiative

Develop precedent documents for the ten core documents used by the corporate group.

Business need

Our clients expect consistency and high quality in our documents across all our offices.

There is a high risk of giving bad advice associated with inconsistent language in our documents.

Our partners need to leverage their expertise and find ways to delegate work to junior staff.

Current Situation

Lawyers use different forms of documents, resulting in inconsistent work product across the practice.

Our group has no way of managing our risk exposure due to bad language in documents produced by our lawyers.

Clients complain that they receive inconsistent documents from our firm, damaging our client relationships.

Partners have difficulty delegating work to junior lawyers and must spend more time than necessary on drafting and reviewing documents.

The group must write off a large amount of time associated with inefficient drafting processes.

Benefits

- Enables partners to delegate drafting to junior lawyers, freeing partners to focus on high-value work and generate greater revenue
- Increases consistency in documentation
- Reduces drafting time, resulting in lower write-offs
- Improves the quality of work product, resulting in lower risk exposure

Timeline

Six months for completion of ten precedent documents

Investment

- One full time partner for 6 months
- Lawyers to contribute sample work product
- Professional support lawyer to assist partner in drafting and to manage the project
- Precedents team to help administer development of documents

Critical success factors

Corporate lawyers provide best practice documents as a starting point for precedent development.

Corporate partners agree on precedent document language and format.

The precedent drafting partner is able to leave his client work for 6 months.

The professional support lawyer is able to dedicate adequate time to assisting the partner.

The precedents team has available resources to assist the corporate group.

Criteria for measuring value

- ♦ Usage of precedents
- ♦ Level of consistency in documentation
- ♦ Level of quality of documentation
- ♦ Amount of write-off time
- ♦ Delegation of work by partners to junior staff
- ♦ Avoidance of risk
- ♦ Ease of drafting

It considers the business need for precedents, reviewing the gap between the current situation and the desired outcome. It also considers the investment required to address that business need. The partners conclude that having a core set of precedents is a business imperative for the group and it identifies this as a short term knowledge management initiative.

After each practice group has identified its top three knowledge management initiatives and demonstrated why these initiatives should be pursued, you should look for similarities among the practice groups and find opportunities for practice groups to collaborate on their initiatives. Thus, the central knowledge management organization can help the practice groups efficiently implement knowledge management by reducing duplicative development efforts.

You should also identify opportunities for the core knowledge management functions, such as the precedents group, library and intranet team, to provide assistance to practice groups in addressing their knowledge management needs. This will help practice groups to take a consistent approach to knowledge management.

Finding similarities also enables your firm to define the minimum knowledge management standard for each practice group. Consider the following illustration.

The knowledge management organization of a law firm asks its eight practice groups to define their top three knowledge management initiatives. The knowledge management organization has emphasized the importance of pursuing "quick wins" and asked each practice group to determine their three initiatives based on high value and low complexity.

While there are vast differences in the work of each practice group, it becomes evident that there are certain common threads in the knowledge management needs of each group. The most commonly defined initiatives are:

- ◆ Developing a set of precedents
- ◆ Creating a repository of best practice documents
- ◆ Enhancing or developing a professional development program

♦ Building a practice group intranet site.

When the knowledge management organization sees this, it decides that all practice groups should pursue these four initiatives in one form or another.

Naturally, the differences in each practice group will influence the relevance of each of the above initiatives, though the firm is confident that each group:

♦ Produces some degree of repetitive documentation, and will benefit from a set of precedents.

♦ Conducts research on prior work before advising clients, and would benefit from a repository of best practice documents.

♦ Has junior lawyers who need to develop into senior lawyers and would benefit from a professional development program.

♦ Has lawyers located across multiple offices who would benefit from having a common interface into the group's knowledge resources, via an intranet site.

For these reasons, the firm introduces a minimum standard for knowledge management across all practice groups, requiring each practice group to focus on these four initiatives.

The minimum knowledge management standard

Since knowledge management is about making your law firm leverage its knowledge across all practice groups to make your firm achieve its business objectives, it is critical that practice groups progress at a consistent level. Having knowledge management systems and processes in only some of your practice groups all but guarantees failure in your knowledge management efforts.

Some practice groups are more advanced than others

As practice groups begin to implement their initiatives, it may become evident that some groups progress their initiatives quicker than others. The challenge for your knowledge management organization is to strike a balance between:

♦ Ensuring practice groups progress to achieve the minimum standard.

♦ Enabling advanced practice groups to implement more sophisticated initiatives.

The minimum standard approach assumes that some practice groups will not necessarily embrace the importance of knowledge management in the short term, and may hold back the firm's knowledge management efforts. Just as some practice groups may be slow on the uptake, some practice groups may be lengths ahead of others in their adoption of knowledge management systems and processes. These practice groups should not be held back from pursuing more sophisticated knowledge management initiatives.

One way of managing the balance described above is for the knowledge management organization to work with advanced practice groups on implementing more sophisticated knowledge management as pilot initiatives.

Pilot knowledge management initiatives

When an advanced practice group identifies a sophisticated knowledge management initiative that may have wider application throughout the firm, you should treat it as a pilot initiative. This means working with the practice group to implement the initiative, with a view to possibly implementing it across other practice groups at a later date. Consider the following illustration:

> The corporate group in the law firm described above has already achieved the minimum knowledge management standard set by the firm's knowledge management organization. It has a well-maintained library of precedents and best practice documents, a market leading professional development program, and a comprehensive intranet site.
>
> The corporate group sees great value in focusing on the tacit knowledge acquired by its lawyers during a matter. The group therefore wants to develop a debriefing process as its knowledge management initiative.
>
> The knowledge management organization recognizes that conducting debriefing sessions at the end of a matter is an excellent example of how to leverage both the tacit and explicit knowledge acquired during a matter. The knowledge management organization sees great value in introducing debriefing to all practice groups, but knows that it would be premature to introduce it to other practice groups at this time.
>
> The knowledge management organization works closely with the corporate group to design the debriefing process, conduct debriefing sessions at the conclusion of three matters, determine how best to capture the gathered information, and refine the debriefing process based on lessons learned during the pilot.

> The final product is a debriefing methodology that is then introduced to other practice groups across the firm.

Running a pilot enables the knowledge management organization to leverage a very good idea from one group across the firm. By working closely with the practice group, it ensures that best practice knowledge management methodologies are applied to the development of the pilot initiative.

Implement knowledge management initiatives

Once the knowledge management organization has worked with practice groups to draft the project plans and business cases for their initiatives, it should monitor the progress of those initiatives. The key is to let practice groups own the initiatives, while the knowledge management organization provides guidance on how to progress the initiatives.

Where a law firm has a well-developed team of knowledge management staff at the practice group level, such as professional support lawyers, knowledge managers and information officers, implementation is typically managed at that level. Central knowledge management staff are aware of the initiative but are only peripherally involved in its implementation.

Peripheral involvement should mean managing the direction and progress of initiatives so that the practice groups are consistent in their approach to knowledge management. Regular meetings between knowledge management staff in different practice groups and central knowledge management staff are critical. These meetings ensure that staff discuss the progress of initiatives, agree on the direction initiatives should take, share best practices and identify opportunities for practice groups to collaborate.

Where a law firm has a smaller knowledge management organization, the head of knowledge management and other central knowledge management staff must play a more active role in implementation.

Throughout implementation, the knowledge management organization should be clear on the progress of all practice groups, with the goal of bringing all practice groups to a high standard of knowledge management.

From short term to longer term

If practice groups successfully implemented their short term knowledge management initiatives, they built a strong foundation for knowledge management, which will form the basis for more sophisticated knowledge management. They also should have created a strong appetite among staff for more sophisticated knowledge management.

In the mid to long term, practice groups should build upon the initiatives they implemented in the short term and move toward more sophisticated high value knowledge management systems and processes that go further in meeting the firm's business objectives. Consider the following example.

> The eight practice groups in the firm described earlier work hard to develop precedents, a library of best practice documents, market leading professional development programs and intranet sites. After 18 months, the knowledge management organization reviews the progress of each group, and is confident that all groups have reached the firm's minimum knowledge management standard.

Now that the practice groups have created the foundation for knowledge management, they see the value in working smarter and are keen to pursue more complex knowledge management initiatives that build upon their initial work.

Having precedent documents is very helpful, but the groups soon realize that only part of their knowledge is captured in a precedent document. Without further explanation, a lawyer must know the context in which to use a precedent document.

In the past, a lawyer typically learned the context in which to use a precedent by relying on more experienced colleagues. With the creation of comprehensive professional development programs, lawyers now learn about the context in which a specific precedent should be used, as they learn about a particular process.

The practice groups realize that by combining the professional development program with the precedent documents in the form of a know-how file, they can give lawyers the context in which to use a precedent. Combining the precedent library with the professional development program creates a much more powerful knowledge management tool than each provides separately.

Developing know-how files for all key work processes in the practice groups becomes a major focus of the next phases of knowledge management at this firm. The firm could not have pursued the development of know-how files without the foundation work of the short term phase.

Some tips for working with practice groups

There are some patterns that should be kept in mind throughout every phase of knowledge management implementation:

1. Practice groups need guidance from the knowledge management organization on applying business rigor to their knowledge management initiatives. Drafting **business cases** and **project plans** provide practice groups with the tools to ensure knowledge management initiatives are closely tied to your business. They also ensure that practice groups commit to providing the resources and investment necessary for implementing those initiatives.

2. Practice groups should be able to identify their own knowledge management initiatives, though groups may differ in their enthusiasm for knowledge management. Allowing practice groups to identify their knowledge management initiatives and then defining a **minimum knowledge management standard** across the firm strikes a balance between flexibility and consistency. The minimum knowledge management standard ensures that there is a basic level of consistency in how practice groups adopt knowledge management principles.

3. As practice groups identify their knowledge management initiatives, it may become evident that some initiatives should be implemented across the firm, and would be better managed at the firm level. The key is not to alienate practice groups by taking their knowledge management ideas out of their hands. Working closely with the practice group which identified the initiative to implement the initiative as a **pilot** for other groups is a good approach. It addresses the practice group's desire for the initiative, while ensuring that other practice groups will ultimately benefit from it.

Other Elements of Implementation

Identifying initiatives, assessing their value and complexity, prioritizing their implementation and taking a phased approach to implementation are the logical steps you should take for a smooth implementation. However, there are many other issues affecting a smooth implementation that you also must consider.

Obtaining sufficient funding, communicating progress, involving management, gaining wide support and demonstrating value are critical elements of implementation you should think about.

Budget

The amount of money you have to spend on knowledge management will determine the scope of your implementation efforts. During the strategy phase, you would have provided a high level cost estimate for implementing the strategy. It is difficult to produce a more detailed estimate until you have defined specific initiatives.

Ideally, when management adopted the strategy, it should have created a knowledge management budget. With this budget, the knowledge management organization can apply funds to knowledge management initiatives that implement the firm's knowledge management strategy.

When you define specific initiatives to implement your strategy recommendations, you should produce a business case and a project plan for each initiative, as outlined earlier in this Chapter. The project plan is a tool that defines the time, resources and costs associated with a specific initiative. You should create a project budget based on the project plan.

The business case is a tool to define the business need and describe how a specific knowledge management initiative meets a business need. The business case should provide you with the justification for your project budget.

Applying this discipline to the distribution of funds ensures that the firm invests in initiatives that directly drive the achievement of the firm's knowledge management and business objectives.

Communication

Knowledge management involves a significant shift in how most law firms operate. To successfully introduce any significant change into a law firm, you must communicate the benefits of the change to every person in the firm. Communication surrounding knowledge management is therefore a critical success factor of implementation.

Communicating the efforts of the knowledge management organization to the entire firm raises awareness about knowledge management and manages staff expectations surrounding the speed and scope of knowledge management implementation.

As you implement knowledge management systems and processes in your firm, you must pay careful attention to continually reinforcing the benefits of knowledge management to all staff.

Management involvement

Management involvement is crucial for knowledge management to succeed. Just as management is needed to adopt your firm's knowledge management strategy, it must remain involved in the implementation of that strategy.

Ideally, management should become the voice of knowledge management—continually reinforcing the relationship between knowledge management and the firm's business objectives. When communications about knowledge management are distributed across the firm, they should be delivered by your firm's senior management.

Talking about the benefits of knowledge management is not enough. Management must provide appropriate funding for the implementation of knowledge management initiatives.

Management involvement is also crucial to realizing the cultural change necessary for knowledge management to succeed. Management play a critical role in addressing the cultural barriers to knowledge management and achieving the target knowledge management culture described in Chapter 6.

Relationship between knowledge management and administrative functions

Many of the initiatives you identify will involve drawing upon knowledge currently maintained in several isolated forms across different parts of your firm. These and other initiatives will require administrative functions to dedicate resources to their implementation. Thus, you need to develop close relationships with the administrative functions of the firm. In Chapter 5, I described how the knowledge management organization must work closely with the administrative functions in your firm.

As you develop project plans for initiatives, you will identify the steps involved in the initiative and the resources needed from administrative functions. It is wise to engage the relevant administrative function in the project planning process as early as possible.

Measuring and demonstrating value

Drafting project plans and business cases for each knowledge management initiative attaches business rigor to the process—ensuring that knowledge management is directly tied to the firm's business objectives. The business case predicts the value of the knowledge management initiative by tying it closely to a business need.

Measuring the value of an initiative should therefore be a critical step at the conclusion of implementing an initiative.

As you draft your business case for each knowledge management initiative, you should define criteria for measuring value. This should include both hard and soft measurements of value.

The fundamental questions to ask are:

♦ Did the knowledge management initiative meet our immediate business need?

♦ Did the knowledge management initiative help meet our firm's business objectives?

Measuring the value of your knowledge management initiatives ensures that the firm stays on track and only focuses on knowledge management initiatives that directly relate to the firm's business objectives.

Once you measure value, you must demonstrate that value to the firm. This is a great way of raising awareness about the value of knowledge management.

You will need to continually demonstrate the value that knowledge management brings to your firm—until its value is so obvious, nobody asks.

Chapter 10 deals with measuring and demonstrating the value of knowledge management in more detail.

Common Implementation Issues

As you move toward implementation of your firm's knowledge management strategy, you may face some of the issues commonly faced by law firms. Unfortunately, this is not an exhaustive list, but it serves to demonstrate the sort of issues you may face, and how you might address them.

Management does not participate

Without vocal and substantive management support for knowledge management, there is a limit to what your firm can achieve. If management is not engaged in knowledge management efforts, you need to address why that is the case. It may mean that you need to spend more time articulating the benefits of knowledge management to management. If management understands the benefits of knowledge management, you need to emphasize why management involvement throughout implementation is critical.

You should engage management throughout every step of implementation—from presenting an implementation plan to reporting on the successes of implementation.

There is no way to sugar coat the impact management's lack of participation has on knowledge management. Without its support, at best your firm will only make limited progress in knowledge management.

Our firm does not have the budget to implement initiatives

As with management support, having funds to implement knowledge management initiatives is critical to achieving your firm's knowledge management objectives. If the firm is strapped for funds, start off small. Focus on simple, high value knowledge management initiatives that demonstrate the value of knowledge management. Hopefully, these initiatives will serve to demonstrate how much more could be achieved with more funding.

Knowledge management initiatives are competing with other firm projects

It is unlikely that knowledge management is the sole initiative of your law firm. Your firm may have several major projects being implemented at the same time, all competing for finite resources. As you draft project plans and business cases, you should seek the input of administrative functions and practice groups across the firm. During your project planning stage, you should understand the environment in which the firm is operating and plan your implementation accordingly. Trying to implement initiatives when people are focused on other initiatives is a recipe for failure.

Administrative functions do not participate in knowledge management

Administrative functions may be so busy implementing their own initiatives, they cannot dedicate the time or resources needed for knowledge management initiatives. The best way to manage this is to engage administrative functions during the project planning stage. You should present your project plans in draft form to administrative functions affected by the project and seek their input in the project planning process. Their input may well affect the prioritization of initiatives. Delaying implementation is better than beginning implementation prematurely and then failing.

Practice groups progress at different stages

It is likely that some practice groups will be slow to adopt knowledge management systems and processes, while other groups will take to knowledge management in leaps and bounds. There are two challenges you face:

  ◆ What do you do with groups that just won't participate?

♦ How do you handle advanced groups who want to pursue more sophisticated initiatives without being held back?

The answer to the first question is to build knowledge management into the firm's business processes. When knowledge management becomes a criterion in partner and lawyer performance reviews, affecting compensation and career progression, lawyers will be very interested in knowledge management.

The answer to the second question is that advanced groups should be encouraged to pursue more sophisticated knowledge management initiatives. With that said, the knowledge management organization should be careful to manage the widening gap between practice groups that may result from this. The best approach is to work with advanced practice groups to implement their knowledge management initiatives, treating those initiatives as pilots for the rest of the firm.

Implement Knowledge Management at Your Firm

As you move from strategy to implementation, ask yourself these questions:

1. Have you turned your knowledge management strategy into specific initiatives?

2. Have you developed a project plan for each initiative, identifying the time, resources and cost

associated with the initiative? Have you defined the critical success factors affecting the initiative?

3. Have you drafted a business case for each initiative, describing the business need, current situation and benefits associated with the initiative? Have you identified criteria for measuring the value of the initiative? Have you included the level of investment and critical success factors drawn from the project plan?

4. Have you prioritized your initiatives based on their value and complexity?

5. Have you taken a phased approach to implementing knowledge management, defining short term, mid term and long term initiatives?

6. In the short term, have you focused on implementing simple initiatives that will form the basis of more sophisticated systems, and will raise awareness among your staff about the benefits of knowledge management?

7. In the mid term, have you focused on implementing more complex knowledge management initiatives that build upon the work achieved during the short term?

8. In the long term, have you focused on developing sophisticated knowledge management systems and programs that achieve the firm's knowledge management vision, as stated in the knowledge management strategy?

9. Have your practice groups identified their knowledge management initiatives?

10. Have your practice groups drafted business cases and project plans for each initiative?

11. Have you identified similarities in the knowledge management initiatives identified by the practice groups?

12. Have you defined a minimum knowledge management standard for all practice groups?

13. Have you managed practice groups' different rates of implementation?

14. Have you implemented pilots for advanced practice groups?

15. Have you managed the implementation of practice group knowledge management initiatives by providing overall guidance and meeting regularly with the practice groups?

16. Do you have an adequate budget for knowledge management initiatives?

17. Do you communicate the value of knowledge management to the firm regularly?

18. Is management involved in implementing knowledge management?

19. Have you developed strong working relationships with administrative functions at the firm?

20. Do you measure and demonstrate the value of specific knowledge management initiatives?

The Value of
Knowledge Management

Chapter Contents

Two partners in the banking group of a large, dispersed law firm decide to develop a database of the practice group's work product. The partners define the database requirements without consulting other members of the practice group, and instruct the IT department to build the database based on their requirements definition.

The database is intended to contain every document produced by the lawyers in the banking group. There are no guidelines about which content should be placed in the database, and no review of the quality of content.

Building the database is a major undertaking. The IT department initially develops the database based on poorly defined criteria. The partners continually revise their requirements, and consequently, the development phase is slow and expensive.

Once the database has been developed, the partners promote the database at a series of practice group meetings in different offices and ask lawyers to contribute their work product. Over time, it appears that the only office using the database is the office in which the two partners work. Over the course of two years, the database grows to a collection of more than 2,000 documents. There is no workable retrieval system or method of classification of these documents or the information contained therein.

Not surprisingly, few people use the database. In time, its use has deteriorated to become an instrument for the two partners and their direct reports. The database comes to be regarded as a failure among the wider banking group.

When the newly formed knowledge management organization learns of the database, it suggests a review of its use to ascertain its value to the banking group. In its review, the knowledge management organization learns that few people use the database because they have little confidence in the quality or relevance of content.

On closer examination, it becomes clear that the banking group was never asked to define their knowledge and business needs. Indeed, when the knowledge management organization learns about the work of banking lawyers, it ascertains that lawyers rarely refer to prior work product. The terms in final documents are sometimes so heavily negotiated that to re-use these documents for new work product would be risky. Instead, lawyers tend to maintain their own sets of precedent documents, which they use as a starting point for each new transaction.

Because the two partners never consulted with their lawyers to understand what their knowledge and business needs were, they developed an expensive database of little value to their lawyers.

Knowledge is at the core of the business and practice of law. It is the most important asset of a law firm. Knowledge management is a business imperative. If done well, knowledge management enables your firm to increase revenue, decrease costs, increase profitability and achieve its other business objectives.

The arguments for knowledge management in a knowledge-based business are obvious. Some may even argue that the relationship between knowledge management and a firm's business objectives is so obvious that there should be no need to measure and demonstrate its value. However, since knowledge management is a new concept at many law firms, requiring heavy investment and significant cultural change, you need to measure and demonstrate the value of knowledge management to your firm at every step—at least in the early stages of implementing knowledge management. If you cannot demonstrate the value of a knowledge management initiative to your firm's business objectives, the initiative is doomed to failure.

Measuring the value of knowledge management means ensuring that every knowledge management activity supports your firm's knowledge management strategy and business objectives. Measuring the value of that initiative may be in the form of seeking feedback from staff and clients about how the initiative addresses a specific need or achieves a business objective.

To ensure that knowledge management addresses a business need and facilitates the achievement of your business objectives, you should do the following:

- Define a business objective or need

- Identify a specific knowledge management initiative that addresses that objective or need, defining a project plan and business case

- Define criteria for measuring the value of that initiative in meeting that objective or need, including a range of hard and soft measures

- Measure the value of the initiative

- Demonstrate the value of the initiative

- Apply lessons learned to future knowledge management initiatives.

Any initial skepticism surrounding the value of knowledge management will soon give way once people can see how knowledge management initiatives address a business need and support the firm's business objectives. This is no different from initial skepticism surrounding any new function or concept in a law firm. Consider the evolution of the marketing department in law firms. Initially, partners needed to be convinced of the value of an in-house marketing function. Over time, the marketing department has become a core function in law firms.

In this Chapter, I describe why knowledge management is a business imperative, and the many benefits that knowledge management brings to a law firm. I then describe the process of ensuring that knowledge management continually brings value to your firm.

Knowledge Management Is a Business
Imperative

In Chapter 1, I described why knowledge management is so critical to a law firm, namely:

♦ Clients place increasing pressure on law firms to provide efficient, proactive, commercially focused legal services at a lower cost.

♦ Technology creates an expectation of faster and alternative legal services.

♦ The information age has led to an explosion of information that lawyers must digest.

♦ Lawyers can pursue alternative career paths, making it a challenge to retain them.

♦ Consolidation of law firms has led to multi-office, multi-practice organizations and many associated diseconomies of scale.

♦ Global consolidation and the entry of multi-disciplinary practices have increased competition.

Law firms can no longer depend on long-standing relationships with their clients, lawyers who will stay with the firm throughout their careers or a predictable number of market competitors. The pressures facing law firms mean that firms must carefully examine their business models and find smarter ways to work. They need to find ways to keep and grow their client relationships. They must find ways to differentiate themselves in their market and enter new markets. They must develop and maintain a team of talented individuals. Ultimately, they need to lower costs, increase revenue and increase profitability.

Let's consider how knowledge management addresses these pressures, and then look at the relationship between knowledge management and lower costs, greater revenue and greater profitability.

Clients expect efficient, proactive, commercially focused legal services at a lower cost

Clients place a value on the work they outsource to law firms. They will not pay for duplicative work product, senior time spent on junior tasks or too much time spent on simple processes.

They expect their lawyers to be market leaders who deliver high quality legal services that meet their particular needs. They also expect their lawyers to act like a cohesive firm. A client assumes that its multi-disciplinary law firm can easily pull together a cross-disciplinary team of experts—or that information shared with one lawyer is passed on to the client's other lawyers in the firm.

Knowledge management is about identifying opportunities to work more efficiently by leveraging the knowledge of senior lawyers by providing tools that enable delegation to junior lawyers. Through the creation of best practice document repositories, precedent documents, and methodologies, senior lawyers confidently delegate tasks to junior lawyers. This frees up senior lawyers to develop their expertise and continually grow as market leaders. These tools also help a firm reduce the amount of non-billable time spent on duplicative work and ensure a high quality standard throughout the firm.

Knowledge management is also about sharing knowledge across a broad organization. Through building a culture of knowledge sharing, and developing knowledge management systems and processes, such as skills and expertise locators, or communities of interest across practice groups, a law firm can truly act like the multi-disciplinary firm its clients expect, rather than a loose collection of separate businesses.

Managing knowledge about clients and their industries also enables lawyers to be aware of their clients' needs and proactively tailor legal services to meet those needs.

If clients perceive that they are not receiving value for money from their firms, they will take their business to another law firm. Using knowledge management can directly result in the retention or acquisition of a client.

Technology creates an expectation of faster and alternative legal services

Lawyers are increasingly under pressure to deliver faster legal services via instantaneous communication tools. Introducing e-mail and extranets is not enough to meet this expectation. Lawyers must be able to produce documents in a faster turnaround time than ever before.

Knowledge management provides a means of creating high quality work product in a reduced time frame. Leveraging the firm's knowledge, through the use of methodologies, best practice documents and precedent documents, can significantly reduce the time taken to deliver legal services to clients. Knowledge management directly enables a firm to deliver faster legal services.

Law firms are also under pressure to use technology to deliver alternative legal services. Beyond using technology as a delivery tool, law firms are examining how e-business can transform the way they deliver legal services. Some global law firms have already developed sophisticated on-line legal advisory tools. Many firms offer client extranets to share knowledge with their clients.

There is a direct link between the knowledge management efforts of a law firm and its ability to build and maintain market leading e-business tools. Since the content of an e-business tool has to be drawn from the knowledge of the firm, the success of the tool depends almost entirely on the firm's internal knowledge management systems and processes.

The information age has led to an explosion of information that lawyers must digest

In this information age, lawyers face an exponential increase in the volume of information they must digest. The high volume of content that passes a lawyer's desk every day presents a challenge to identify which information is critical, and then how to digest that information. Lawyers can easily become overwhelmed with the amount of new information they must absorb. There are, however, enormous risk implications associated with lawyers missing a critical piece of information.

Law firms must find ways to deliver information and knowledge to lawyers in a form that ensures lawyers will absorb the information. The goal of knowledge management is to present the knowledge lawyers need when they need it, in an easily digestible form.

Lawyers can pursue alternative career paths

With the wide range of career options open to lawyers today, lawyers spend a significantly shorter period of time working with a law firm than in the past. At the same time, the salaries of lawyers (especially new graduates) have risen dramatically. The classic law firm scenario is where the firm invests in the professional development of a junior lawyer for the first two years, and in the third year, the lawyer leaves the firm. Since the lawyer only becomes profitable in his third year, the firm never realizes the return on its investment.

Since the profitability of lawyers is low in the early stages of their career, law firms must focus on how to accelerate the learning curve to increase their profitability. Better trained lawyers mean a reduction in non-recoverable time and a faster climb to a higher billing rate.

Law firms must also find ways to retain staff. This means decreasing the time spent on low value added tasks, providing a better learning environment and creating a better work/life balance. Indeed, the firm can even provide one of those alternative career paths by offering lawyers the opportunity to join the firm's knowledge management organization.

Knowledge management can help your firm improve its lawyer retention rates and accelerate the learning curve. Professional development programs, methodologies, best practice document repositories and precedent documents are all examples of specific knowledge management initiatives that accelerate the learning curve. They should also help improve lawyer retention rates by providing lawyers with the tools to work more efficiently. Most importantly, finding smarter ways to work through the implementation of knowledge management systems and processes also frees up lawyers to undertake more challenging work.

Consolidation of law firms has led to multi-office, multi-practice organizations and many associated diseconomies of scale

When a law firm grows, there is an expectation that the benefits derived from growth will far exceed any newly incurred costs. In reality, as law firms grow, they often do not leverage their larger infrastructure. Lawyers rarely work with colleagues outside of their practice group or floor. Practice groups do not look for opportunities to form multi-disciplinary teams or to refer work to other practice groups. Instead, firms carry the burden of an enormous infrastructure without realizing the benefits of building this infrastructure.

Knowledge management focuses on leveraging the knowledge of your staff across the entire firm and gaining the benefit of a growing infrastructure. Initiatives such as skills and expertise locators, an intranet, communities of practice and staff retreats are all designed to facilitate knowledge sharing across a law firm. Knowledge management is key to leveraging the benefits of a large infrastructure while minimizing the diseconomies of scale associated with growth.

Global consolidation and the entry of multi-disciplinary practices have increased competition

In the past, law firms could be reasonably certain about their market position and their competitors. This has changed and continues to change. Law firms now face competition from non-traditional sources, such as foreign or global law firms and multi-disciplinary practices. Law firms must have a very clear understanding of their market position, and how best to differentiate themselves from their competitors. Knowledge management is critical to this process. By managing knowledge about a firm's market strengths, a firm can identify where it should be focusing its marketing energies. By managing knowledge about a firm's market weaknesses, the firm can closely examine how best to address them.

Law firms also need to be aware of the service offerings of their competitors. Many law firms are proactively seeking out ways to offer a better client service. For example, your competitors may already be analyzing how their clients' legal needs may evolve in the next five years, and planning how best to offer legal services to meet those needs. Managing knowledge about your clients and their industries—a key focus of knowledge management—enables you to plan ahead and to ensure that you stay one step ahead of your competitors.

Your competitors may already be providing clients with access to their internal knowledge management systems and processes. If you don't offer similar tools to your clients, you may be giving away your competitive advantage.

Knowledge management enables law firms, whether their work is routine or highly specialized, to become competitive through the efficient delivery of legal services. For the firm that handles routine matters, knowledge management involves developing standard documentation and methodologies so that work can be delegated to more junior staff. One outcome of delegation is to reduce the costs associated with doing the work, allowing the firm to be competitive in its market.

What of the law firms focusing on high-end client work, where firms differentiate themselves from their competitors based on the quality of legal knowledge? At these firms, the focus of their marketing efforts is on building and maintaining a reputation of legal excellence. Knowledge management is also key to these firms. Knowledge management systems and processes, such as professional development programs, current awareness tools and communities of practice, can improve the level of expertise and the quality of legal knowledge within the firm. Implementing knowledge management processes and systems that diminish the time a lawyer has to spend on repetitive tasks frees that lawyer to be innovative and develop new skills and expertise.

Knowledge management therefore enables all kinds of law firms to be competitive in their market.

Lower Costs, More Revenue, Greater Profitability

Lower costs

Knowledge management can directly drive lowering the cost of:

- Maintaining the same knowledge in multiple sources
- Writing off time that cannot be billed to a client

♦ Poor risk management

The cost involved in maintaining the same knowledge in multiple sources. If knowledge is stored in multiple technology systems, consider how much it costs your IT department to develop and maintain those systems. If the knowledge is not stored in a system, but resides in the heads of your staff, consider how much it costs in time wasted by your staff as they try to access this knowledge. The following example should be familiar to many lawyers and marketing people.

The projects group of a law firm is preparing a bid to represent the builder of an electricity plant. At the eleventh hour, the group asks the marketing department to help prepare its bid. The group must present its credentials, including a list of major projects that the firm has been involved in, together with the skills and expertise of the proposed legal team. The projects group does not record information about their past projects or maintain an inventory of the skills and expertise of its lawyers. When the group needs to prepare a bid, it scrambles to find a description of prior projects, relying on partners' recollections about past work. The same applies to providing a description of the skills and expertise of staff. Since there is no record of staff skills and expertise, the partners must first remember which lawyers should be involved in the bid team, and then create a description of their skills and expertise.

The marketing department maintains a database containing a description of the firm's prior projects, and a record of the firm's prior bids. The content of this database reflects the level of involvement the marketing department has in the preparation of a bid. Since the projects group does not typically engage the marketing department to assist in bid preparation, the database contains little knowledge relating to the projects group. If the marketing department had project group information in its database, it would take two days to prepare a bid. Because of the lack of captured knowledge needed for this bid, this bid takes a week to prepare.

Knowledge management means providing efficient access to accurate, high quality knowledge to your staff. Knowledge management therefore drastically reduces the cost associated with having to locate knowledge from multiple sources.

The cost of writing off time that cannot be billed to a client. Think about how many hours a partner must write off because he cannot charge a client for unproductive time. Consider the following example:

A partner asks a junior lawyer to produce the first draft of a letter of advice to a client. The client is a top 10 client of the firm, sending millions of dollars in work to the firm each year. Since this is the first time the junior lawyer has been asked to write a letter of advice, he pours over the exercise, spending countless hours researching the question of law, then perfecting his writing style until he feels it is appropriate for partner review.

> The firm does not have a repository of best practice letters of advice. The firm also has limited legal research tools. With limited knowledge resources available to him, the lawyer spends 40 hours drafting the letter.
>
> When the partner reviews the time spent on this exercise, he realizes that it is only worth 20 hours of work. The partner knows he can only charge the client for 20 hours of the junior lawyer's time. The remaining 20 hours must be written off.

Knowledge management involves identifying and leveraging opportunities to work more efficiently. In the above example, the junior lawyer would have spent far less than 40 hours on his drafting exercise if he had access to best practice letters of advice and better legal research tools. He probably could have benefited from a professional development program that taught him how to write letters of advice—or a mentoring program that encouraged him to ask a senior lawyer for help.

The cost of poor risk management. Lawyers must ensure that their advice is accurate. This sounds obvious, though with a rapidly changing legal environment, it becomes increasingly challenging for lawyers to be aware of every development in the law. If a law firm gives bad advice, its client may sue, resulting in monetary damages and damage to the firm's reputation. Knowledge management is a critical risk management tool. If a firm manages the skills and expertise of its staff, inexperienced people can direct legal issues to the expert, rather than attempting to address the issues alone. Where the law changes rapidly, the firm can introduce current awareness tools, such as daily alerts that present a digest of judgments, rulings or legislative and regulatory changes, to ensure that lawyers are kept abreast of developments in the law.

Increased revenue

Knowledge management directly contributes to increased revenue in a law firm in several ways:

- ◆ More efficient use of time means a greater recovery of time recorded.

- ◆ More consistent, best-in-industry service to clients builds client loyalty and supports a firm's future client revenue stream.

- ◆ Better knowledge management tools enable delegation of work to more junior staff at a higher billing rate.

- ◆ Delegating work to junior staff allows partners and senior lawyers to concentrate on high quality work and charge premium rates.

- ◆ Delegating work to junior staff and better knowledge management tools create more opportunity to develop new services and products.

More efficient use of time means a greater recovery of time recorded. Recording time spent on a client matter is one thing. Deciding how much of that time can be billed to a client is another. Law firms cannot charge clients for inefficient work processes. Consequently, it is common for a percentage of time recorded never to be recovered. Knowledge management is about eliminating inefficient work processes and allowing staff to focus on value added tasks. This should therefore reduce the amount of recorded time that is written off. By reducing the amount of write-off time, and increasing the percentage of time recorded that can be billed, knowledge management directly increases the revenue of the firm.

More consistent, best-in-industry service to clients builds client loyalty and supports a firm's future client revenue stream. Marketing professionals will tell you that it is much easier to develop existing clients than to bring in new clients. Building and maintaining client loyalty is key to your future revenue stream. In an environment where clients are savvy purchasers of legal services and can choose from many options, law firms must find ways to keep their existing client base. They will do this if they continually provide efficient, proactive, commercially focused legal services at a lower cost. Knowledge management systems and processes enable a law firm to provide the legal service that clients are looking for.

Better knowledge management tools enable delegation of work to more junior staff at a higher billing rate. A strong focus of knowledge management is on finding ways to take the expertise of your senior lawyers and impart that expertise to more junior staff. The billing rates of junior lawyers are based on their value to your clients. If you can develop your lawyers in a shorter time period, they quickly become more valuable to your clients. This means that you can increase their billing rate. While their salaries may also increase, law firms should continually look for ways to increase the revenue:cost ratio of your lawyers through delegating work to more junior staff. Knowledge management is about leveraging your staff by finding opportunities to delegate work while building the skill base, and increasing the value, of your lawyers.

Delegating work to junior staff allows partners and senior lawyers to concentrate on high quality work and charge premium rates. Since senior lawyers now more often delegate work to junior staff, senior lawyers have time to focus on the high-end work for their clients. Where the skills required for a particular matter are so specialized that they are not readily available in the market, and where the outcome is critically important to the client, there may be an opportunity for your firm to charge premium rates. Where premium rates for specialized work are possible (e.g., corporate mergers and acquisitions), the more time a partner or senior lawyer has to focus on high-end work, the more opportunity there is to recover these premium rates. Knowledge management is all about confidently delegating work to junior associates, so that your senior staff are free to concentrate on high value, highly compensated work.

Delegating work to junior staff and better knowledge management tools create more opportunity to develop new services and products. Just as delegating work to more junior staff frees up partners to concentrate on high value work, it also provides partners with the time to develop new services and products. The future revenue stream of the firm will depend upon your firm's ability to tailor your legal services and products to keep up with the changes in the legal and regulatory environment. Indeed, you will be at a greater competitive advantage if you can introduce new services and products ahead of your competitors.

Managing knowledge about the legal and regulatory environment in which you operate, together with knowledge about your clients and their industries, also enables your firm to develop new services and products based on a clear understanding of market forces. Consider the following illustration:

> The banking group of a global law firm predicts that the banking industry will change dramatically in the next five years. The group wants to make sure that it stays ahead of the curve, adapting its legal services to meet the changes in the banking industry. The group establishes a task force of five partners from different offices to examine the likely changes in the banking industry and to strategize about how legal services will need to adapt to meet banking client needs. Among its many recommendations, the task force suggests developing

on-line advisory tools and documentation packages, establishing several communities of interest to develop expertise in specific industry developments, and creating key client relationship partners to ensure the group meets client expectations. Strategizing about the banking industry enables the firm to respond quicker than any of its competitors to industry changes, and ultimately establishes the firm as number one in this industry.

Increased profitability

The purpose of knowledge management is to enable lawyers to work smarter in response to market pressures, and in turn, decrease costs, increase revenue and ultimately, increase the profitability of the firm.

Align Your Knowledge Management Strategy with Your Business Strategy

In Chapter 8, I described how the knowledge management strategy should be drafted in the context of your firm's current position and its business objectives. In doing this, it should lay out the key challenges facing your firm, and describe how knowledge management will help the firm address those challenges. As you draft your knowledge management strategy, consider:

1. What are our business objectives?
2. What are the current challenges facing our business?

3. How can knowledge management help us address those challenges and achieve our business objectives?

Define the Measurements of Value of Knowledge Management

In Chapter 9, I described the importance of defining a business case and project plan for every knowledge management initiative. This process ensures that every knowledge management initiative is strongly tied to the firm's knowledge management and business objectives, and therefore brings value to the firm. Of course, at the business case and project plan stage, you can only predict the value an initiative will bring to your firm. As you implement initiatives, you should measure the value of each initiative to ensure that each actually helps achieve the firm's knowledge management and business objectives.

Define specific criteria for measuring the value of each knowledge management initiative

Criteria should be based on the desired outcomes of the initiative, which in turn, should be strongly linked to the business need or business objectives the initiative is intended to address.

You need to keep your criteria simple and specific. You should be conscious of moving from high-level strategic statements about the value of knowledge management to tangible, measurable components. In Chapter 9, I described how a corporate group defined its business case and project plan for developing a set of precedent documents. Consider how the corporate group described in Chapter 9 defines its criteria for measuring value:

In its business case for drafting precedent documents, the corporate group defined a number of business needs addressed by developing precedents, as well as the benefits that they hope will result from this initiative.

The business needs addressed by developing precedents are as follows:

- Our clients expect consistency and high quality in our documents, across all our offices.
- There is a high risk of giving bad advice associated with inconsistent language in our documents.
- Our partners need to leverage their expertise and find ways to delegate work to junior staff.

The benefits resulting from developing precedents are listed as:

- Enables partners to delegate drafting to junior lawyers, freeing partners to focus on high-value work and generate greater revenue
- Increases consistency in documentation
- Reduces drafting time, resulting in lower write-offs
- Improves the quality of work product, resulting in lower risk exposure.

The corporate group should look at each specific business need and benefit and decide how to measure whether developing precedents addresses the business need, and results in the benefits listed in the business case, as follows:

1. Our clients expect consistency and high quality in our documents, across all our offices.

   Measure value by:
   - Seeking client feedback on quality of work product and its consistency.
   - Examining whether there is an increase in client work by analyzing financial data.

2. There is a high risk of giving bad advice, associated with inconsistent language in our documents.

   Measure value by:
   - Seeking partner anecdotal evidence of avoided risk issues as a result of having the precedent documents.

3. Our partners need to leverage his expertise and find ways to delegate work to junior staff.

   Measure value by:
   - Seeking partner feedback on his ability to delegate work
   - Seeking lawyer feedback on the ease of drafting as a result of the precedent documents
   - Examining whether there has been a decrease in time that is written off by analyzing time sheets and client bills
   - Examining usage of precedents by generating precedent usage reports.

Use hard and soft measurements

The above example illustrates how a firm uses both hard and soft measurements of value. Hard measurements mean data, including financial data and usage data.

Examples of hard measurements may include analyses of:

♦ Time sheets against bills to determine the recovery rate.

♦ Time sheets to determine how lawyers are spending their time.

♦ Client revenues to determine whether the client relationship is stronger or weaker.

♦ Partner revenues to determine increases or decreases.

♦ Usage of knowledge management resources such as the intranet, precedents and best practice documents.

In the above example, the corporate group uses financial data to analyze whether there is an increase in client work. It also analyzes client billing information and time sheets to examine whether there has been a decrease in time written off.

Soft measurements involve seeking oral and written feedback from staff or clients on desired outcomes. Feedback is usually sought through interviews or surveys. In the above example, the corporate group seeks client feedback on the quality and consistency of work product. It interviews partners to find out whether any risk issues have been avoided, and about their ability to delegate work. The group also interviews lawyers about whether drafting has become easier as a result of the precedent documents.

Measure the Value of Knowledge
Management

After a reasonable amount of time has elapsed since you completed implementing an initiative, you should measure the value of the
initiative, based on the measurements you defined at the beginning
of the initiative.

Six months after the precedent documents have been
developed and released to the corporate group, the
knowledge management organization works with the
corporate group to measure the value of the initiative.

It conducts a combination of client interviews and
surveys, partner interviews and lawyer interviews to
ascertain whether the development of precedents
addressed the defined business need and resulted in the
benefits articulated in the business case.

The knowledge management group also seeks hard
data to support the feedback it collects in the surveys
and interviews. It looks at time sheets, client billings and
precedent usage reports.

Partners describe how a significant drop in the time
they spend drafting and reviewing documents has freed
them to pursue more challenging work. One partner
describes how he has been able to focus on higher
value work and charge premium rates. Another partner
describes how he has more time to focus on developing
new products and services. With financial services
reform legislation about to be released, he can now con-

centrate on how best to position the firm as a market leader in reform advisory work.

Clients notice a significant improvement in the quality and consistency of work product. Two clients are so impressed with the quality of documentation that they select the law firm as their preferred provider of legal services, resulting in increased revenue for the group. Another client asks the corporate group to develop a set of client specific precedent documents for a fixed fee, generating even more revenue for the group.

One partner describes how the firm averted a potentially damaging situation because of the precedent documents. A lawyer drafted an agreement based on an old document, which was drafted before a change in the law. The old language would have created a significant tax liability for the client. The partner reviewing the new loan agreement realized that it was not based on the precedent document and picked up on the error. If there had been no precedent document, it is highly likely that the agreement would have included the old language—which would have cost the client and the firm dearly.

Lawyers describe how much easier the process of drafting documents has become. Lawyers no longer feel frustrated as they search for a suitable starting point for documents. They are able to spend less time on producing the first draft of a document and feel more confident in their interactions with partners. They feel more intellectually challenged and positive about their working environment.

In addition to seeking anecdotal evidence, the corporate group also analyzes hard data from the firm's systems. Generating reports from the financial management system, the corporate group notices a significant reduction in time written off and an increase in client billings. Examining timesheets, the partners realize that partners now spend far less time drafting documents and more time focusing on high value work, including client relationship development work. It is also clear from the timesheets that junior lawyers spend more time drafting a greater number of documents than before.

The corporate group concludes that developing the core set of precedents has delivered great value to its practice and the firm.

Demonstrate the Value of Knowledge Management

Demonstrating the value of knowledge management to the firm is especially important in the early stages, as you work to build wide user and management support. Even if management embraces knowledge management as a key business driver, you need to continually demonstrate its value. Knowledge management is iterative, starting with simple, high value initiatives, and moving toward more sophisticated systems. As you move toward these sophisticated systems, your firm may have to increase its investment in knowledge management. The best way to gain support for increased investment is to regularly demonstrate the value of knowledge management to the management of your firm.

Knowledge Management as a Profit Center

The focus of this Chapter has been on how knowledge management drives the achievement of a law firm's business objectives and ultimately helps increase revenue, reduce costs, and increase profitability.

As you build your knowledge management organization, you should examine opportunities to recover the cost of your knowledge management efforts. You may charge clients for knowledge management staff time, just as you charge for lawyer and paralegal time. Where you use precedent documents that significantly reduce the time charged for drafting the document, you may charge a fee for using the precedent.

There are also opportunities to sell your law firm's knowledge management systems and processes to clients. You may develop client specific precedents and methodologies, on-line services or client extranets. Chapter 11 describes how knowledge management can become a profit center, increasing the revenue of your firm.

Ensure That Knowledge Management **Brings Value** to Your Firm

To ensure that your firm's knowledge management efforts bring value to your firm, follow these steps:

1. Have you aligned your knowledge management strategy with your business strategy?

    ◆ Do you know what your business objectives are?

    ◆ Are you clear on the current challenges facing your business?

    ◆ Have you defined how knowledge management can help your firm address those challenges and achieve its business objectives?

2. Have you defined the measurements of value for each knowledge management initiative based on the desired outcomes of each initiative?

3. Have you used hard and soft measurements?

4. Have you measured the value of each knowledge management initiative?

5. Have you demonstrated the value of each knowledge management initiative to your firm?

6. Have you examined opportunities to recover the cost of your knowledge management efforts?

7. Have you examined opportunities to sell your law firm's knowledge management systems and processes to clients?

Knowledge Management and Your Clients

Chapter Contents

In Chapter 1, I described a law firm, currently ranked as the number three firm in its market, with the goal to becoming the number one firm within three years.

To become number one, two parts of its business strategy are to attract the best clients and the best work in its market.

To understand which clients it wants to attract, the firm must first understand its existing client base. The law firm uses its knowledge of its clients and the industries in which they operate. Understanding the needs of its existing clients and the work the firm does for these clients enables management to identify opportunities to win more work from its clients. Comparing the existing client base with the firm's desired client base also highlights gaps in the existing client base and prompts the firm to target new clients.

To attract the best work, the firm must understand which practice groups differentiate the firm from its competitors and identify opportunities to leverage those practice groups. It must also understand where there are opportunities to develop weaker practice groups into market leaders.

To understand which practice groups are the market leaders, the firm uses its knowledge of the market, together with an analysis of revenue and costs associated with each practice group. This helps the firm identify which groups are not only market leaders, but also the most profitable for the firm. It also identifies which practice groups are weaker and need attention.

Management then uses the firm's knowledge to create its business strategy.

Once the firm is clear on the type of clients and work it wants to attract, it focuses on how to attract them. It knows it must provide services that clients want—both now and in the future. The firm's marketing group interviews key clients to learn about their expectations regarding the services offered by their law firms. They learn that clients are looking for the firm to provide value added legal services. Providing traditional legal services is no longer enough. It becomes clear that clients view knowledge management as a critical part of the law firm service offering. Clients want access to billing information and a library of past client work product.

Some clients have developed their own sophisticated approach to knowledge management and want to know how the firm approaches knowledge management, treating this as a good indication of how much the firm is focused on providing the best service to its clients.

> By managing knowledge about clients and their industries, the firm is able to leverage this knowledge to develop its business strategy. The firm's knowledge management efforts also enable the firm to differentiate itself in its market, and attract the best clients and the best work.

Knowledge management plays a key role in your firm's business development efforts in two respects. First, your firm possesses critical knowledge that influences your firm's business development strategy. Second, knowledge management is increasingly becoming a market-differentiating factor for law firms.

In the first part of this Chapter, I describe how law firms can use knowledge management to support their business development efforts. I also describe how knowledge management can be a market differentiator for law firms.

In the second part of this Chapter, I look at the range of approaches firms can take to leveraging their approach to knowledge management with clients, from giving clients access to internal knowledge management systems and processes to developing sophisticated e-business solutions based on internal knowledge management systems and processes.

Knowledge Management and Business
Development Strategy

Law firms possess vast amounts of valuable knowledge that can be managed to assist their business development efforts. Consider the knowledge you possess about:

- ◆ Your clients
- ◆ The industries in which clients operate
- ◆ The legal and regulatory landscape
- ◆ Your competitors
- ◆ Your market position
- ◆ Your revenue
- ◆ Your costs
- ◆ Your profitability

Your firm should be leveraging each of these categories to determine its business strategy.

Your clients

Through your daily interactions with your clients, together with a financial management system, client relationship management system and news feeds, you can develop a clear picture of your clients and your relationship with your clients. For each client, you should understand:

- ◆ Who is your client?
- ◆ What is the size of your client?
- ◆ Which industries does your client operate in?
- ◆ Who are your contacts at the client and what do you know about them?
- ◆ What are the key business and legal challenges your client faces?
- ◆ What type of work do you do for your clients? Is it the high end specialized matters, or commodity work? Is there an emphasis on particular areas of law?
- ◆ How much revenue do you generate from the client?

◆ Who at your firm does work for the client?

◆ Which other law firms does the client send work to?

◆ What legal work does the client send to other firms, and why?

◆ What is the nature of your relationship with your clients? Has your relationship changed since you first signed the client? Why?

◆ What are your client's expectations regarding your firm's service offering?

◆ What added services do you offer to your client?

◆ What will your client look like in five years?

You should use your knowledge of existing clients to formulate your strategy to build and maintain existing client relationships. You should also use your knowledge about your existing client base to help develop your strategy for winning new clients. For example, consider:

◆ Is your firm handling the type of work it wants to?

◆ Does it rely too heavily on a small number of clients?

You can analyze where there are gaps between your existing client base and target client base. Identifying these gaps is the first step in developing a strategy to win new clients.

The industries in which clients operate

You attract clients because you have expertise in applying the law to their particular situations. In other words, clients expect that you are an expert in how the law applies to their industry. Consider the following:

◆ In which industries do you advise?

◆ What are the current issues in each of the key industries you advise?

◆ What are the likely changes to each industry in the next five years?

◆ How will legal services change to meet the demands of industry changes in the next five years?

Your knowledge about the industries in which your clients operate enables your firm to take a proactive, strategic approach to the services and products it offers its clients.

The legal and regulatory landscape

Law firms must quickly respond to legislative or regulatory changes. Changes to the legal and regulatory landscape create major opportunities for firms to steal the thunder from their competitors and establish themselves as market leaders in understanding and advising on the impact of the changes. A firm that carefully manages its knowledge about legal and regulatory changes is at a distinct advantage over its competitors. Consider:

◆ What is the change to the legislative or regulatory environment?

◆ What is the impact of the change?

◆ Who are the experts in your firm who can advise clients on the change?

◆ How are changes monitored and disseminated throughout your firm?

◆ What new services should you offer as a result of the change?

Your knowledge about the legal and regulatory landscape enables your firm to develop a strategy to address legal and regulatory changes.

Your competitors

Just like any other business, a law firm must know everything it can about its competitors. While your marketing department possesses a good deal of market intelligence, your lawyers also acquire knowledge about their competitors in their daily interactions with clients. You should know:

- Who are your competitors?
- What differentiates them, positively and negatively, from your firm?

Your knowledge about your competitors enables you to develop a strategy to differentiate your firm from its competitors.

Your market position

Managing knowledge about your market position highlights the market's perception of your strengths and weaknesses. You should know:

- In which practice areas and industries are you regarded as market leaders?
- What makes your firm a market leader?
- In which practice areas and industries is your firm not regarded as a market leader? Why not?

Your knowledge of your market position enables your firm to develop a strategy to build upon your market strengths and address your market weaknesses.

Your revenue

Your firm typically manages knowledge about its revenue stream in a financial management system. You are able to generate reports that give you a clear picture of revenue generated by practice group, client, industry and matter type.

Understanding where your revenue come from enables your firm to develop its strategy for increasing revenue by practice group, client, industry and matter.

Your costs

Similarly, your firm manages its knowledge about costs in a financial management system. For example, you can generate reports on:

◆ The operating costs incurred by practice group and office

◆ The cost of unrecovered time

◆ The costs associated with conducting a particular matter.

This knowledge can help your firm to formulate its strategy to reduce costs.

Your profitability

Naturally, knowledge about your profitability flows from your knowledge of the firm's revenue and costs. Understanding what makes your firm profitable enables you to develop a strategy to grow your profitability.

★ ★ ★ ★

Managing your firm's knowledge about its clients and their industries, its competitors, market position, the legal and regulatory landscape, revenue, costs and profitability enables your firm to develop a well-constructed business strategy. This is knowledge management at its best—leveraging the knowledge of the firm to understand its current position and help define its future direction.

Knowledge Management as a Market
Differentiator

Clients increasingly want to know what their law firms do to work as efficiently as possible and deliver high value services to the client. They no longer judge their law firms solely on the basis of the core traditional legal services they offer. Increasingly, clients view a firm's approach to knowledge management as a market differentiating factor, seeing their approach as a critical component of the value the firm brings to the client.

Indeed, for many law firms, demonstrating their knowledge management efforts to clients is a business imperative. Many clients already have their own sophisticated approach to knowledge management and expect their law firms to have a similarly sophisticated knowledge management environment.

Beyond simply demonstrating that the firm has knowledge management systems and processes, law firms can take several approaches to leveraging their knowledge management efforts with clients, including:

1. Giving clients access to client related knowledge

2. Giving clients access to the firm's broader knowledge management systems and processes

3. Developing client tailored knowledge management systems and processes

4. Developing market products based on knowledge management systems and processes

Client Access to Client Related Knowledge

At its most basic level, clients want access to your firm's knowledge relating to that client. Your client may ask your firm to provide access to transaction documents, litigation documents, or letters of advice drafted by the firm for the client. Clients may want access both to draft documents and final documents.

Clients will also value access to client billing information and matter progress information, so that they can track the costs associated with a matter, as well as the progress of that matter. This is critical information to a client who must manage its organization's legal spending and report to management on the progress of legal matters impacting its organization.

Providing clients with access to this knowledge should be a basic service offering, and it is unlikely that you can charge your client for this. Though giving clients access to their knowledge seems simple, there are also a number of issues you need to consider. You need to provide secure access to this knowledge, ensuring that only authorized client staff can access knowledge. You also must protect the confidentiality of your other clients, ensuring that one client cannot access knowledge relating to other clients. Once you create this service, you need to maintain the service, ensuring that all content is up to date.

Client Access to Law Firm Knowledge
Management

When clients know that you have the means to provide them with client related knowledge, and that you have sophisticated knowledge management systems and processes, they may want access to these systems and processes, including:

♦ Precedents

♦ Best practice documents

♦ Legal research systems, e.g., on-line services and library systems

♦ Methodologies

♦ Staff skills and expertise

♦ Professional development courses

This is not about tailoring your knowledge management systems and processes to meet the specific needs of a client. This is simply about giving clients access to your internal knowledge management systems and processes. You therefore need to determine the level of access you feel comfortable giving a client to your internal knowledge management systems and processes. Since this involves giving a client access to some of the most valuable knowledge of the firm, you need to manage this process very carefully. Consider the following issues:

♦ How do you protect your duty of confidentiality to other clients?

♦ How should you charge clients for access to your knowledge management systems and processes?

♦ How do you ensure secure access to your knowledge management systems and processes?

♦ What is your risk exposure if you give clients access to your knowledge management systems and processes?

    – Is the content up-to-date?

    – What if the client incorrectly uses knowledge?

Despite the risks, you should view giving your clients access to your knowledge management systems and processes as an opportunity to further cement your relationship with your clients.

There are opportunities to generate revenue from giving clients access to your general knowledge management systems and processes. Deciding what to charge clients for this access depends largely on the value of the knowledge. In the knowledge pyramid, described in Chapter 3, the highest value knowledge is that which is unique to your firm and is not readily available in the market, represented by the top tier. It is access to top tier knowledge that will most likely generate revenue for your firm. For example, if you give a client access to a precedent document, you should consider charging a fee for the use of that document. There may also be opportunities to generate revenue from giving access to knowledge in the bottom tier if your firm has to pay for it. For example, where your firm pays a direct charge for access to on-line services, and is contractually able to give clients access to those services, it should pass that charge on to clients.

Client Tailored Knowledge Management

Once you have built a market-leading knowledge management environment, you should identify opportunities to tailor your knowledge management systems and processes for a specific client need. This is a great example of leveraging your knowledge management efforts to achieve two common business objectives—(1) to work efficiently and (2) to provide excellent client service. This is also a clear example of how you can directly generate revenue from your knowledge management efforts, since you should charge clients for client tailored knowledge management. Some examples of client tailored knowledge management include:

- ♦ Client specific precedents
- ♦ Client specific work product repositories
- ♦ Client specific methodologies and know-how files

- Client specific skills and expertise locator
- Client specific professional development program

Client specific precedents

Your firm can develop client specific precedents by identifying a client's most commonly used documents and applying your precedent development methodology to those client documents.

Client specific work product repositories

Your firm can develop work product repositories for clients based on its approach to developing the firm-wide work product repository. Developing this client specific repository, tailored to meet the needs of a client, gives the client an important practice management tool. Indeed, to be most useful to the client, the work product repository should manage all of the client's work product, regardless of whether it originates from your firm or from another source.

Client specific methodologies and know-how files

As your firm develops methodologies and know-how files relating to its own common work processes, it can also develop methodologies and know-how files for clients. Your firm can work with its clients to identify common work processes that could be made more efficient if the process was articulated as a series of steps. Your firm then maps the process steps and identifies any related knowledge associated with each step, such as precedents, letters of advice from the firm, and client and law firm contact information. A know-how file or methodology is then developed, outlining the process steps and drawing together all the related knowledge a client must access in performing the process.

Client specific skills and expertise locator

Clients (particularly those that have large, dispersed organizations) may want a means of identifying the skills and expertise of their staff. If your firm has developed a skills and expertise locator, you may be able to adapt it to meet the needs of your client.

Client specific professional development program

Your clients may need to offer their own professional development program to their staff. Also, a corporate law department must often conduct compliance training sessions with the broader organization. Given that your firm has developed an approach to designing and presenting learning programs, you are well placed to develop programs tailored to meet the needs of your clients.

★ ★ ★ ★

The examples described above are just the tip of the iceberg. Clients face many of the same issues as you, so they will be very interested to learn how you have applied knowledge management principles to addressing those issues.

Your clients may not have the means to develop their own knowledge management solutions. As you develop knowledge management systems and processes to address your business and knowledge needs, you should continually look for opportunities to offer these knowledge management solutions as products and services to your clients.

Development of Market Products Based on Knowledge Management

Taking the development of client tailored knowledge management products and services one step further, you should also examine ways to develop generic market products based on your knowledge management efforts. You may sell these products not just to existing clients, but also to new clients. You may also look at selling your market products to a broader customer base. For example, beyond traditional clients, you might want to consider selling your products to other law firms that are not direct competitors.

Examples of market products may include precedents, professional development programs and compliance programs based on area of law or industry.

These client and market products may be technology-based, though some will not. Later in this Chapter, I look at how firms can deliver technology-based knowledge management products to clients and customers—in other words, the relationship between knowledge management and e-business. However, before we turn to e-business, there are some threshold issues that you must consider as you move from an internal focus on knowledge management to selling knowledge management-based products.

Knowledge Management-Based
Products—The Threshold Issues

Developing knowledge management-based products, whether they are client tailored or generic, should generate revenue for your firm—both directly and indirectly. They also require significant investment and carry a certain level of risk. Before you embark on turning your knowledge management work into products, you should be clear on your business objectives, understand the investment and risks associated with developing knowledge management-based products and know what your revenue expectations are.

What are your business objectives?

Developing knowledge management-based products represents a departure from the traditional law firm business model of generating revenue solely from time spent advising clients. Law firms may understandably be nervous about offering knowledge management-based products. The significant investment required, and the risks associated with offering these products, also affects the willingness of a firm to move in this direction. You should first be clear on the objectives of developing these products. Do you plan to:

- Attract new clients to your traditional service offering?
- Attract new clients to new product offerings?
- Enhance service delivery to existing clients?
- Build new revenue streams?

Your responses to these questions will determine the content and purpose of these products and services, the level of investment and your expectations regarding return on investment. You should also research your market to find out what clients want, and what your competitors are doing. In particular, consider whether your competitors' efforts pose a threat to your business.

Can your business model support the development of knowledge management-based products?

You also must consider whether your firm can support the development of products and services based on knowledge management. This means looking at your business model and considering whether you have the infrastructure to build and maintain products.

It may be difficult to shift your business model to accommodate the provision of products based on knowledge management, both for reasons of structure and size. You may want to outsource product development to a third party, enter into a joint venture with a third party or spin off a separate company.

How much revenue can you generate?

Given the significant investment and risks associated with offering knowledge management-based products, you must have a clear picture of the revenue generating opportunities. This means looking at how much revenue a knowledge management-based product can generate and whether the revenue will be generated directly or indirectly.

You can generate revenue directly for a product if the market perceives the content to be valuable enough that it will pay for it. You therefore need to distinguish between knowledge that is freely available in the market from knowledge that is unique to your firm. This means looking at what knowledge your competitors are offering, and whether they charge for this knowledge.

If you want to generate revenue, you should focus on providing knowledge that is not freely available elsewhere. Even if knowledge is unique to the firm, the market may not attach a high enough value to that knowledge that it will pay for it. You therefore need to understand what value your product brings to the market. One question to ask is:

♦ What is the cost to the market if it doesn't use your product?

Generating revenue directly by selling your product is ideal. You should identify how you plan to generate revenue from every knowledge management-based product and then estimate the extent of that revenue. You may also generate revenue indirectly if product users then engage your firm for traditional legal services.

What are the costs associated with developing these products?

Generating revenue for your firm is a great reason to develop knowledge management-based products. However, if the cost outweighs the benefits, you should think twice before investing too heavily in developing products. Given that the development of knowledge management-based products is a radical departure from the traditional law firm business model, you should be clear on the level of investment necessary to develop this new line of business for your firm. Consider:

♦ What is the level of staff time needed to develop these products?

♦ What is the cost of building a technology platform to support these products?

♦ What is the cost of marketing these products?

♦ How much will it cost to maintain these products?

♦ How long do you expect it will take before you recover your costs?

What are the risks associated with developing these products?

Developing knowledge management-based products incurs a certain degree of risk for your firm. You need to protect the confidentiality of your other clients, ensure that only authorized client staff can access content, and protect yourself against clients misusing content when they should be seeking legal advice from your firm.

There are a number of risks your firm must manage if it decides to develop knowledge management-based products for clients and the broader market. Consider:

♦ How do you protect client confidentiality?

♦ How do you protect your firm against client misuse of content?

♦ How do you ensure that content is kept up-to-date?

♦ How do you limit access to licensed users?

What are the risks associated with not developing knowledge management-based products?

As your competitors become more sophisticated in their knowledge management efforts, you may no longer have the luxury of deciding whether it is beneficial for you to offer knowledge management-based products. It may simply become a business imperative. The key question you should ask is:

♦ What are the risks associated with not developing knowledge management-based products?

Knowledge Management and E-Business

E-business has become a hot topic for lawyers in recent years. For many law firms, e-business means building a website or offering extranets to clients. To these firms, e-business means using technology to deliver traditional legal services more efficiently. However, true e-business is the transformation of your traditional business through the use of technology. Neither websites nor extranets are market transforming. On-line products may be. There are four levels of e-business evident in law firms as described below.

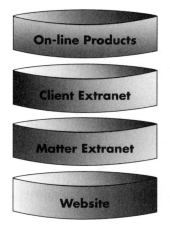

The Law Firm Website

Law firm websites have evolved in recent years but essentially remain electronic brochures, providing information to the public about the law firm. They typically contain office address details, a staff directory, a description of the firm's practice groups, the firm's philosophy and electronic copies of the firm's publications. Since law firm websites are commonplace, it is difficult for a website to differentiate your firm from its competitors. From a knowledge management perspective, the website only publishes freely available knowledge. As an e-business initiative, law firms receive a very small return for their investment. On the other hand, since most firms have a website, it is a business imperative for your firm to have one.

Matter Extranets

Matter extranets or deal rooms are secure web-based workspaces, accessible only to defined parties involved in a matter. A matter extranet typically has a limited lifespan, established at the beginning of a matter and dismantled at the conclusion of the matter. There are variations in the features of extranets, depending on the investment a firm makes in building its extranet capability. A typical matter extranet may include party contact information, draft documents, news items relating to the deal, matter progress and billing information. These basic extranets are essentially a content delivery tool that enable the posting of content from other systems. More sophisticated extranets may feature document collaboration functionality, so that parties involved in the matter can also edit content via the extranet.

While the matter extranet is not exactly market transforming, there are a number of benefits. Using an extranet lowers the risk of parties working with inconsistent knowledge, since all parties access the same content at the same time. Costs associated with the matter are also reduced, as the use of traditional forms of delivery, such as fax or courier, are significantly reduced. Extranets are also very convenient, allowing parties to access content from any location at any time.

If your firm offers matter extranets, you should consider the following:

- Who hosts the extranet?
  - Is it your firm or another firm?
  - Do you use a third party?
- Does your infrastructure enable integration between the extranet and your internal knowledge management systems and applications?
- What happens to the content at the end of the matter?

Client Extranets

Using the same technology framework as the matter extranet, law firms can develop client extranets. These extranets have a longer lifespan than a matter extranet and can be used as the principal means of delivering client related knowledge management services and products. As discussed earlier in this Chapter, you may want to provide your client with access to:

1. Client related knowledge
   - Client transaction documents
   - Client litigation documents
   - Client letters of advice
   - Billing information
   - Matter progress information
   - Law firm contact information

2. Law firm knowledge

◆ Precedents

◆ Best practice documents

◆ Legal research systems

◆ Methodologies

◆ Staff skills and expertise

◆ Professional development courses

3. Client tailored knowledge management

◆ Client specific precedents

◆ Client specific work product repositories

◆ Client specific methodologies and know-how files

◆ Client specific skills and expertise locator

◆ Client specific professional development program

The benefits and the issues associated with developing a client extranet are generally the same as those relating to matter extranets. However, there is one distinct difference. A matter extranet has a single purpose of facilitating knowledge sharing during the life of a matter. The client extranet, on the other hand, forms the basis of a more permanent and valuable knowledge-sharing tool. Of course, it is your client who decides whether the client extranet is a valuable tool. Clients will have an even higher standard of what they consider valuable if they must access several different law firm extranets. To ascertain whether your clients see the client extranet as a valuable tool, you should ask the following:

◆ Does the extranet actually provide useful content to the client?

◆ What content would be useful to the client?

On-Line Products Based on Knowledge Management

Earlier in this Chapter, I described how law firms face extraordinary opportunities to truly transform their business model through the development of knowledge manage-

On-line Products

ment-based products. While some of these products may not involve technology at all (for example, client professional development programs), many will rely heavily on technology. It is the delivery of knowledge management-based on-line products that represents true market transforming e-business for law firms. In this venue, firms can build new markets by leveraging their knowledge management efforts. Building new markets means selling your services and products to a new client base. If your firm only sells traditional legal services to Fortune 500 companies, it may be able to sell on-line products to small to medium size businesses. If your firm's traditional client base is in one city, it may be able to sell on-line products across the country.

In the knowledge management-based on-line products industry, there is a strong interrelationship between client products and market products.

Firms can take two approaches:

Client Tailored
On-line Products

Generic
On-line Products

A firm might begin with developing a knowledge management-based product for a particular market and then look for opportunities to create client tailored versions of the product.

A law firm develops an on-line advisory system for the banking industry. The system provides law departments in the banking industry with comprehensive knowledge about U.S. and European regulation of derivative instruments. The system costs $2 million to develop and $500,000 a year to maintain. Many of the world's major banks subscribe to this system, generating over $5 million in revenue for the firm each year.

Given the success of the system, the firm explores opportunities to further develop it. In particular, it explores the opportunity to develop a client tailored version of the system. It learns that after a client has queried the on-line advisory system, it typically generates a document based on the answer to that query. At the moment, lawyers generate those documents in a separate system. Based on its research, the law firm decides to build a document generation capability into the on-line advisory system. Leveraging its own precedent drafting methodology, the firm can develop the client specific precedent documents that form the basis of any new documents generated by the system. Seeing the great value in combining advice with document generation, five subscribers to the original on-line advisory system purchase the client tailored version. The law firm works with each client to identify and develop its own set of client-specific precedent documents. The precedent documents are then built into a tailored version of the on-line advisory system.

The client tailored on-line advisory system is a powerful knowledge management tool, enabling clients to

> manage the process of researching a question of law and then generating accurate documents based on the advice they receive.

The second approach a firm can take is to begin with a client tailored knowledge management–based product and then look for ways to create a broader market version of the product.

> A law firm advises a client on the development of a shopping mall. The firm drafts a series of agreements, each containing many client commitments relating to the development of the shopping mall. Knowing that there are hundreds of commitments that must be met during the estimated three years of the development, the client asks the firm to suggest a way for the client to manage the execution of its commitments. The firm offers to build a contract management system to alert the client of its commitments when they arise. The firm identifies all commitments contained within the agreements and builds a means of alerting the client of its commitments into an on-line contract management system.
>
> The contract management system is a great success and further cements this client relationship. The firm believes that the contract management system would have a wider application to a broader market. Based on the original client contract management system, it develops a generic version, selling it to other clients.

Succeeding at E-Business

E-business represents a fundamental shift in the traditional law firm business model. Law firms traditionally take a short term tactical approach to their business, focusing on revenue based solely on hours billed. There is little room for investment in a longer term strategic approach. There is also little investment in finding alternative methods of revenue generation. Put simply, the emphasis is on short term gains, rather than longer term growth.

The focus on the billable hour is the biggest challenge to transforming your business. Until law firms commit to moving away from the time-based billing model, it will be extremely difficult to explore the revenue generating opportunities that e-business offers.

To succeed at e-business, you must have management commitment to long term investment in the growth of the firm. Management must not only realize the great revenue generating opportunities that lie outside of the billable hour. Management must also be willing to accept that significant investment—and time—are necessary to succeed at e-business.

Ensure Knowledge Management Supports
Business Development at Your Firm

To ensure that your firm's knowledge management efforts support your business development efforts, follow these steps:

1. To support your business development efforts, do you manage your knowledge about:
    ♦   Clients?
    ♦   The industries in which clients operate?
    ♦   The legal and regulatory landscape?
    ♦   Competitors?
    ♦   Market position?
    ♦   Revenue?
    ♦   Costs?
    ♦   Profitability?

2. Do you use this knowledge to develop your firm strategies?

3. Do you leverage your knowledge management efforts to differentiate your firm in its market?

Ensure Your Firm Leverages Its Knowledge **Management** Efforts with Clients

To ensure that you leverage your knowledge management efforts with your clients, follow these steps:

1. Do you promote your approach to knowledge management to your clients?

2. Do you give clients access to client related knowledge?

3. Do you give clients access to your firm's broader knowledge management systems and processes?

4. Do you develop client tailored knowledge management systems and processes?

5. Do you develop market products based on knowledge management systems and processes?

6. Have you considered the threshold issues associated with developing knowledge management-based products?

   ♦ Have you defined your business objectives?
   ♦ Can your business model support the development of knowledge management-based products?
   ♦ How much revenue can you generate?
   ♦ What are the costs associated with developing these products?
   ♦ What are the risks associated with developing these products?
   ♦ What are the risks associated with not developing these products?

7. What is your approach to e-business?

   ♦ Do you have a website?
   ♦ Do you have matter extranets?
   ♦ Do you have client extranets?
   ♦ Do you offer on-line products?
   ♦ Do you have client tailored on-line products?
   ♦ Do you have generic on-line products?
   ♦ Is there a relationship between your client tailored products and generic products?

Knowledge Management for Other Shapes and Sizes

Knowledge Management and the Law Department

The law department of a global pharmaceutical company has over 70 lawyers in ten offices around the world. Until recently, each office operated as a separate law department. When the company underwent a global business reorganization, all ten law departments were merged into one. A New York based General Counsel heads the new law department.

The company has five major lines of business, and operates in 40 countries around the world. To meet the needs of the business, lawyers are aligned both to a region and a business line.

The biggest challenge for the General Counsel is to create a cohesive law department that provides consistent, high quality advice to the business lines across all countries. Essentially, law department staff must present a common face both to the company and to the outside world. This means that they must work closely together and share their knowledge across multiple locations, time zones and cultures. This is no mean feat, but the General Counsel knows that knowledge management is key to creating an effective global law department.

Knowledge management can enable lawyers to take a consistent approach to drafting documents and giving advice. Through developing precedent documents and accessing a best practice work product repository, staff could base their documentation and advice on the same knowledge sources. Both knowledge management tools would be a good starting point for taking a consistent approach.

The General Counsel must also get a handle on the legal risk exposure of the company. He must understand the current legal matters involving the company, and also must identify the areas of high legal risk for the company so he can proactively seek to minimize that risk. A global matter management system will provide valuable knowledge about the legal costs of the organization, as well as trends in legal risk. The General Counsel can use this knowledge to identify areas of high risk and seek ways to minimize that risk. For example, if one division of the company is involved in litigation more significantly than others, the law department can offer compliance training seminars to that division to address some of the behaviors that lead to litigation. The General Counsel can also use the matter management system to control outside counsel costs by comparing the cost of different firms for similar work, and then directing work to the lower cost firm.

Pockets of the law department already provide a good foundation for knowledge management. The

Sydney office has developed a repository of best practice agreements. The U.S. offices have used a matter management system for several years.

The General Counsel learns that the company has a corporate knowledge management organization. He meets with the company's Chief Knowledge Officer to discuss the knowledge management activities of the company and to understand the corporate knowledge management strategy. The outcome of that meeting is that the corporate knowledge management organization works with the law department to understand its knowledge needs, and then develops a law department knowledge management strategy that is closely aligned with the corporate knowledge management strategy.

To understand the law department's knowledge needs, the corporate knowledge management organization conducts a knowledge audit of the law department to understand how law department staff work, and what knowledge they use to do their work. The law department also identifies cultural barriers to knowledge management, the need for knowledge management resources and any gaps in the law department's technology platform. At the same time, the law department articulates its business objectives. Some objectives relate to the company such as:

- ◆ Manage the company's legal risk exposure
- ◆ Provide consistent, high quality advice that facilitates business activities
- ◆ Reduce the company's legal costs

Some objectives relate to the operation of the law department:

- ♦ Create a cohesive law department
- ♦ Create a more satisfying work environment
- ♦ Manage the cost of operating the law department

The department then articulates knowledge management objectives that will facilitate the achievement of those business objectives. With the help of the corporate knowledge management organization, the law department drafts its knowledge management strategy.

The strategy describes the scope of knowledge the law department seeks to manage and the scope of its knowledge management initiatives. It contains recommendations for addressing some of the cultural barriers to knowledge management, particularly focusing on the challenges associated with merging ten separate, local law departments into a global law department. Given the size of the law department and its unique knowledge needs, it recommends that the law department develop its own knowledge management organization based on the corporate knowledge management organizational model.

The strategy also includes recommendations for the law department knowledge management system. The strategy recommends that the law department leverage its existing technology tools (the matter management system and repository of best practice documents) and implement other existing corporate technology tools not yet used by the law department, including a corporate document management system, a corporate intranet and an enterprise wide search engine. The goal is to build a single user interface knowledge management system which manages all content stored in the department's underlying systems and applications.

The General Counsel looks to his panel of outside counsel who may have their own knowledge management systems and processes. He approaches each law firm to provide knowledge management solutions. For example, he asks outside counsel to provide electronic copies of all documents drafted by the firm for the company. He wants training courses offered by the law firm, and access to the on-line research tools of the firm. He wants law firms to draft certain precedent documents so that in-house lawyers can create commonly used documents internally rather than outsourcing this drafting.

Once the law department has developed its strategy, it turns to implementation. This means defining specific knowledge management initiatives that deliver high value to the department. The law department rolls out a global matter management system and a standard approach across all offices to capturing knowledge about the company's legal matters. This initiative enables the General Counsel to understand the legal issues impacting the company.

Another priority is getting staff to give consistent advice. A high value and simple initiative is to roll out the best practice document repository to all offices and introduce a process for law department staff to identify, capture and store best practice documents.

Creating a cohesive law department is also critical. The General Counsel introduces an annual global law department retreat for all lawyers to meet and form relationships. While lawyers are aligned by business line and location, the General Counsel recognizes that there should be a way to group lawyers according to other common interests. He creates "communities of practice," drawing together lawyers working in the same area of law or on the same matter. To build relationships throughout the department, he introduces regular video-conferences for lawyers and staff.

The law department also examines whether it can leverage any of the company's knowledge management systems and processes. Seeing great value in the corporate document management system and search engine, the law department works with the corporate knowledge management organization to roll out these systems in the law department.

It develops a law department intranet based on the corporate intranet. This becomes the principal knowledge sharing tool of the law department, providing the interface into the department's matter management system, best practice document repository, law department news and legal current awareness.

The law department builds its own knowledge management organization to build and maintain these knowledge management initiatives. Initially, the department employs a knowledge manager, an information officer and an intranet content manager. The knowledge manager reports to the General Counsel and the corporate Chief Knowledge Officer, while the information officer and the intranet content manager report to the knowledge manager.

The law department also focuses on addressing the cultural barriers to knowledge management. In particular, it must overcome differences in regional cultures and in practice area needs. Its biggest challenge is in moving from a decentralized culture of ten separate offices to the centralized culture of a global law department. The General Counsel seeks to overcome these barriers by reinforcing the importance of working together as a team and the value knowledge management brings to this objective. He also makes sure that he regularly acknowledges the contribution of staff to knowledge management.

As the law department identifies specific knowledge management initiatives, it becomes sophisticated in its expectations of how outside counsel can provide assistance. It expects outside counsel to supply:

- Electronic copies of final documentation (both transaction documents and letters of advice)
- Company tailored precedent documents
- Training resources
- Matter updates

While the initial focus is on creating knowledge management tools for internal law department knowledge sharing, the department works hard to leverage these tools with internal clients. Over time, it looks for

> ways to make these tools available to its clients. For example, it makes basic documents available on the corporate intranet. It also enables clients to track the progress of matters in which they are involved.
>
> For every knowledge management initiative, the General Counsel focuses on how knowledge management achieves the law department's business objectives. There must be a solid business case for each knowledge management initiative, with defined criteria for measuring value. At various points of implementation, the General Counsel examines the value of the initiative. The General Counsel recognizes that knowledge management helps achieve the business objectives of the law department and the company.

For a law department, knowledge management is the leveraging of your department's collective wisdom by creating systems and processes to support and facilitate the identification, capture, dissemination and use of your department's knowledge to meet your business objectives. It is simply about working smarter.

Knowledge management is as important for law departments as it is for law firms. Like law firms, law departments must provide their clients with high quality, commercially sound, consistent legal advice in an efficient manner. Although they may not be driven by revenue like their law firm counterparts, they are under constant pressure to demonstrate their value. Their value is usually measured in terms of their ability to manage the legal risk exposure of their organization. How well does the law department facilitate commercial transactions and minimize the legal costs of the organization? There is a direct link between a law department's knowledge and its ability to manage the legal risk exposure of its organization. Knowledge is therefore at the heart of a law department.

Throughout the preceding Chapters of this book, I have described how law firms should approach knowledge management. Where there are similarities between law firms and law departments, I refer you to the relevant Chapters. There are, however, some important differences that affect how a law department should approach knowledge management. This Chapter highlights those differences, and describes how they may affect a law department's approach to knowledge management.

First, the business objectives of a law department differ from those of a law firm. Unlike a law firm, a law department is not focused on increasing revenue and profitability. On the other hand, a key business objective is managing the organization's legal costs: litigation and settlement costs, outside counsel costs and the cost of the law department itself. Another common law firm business objective is to differentiate itself from other law firms. A law department is not competing with other law departments for its client's work. However, the law department still must demonstrate its value to its organization. It is important to understand these differences, since your approach to knowledge management is so intrinsically linked to your business objectives.

Second, since most law departments do not record time or charge back to clients, they do not face the biggest cultural barrier to knowledge management in law firms—the time-based billing model. Also, since lawyers are not competing for compensation based on the revenue of the law department, as they do in a law firm, it should be less of a challenge to get lawyers to work together and share their knowledge.

Third, a law department is part of a wider organization that may already have a knowledge management strategy. If so, the law department must adopt an approach to knowledge management that is consistent with the organization's approach. It should also look at how to leverage the work of the wider organization. Are there knowledge management resources you can use? Are there knowledge management technology tools you can implement? Are there knowledge management initiatives that apply to the law department?

Fourth, law departments are in the enviable position of being able to derive the benefit of their outside counsel's knowledge management efforts. Law departments should look to their law firms to provide knowledge management products and services that meet the needs of the law department.

Although there are major differences between a law department and a law firm, like a law firm, before you develop your approach to knowledge management, you should be clear on your law department's business and knowledge management objectives. You should also look closely at the influence your organization's approach to knowledge management has on your law department.

Even if your organization has a knowledge management strategy, you should draft a separate one for the law department. This strategy should align with your organization's strategy and reflect the business and knowledge management objectives of your law department. In that strategy, you should focus on the broad range of issues relating to knowledge management—defining the scope of knowledge and knowledge management, creating a knowledge management organization, building a culture to facilitate knowledge management, and developing a knowledge management system.

Most importantly, as you implement knowledge management, you should apply business rigor to every knowledge management initiative you pursue—from developing a business case to measuring and demonstrating the value of that initiative.

Getting Started

In Chapter 2, I described how a law firm should get started in knowledge management. The steps are similar for a law department, namely:

◆ Learn about your organization's approach to knowledge management.

◆ Gain high level support for knowledge management from law department management.

◆ Form a knowledge management team to build awareness about knowledge management throughout the law department and develop a knowledge management strategy.

◆ Get management to send a clear message of the importance of knowledge management to the law department.

◆ Understand the knowledge needs of the law department.

◆ Draft a knowledge management strategy.

◆ Implement specific knowledge management initiatives.

◆ Apply business rigor to every phase and every initiative.

◆ Measure and demonstrate the value of knowledge management.

What Is Your Organization's Approach to Knowledge Management?

You should examine your organization's approach to knowledge management before you undertake any significant work in this area. There is a good chance that your organization has a knowledge management strategy. Find out whether your organization has a Chief Knowledge Officer and a knowledge management organization. Explore what technology systems and applications have been implemented by your organization to support and facilitate knowledge management.

If your organization has a well-defined approach to knowledge management, you should develop a law department knowledge management strategy that aligns with that of the organization. When you move to implementation of knowledge management initiatives, you should seek to leverage organization-wide knowledge management systems and processes. From a pure cost standpoint, it will be an easier sell to your law department management if you can leverage the knowledge management efforts of the wider organization.

Gain High Level Law Department
Management Support

Once you have learned about your organization's knowledge management efforts, you should gain high level support for knowledge management from law department management. (Depending on the size of your law department, it may only be the General Counsel you need to convince. However, if your law department is large and dispersed with a management team consisting of deputy general counsels, division heads or country heads, you will need to gain support from this larger group at this early stage.) To gain its support, law department management should have at least a cursory understanding of the value of knowledge management. Since knowledge management is a relatively new concept, management may not know what knowledge management actually is and will probably need to be convinced of its value to the law department.

A law department's initial interest in knowledge management may be limited to a few senior people in the department who recognize the value of knowledge management and believe strongly in the department's need to focus on this area. These people must, with the help of your organization's knowledge management staff, place knowledge management in the context of the law department's business objectives and demonstrate how knowledge management can drive the achievement of those business objectives. Consider the law department in my earlier illustration, and these two simple examples of how knowledge management can support the department's business objectives:

BUSINESS OBJECTIVE

The ten law departments of a global pharmaceutical company have recently merged into one large global law department. One of the biggest challenges for the General Counsel is to create a cohesive law department. Law department staff must work closely together and share their knowledge across multiple locations, time zones and cultures to assist the business lines.

KNOWLEDGE MANAGEMENT SOLUTION

Building a law department intranet that publishes knowledge about different practice areas, regions and business lines is an effective first step in sharing knowledge across the law department.

BUSINESS OBJECTIVE

Lawyers spread across the global law department described above must provide consistent, high quality advice to all business lines in all countries.

KNOWLEDGE MANAGEMENT SOLUTION

Developing a precedent documents database provides lawyers with a standard starting point for all new documentation. This ensures a high degree of consistency and quality in the work product of the law department across all locations.

You need to get law department management to conceptualize knowledge management in broad terms. This is not just about day-to-day legal work. This is also about how management gathers and uses its knowledge to operate the law department and minimizes the legal risk exposure of the organization. You will get management's attention by drawing the lines connecting knowledge management and business objectives.

Form a **Knowledge** Management Team

Your department should create a law department knowledge management strategy team. The team should consist of a small number of representatives from the lawyers, administrative staff and IT staff. The team should work closely with the wider knowledge management organization, if one exists. The purpose of the team is to build awareness about knowledge management throughout the law department and develop the law department's knowledge management strategy.

Management Sends a Clear Message

Once management understands the importance of knowledge management to the law department, it must send a clear message of support to the department. The rhetoric of management regarding knowledge management will set the tone for the department's approach to knowledge management. It will help build awareness throughout the department about what knowledge management is and why it is important. People are more inclined to adopt change if they understand why they need to change. As with law firms, law department staff need to understand how knowledge management will not only improve the department's overall performance, but will also make their lives better.

Understand the Knowledge Needs of the Department

To develop a knowledge management strategy that meets the needs of your law department, you must first understand the knowledge needs of the department and look at how staff currently address those needs. In Chapters 2 and 8, I described an approach for identifying the knowledge needs of law firm staff. This approach applies equally in law departments:

Conduct a "knowledge audit"

A knowledge audit enables you to understand the knowledge needs of the department—and to identify what knowledge management systems and processes the department already has.

In Chapters 2 and 8, I described conducting focus sessions with lawyers and support staff to learn about how people work and how they use knowledge to do their work. I suggested that focus sessions should be practice group-centric. In a law department, rather than being aligned by practice group, lawyers may be aligned by business line or industry. The key is to group focus session participants according to a common interest. These focus sessions will help the knowledge management team to understand how people work and how they use knowledge to do their work, and to identify existing knowledge management practices.

You should also conduct sessions with administrative staff. These sessions should focus on understanding how specific systems and processes supporting knowledge management are maintained. For example, secretaries can provide insight into how lawyers create documents, maintain outside counsel contact information or communicate with their internal clients.

Since law departments exist to serve the needs of the wider organization, you should also ask your clients in the business lines about their expectations regarding the law department.

Analyze results and identify the key findings

The focus sessions will help you identify the specific knowledge needs of staff, opportunities for knowledge management, and any barriers to knowledge management. The barriers may be cultural impediments, such as differences in regional cultures. They may be organizational barriers, such as lack of resources. They could also be technological impediments, such as insufficient systems and applications to manage knowledge.

Identify knowledge management best practices

As you analyze how your department currently uses knowledge to operate, your knowledge management team should look at industry best practices. The team should then consider the key issues facing your department in the context of knowledge management best practice.

Test the findings from the focus sessions

Your knowledge management team should report the results of the focus sessions to the department. In Chapter 8, I described drafting a findings report. The purpose of testing findings with the department is to ensure that the knowledge management team has a clear understanding of the department's knowledge needs before drafting the knowledge management strategy.

With the department's confidence that the knowledge management team understands its knowledge needs, the team should develop its knowledge management strategy.

Draft a Knowledge Management Strategy

The knowledge management strategy should reflect the knowledge needs and work processes of all staff, as well as your department's culture and its business strategy. If your organization has a knowledge management strategy, your strategy must align with it. As you develop your strategy, you should look at what knowledge management systems and processes your outside counsel can offer.

In Chapters 2 and 8, I described how lawyers should develop a strategy that acknowledges the many facets of knowledge management. The strategy should define the scope of knowledge that you will manage and the scope of knowledge management initiatives you will implement. It must focus on building a culture of knowledge sharing, creating an organization to support and facilitate knowledge sharing, developing a technology platform for the knowledge management system and ensuring that knowledge management initiatives facilitate the achievement of business objectives.

The strategy should describe the department's knowledge management objectives and highlight its current approach to knowledge management. It should contain recommendations to move the department to the achievement of its knowledge management objectives, but be flexible enough to enable different groups within the department to develop knowledge management processes and tools that meet their needs.

Following are the key issues your department should address in its knowledge management strategy. Consider:

♦ **What are the department's business objectives?**

   Since knowledge management is a key business driver, the knowledge management strategy should align with the department's business strategy.

♦ **What are the department's knowledge management objectives?**

   The department's knowledge management objectives should articulate exactly how knowledge management will support the department's business objectives.

♦ **What is the organization's approach to knowledge management?**

   Does the organization have a knowledge management strategy? Does the law department knowledge management strategy align with the organization's knowledge management strategy?

♦ **What is the scope of knowledge you will manage?**

Is the focus on managing legal knowledge or all knowledge used in a law department? Will the department manage only explicit knowledge or examine ways to address tacit knowledge?

♦ **What is the scope of knowledge management initiatives you will pursue?**

Will knowledge management initiatives be purely technology driven, or will the department implement technology and non-technology systems and processes to manage knowledge? Will the department focus only on implementing systems to capture and share knowledge, or will it focus on building an organization and address cultural barriers to knowledge sharing?

♦ **What are the strengths of your culture?**

Since knowledge management becomes part of the way your department works, it should reflect your department's culture. If a key strength of your department is its culture of autonomy at the regional level, your department's approach to knowledge management must reflect this. As you develop an overarching department-wide knowledge management strategy, you should acknowledge that there may be some region-specific knowledge management initiatives that will be implemented at the regional level, consistent with the department's approach to knowledge management.

♦ **What are the cultural barriers to knowledge management you need to address?**

Do lawyers see the value in sharing their knowledge with others? Do you have a decentralized culture? Are there differences in regional cultures?

♦ **What approach will your department take to knowledge management?**

Will knowledge management be managed centrally? Will it be completely decentralized? Will your department adopt a hybrid model?

♦ **What will your knowledge management organization look like?**

Who will lead it? Will you form your own knowledge management organization or will you rely on the wider knowledge management organization? How many knowledge management staff will there be? What will be their roles? Are there existing functions in the law department that will form part of the knowledge management organization?

♦ **How will the knowledge management organization be positioned in the department?**

Who will the head of knowledge management in your law department report to? What is the relationship between the law department knowledge management organization and the wider knowledge management organization? What is the relationship between the knowledge management organization and law department staff?

♦ **What will your knowledge management technology system look like?**

Will the department develop a single user interface into multiple applications? Will the department focus on developing a heavily vetted work product repository?

♦ **What technology tools do you have?**

Does the department have the fundamental components of its knowledge management technology platform? Is each tool already leveraged, or are there opportunities to improve use of the existing tools?

♦ **What technology tools do you need?**

Are there clear gaps in your department's technology platform? What technology systems does the organization have that you could leverage?

♦ **How will your outside counsel support your knowledge management efforts?**

Will you look to your outside counsel to provide knowledge management solutions to your department?

♦ **Will your department give its internal clients access to its knowledge management systems and processes?**

What knowledge will you make available to clients on your intranet? Will you enable clients to track the progress of matters? Will your department give internal clients access to its work product repositories? Will your department make precedent documents available to the organization?

♦ **What are the critical success factors?**

What are the key cultural, organizational and technological factors that may affect the success of knowledge management in your department?

♦ **What will knowledge management cost?**

Consider the cost of creating a knowledge management organization and implementing technology tools or non-technology programs. Consider also the cost of not doing knowledge management.

♦ **What value will knowledge management bring to your department?**

How will you measure the value of knowledge management to your department? What hard measures, such as financial and usage data, will you use? What soft measures, such as anecdotal feedback about value, will you use?

The critical elements of the knowledge management strategy are:

- Scope, described in Chapters 3 and 4
- Organization, described in Chapter 5
- Culture, described in Chapter 6
- Technology, described in Chapter 7

The Scope of Knowledge

In Chapter 3, I distinguished knowledge from information and data and described the importance of both explicit and tacit knowledge. I highlighted how lawyers typically place a heavy emphasis on core explicit legal knowledge, such as:

- Case law, commentary and interpretation
- Legislation and commentary
- Best practice (or model) documents
- Precedent (or form) documents

Lawyers, however, use a broader range of knowledge—knowledge relating to the business of law, as I described in Chapter 3. Lawyers in law departments have similar broad knowledge needs. In particular, it is critical that in-house lawyers be commercially minded, giving advice that applies the law to the commercial needs of the business. A law department possesses knowledge about:

◆   The nature of legal issues affecting the organization

◆   The progress of legal matters affecting the organization

◆   The legal costs of the organization

◆   Areas of potential legal risk

◆   The business of the wider organization

◆   The skills and expertise of law department staff

◆   Internal clients

◆   Outside counsel and other third parties

Consider each of these categories:

The nature of legal issues affecting the organization.
How are these legal issues best managed? Managing this knowledge allows the law department to tailor its services to meet the needs of the organization.

The progress of legal matters affecting the organization. What is the progress of legal matters to be litigated? How many matters has the department settled? What is the progress of commercial transactions? This knowledge enables the General Counsel to advise management on the legal issues affecting the organization.

The legal costs of the organization. How much do you spend on litigation and on settlements? How much do you spend on outside counsel? How much does it cost to operate the law department? Understanding the legal costs of the organization is the first step in managing those costs.

Areas of potential legal risk. What are the recurring legal issues? Which areas of the organization generate the most legal issues? What are the legislative and regulatory changes that may affect the organization? Highlighting the areas of potential legal risk enables the law department to proactively manage those potential risks.

The business of the wider organization. What are your lines of business? In which industries do you operate? What are the key trends in those industries? What areas of law are relevant to the lines of the business? This knowledge enables lawyers to offer commercially focused legal counsel to its internal clients.

The skills and expertise of law department staff. Who are your lawyers? Who are the experts in an area of law, geographic region, business line or industry? This knowledge enables the law department to provide the best service to the organization by directing legal issues to the appropriate law department resource. This is a particular challenge for a large, dispersed law department.

Internal clients. Who are your clients? What are their legal needs? What is your relationship with your clients? A law department needs to understand its internal clients and their expectations in order to best meet their needs.

Outside counsel and other third parties. Who are your outside counsel? When do you use outside counsel? Do you use specific outside counsel for specific matters? Do you use third parties? A large part of managing a law department is managing its use of outside counsel. In-house lawyers must therefore know about their outside counsel and have a clear understanding of which firms to use in particular circumstances. This also applies to the use of third parties, such as expert witnesses.

You should take a broad view of the categories of knowledge used by all staff in your law department, including both knowledge for the practice of law (advising clients on a day-to-day basis) and the business of law (managing the legal risk exposure of the organization and related costs). As described in Chapter 3, you should manage both tacit and explicit knowledge.

Once your department is clear on the scope of knowledge it should manage, it should assign a value to that knowledge. The value of knowledge determines the effort your law department should put into managing that knowledge. Also, you should be clear

KNOWLEDGE MANAGEMENT
AND THE LAW DEPARTMENT

on who owns the knowledge you seek to manage. Chapter 3 contains a chart to help determine value and ownership of knowledge.

The Scope of Knowledge Management

In Chapter 4, I described four principles law firms should follow in defining the scope of knowledge management. These also apply to law departments:

1. You need to understand what knowledge you must manage before you can find the best way to manage that knowledge.

2. Do not limit your thinking on the scope of initiatives that can help you manage that knowledge.

3. Base your investment in knowledge management on the value of the knowledge to your practice and your business. The more valuable the knowledge, the greater the investment in knowledge management.

4. Begin with simple, discrete knowledge management initiatives, and over time, draw them together into more complex knowledge management tools and processes.

Chapter 4 provides a detailed definition of knowledge management and the scope of knowledge management initiatives that apply to any legal practice—whether a law firm or law department. The most important distinction for a law department is that your organization may have already implemented knowledge management initiatives that can apply to your department. Your department could derive the benefit of the work already done by the knowledge management organization, and simply adapt broader knowledge management initiatives to meet your department's needs. It is often easier (and more cost effective) to adapt an existing initiative than to implement one from scratch. As you look at the scope of knowledge management initiatives your department will implement, you should consider how the knowledge management initiatives of your wider organization might apply to your department.

Knowledge Management Organization

Knowledge management may be the responsibility of everyone in your law department, but it also requires a dedicated team. You need staff dedicated to the tasks of identifying, capturing and disseminating knowledge in a form that others can use. In Chapter 5, I described three critical factors—size, composition and positioning of the knowledge management organization. The discussion of these factors applies to law departments as well as law firms, and I encourage you to read Chapter 5.

Naturally, the size and complexity of your knowledge management organization will be influenced by the size of your law department. You may not be able to justify retaining a head of knowledge management, professional support lawyers, information officers and knowledge managers. However, you should look at each of these roles and identify which will bring the most value to your law department.

As you consider what your knowledge management organization will look like, there is one important distinction to make between law departments and law firms. It is quite possible that your organization has established a knowledge management organization. If this is the case, you should learn about the size, composition and positioning of that knowledge management organization—and see how it applies to your law department. Ask:

♦ Can the broader knowledge management organization support the knowledge management efforts of our law department?

– Does the broader knowledge management organization have enough resources to assist us?

– Do our knowledge management efforts require knowledge management staff with a background in legal practice?

♦ Should we build a separate law department knowledge management organization?

♦ What is the relationship between a separate law department knowledge management organization and the broader knowledge management organization?

Knowledge Management Culture

Law departments that do not record time or bill back to internal clients avoid the biggest cultural barrier to knowledge management—the time-based billing model. This means that law departments may have an easier time justifying the investment in finding more efficient ways to work. Indeed, since a business objective of any law department is to control its costs, finding more efficient ways to work is encouraged.

Similarly, since a law department does not generate revenue, lawyers in a law department are not competing with each other for revenue and should therefore be more inclined to work as a team. It should not face the cultural barrier created by revenue-based lawyer compensation models. On the other hand, your career progression and compensation models may still create competitiveness among staff. If this is the case, you need to consider whether those models support or hinder knowledge management.

Chapter 6 describes the major cultural barriers to knowledge management in a legal practice, suggests the target knowledge management culture and illustrates how to address cultural barriers. For a law department, the major cultural barriers tend to relate to how to build a cohesive team that may be spread across different business lines, offices and cultures.

Limited interaction between the divisions of the law department

If your law department is divided into areas of practice or lawyers are aligned to specific lines of business, there may be little interaction between lawyers working in different areas. If your law department is scattered across more than one physical location, it is highly likely that limited interaction will prove a cultural barrier to knowledge management.

When lawyers do not see the value of sharing knowledge outside of their area, they are limiting the department's ability to serve the needs of the entire organization. It also becomes very difficult to implement department-wide knowledge management initiatives. In this environment, lawyers are simply not interested in exploring opportunities outside of their area.

Overlap in areas of practice between lawyers in different areas of the department

Overlap in areas of practice between different areas of the department is often the result of the limited interaction between lawyers. When different areas of the department handle similar matters, they may be giving inconsistent advice to the organization. From a risk management perspective, this can be detrimental as internal clients may seize the opportunity to go "forum shopping." In other words, if an internal client does not like the legal counsel one lawyer has given, he can seek the counsel of another lawyer. This runs counter to the creation of a cohesive law department.

A decentralized culture

Where a law department with multiple offices has a decentralized culture, it is difficult to implement a department-wide approach to knowledge management. Consequently, knowledge management initiatives tend to succeed in small pockets of the department—but the department never gains the full benefit that knowledge management can bring to the department.

Differences in regional cultures

Like a decentralized culture, different regional cultures challenge a department's ability to implement department-wide initiatives. Without a consistent approach to knowledge management, there will usually be inconsistent levels of knowledge management across different offices. From a risk management perspective, it may also mean inconsistencies in the quality of work sent to clients. Global law departments should pay careful attention to understanding how each office works and how it interacts with its clients. In particular, the department's approach to knowledge management must meet the needs of different cultures, while ensuring that the department presents a common face both to the organization and to the outside world.

Lack of senior management support

If senior management does not understand the value of knowledge management, it will not support knowledge management—nor will the rest of your department. Senior management must be engaged in knowledge management—not just understand it, but invest in it and constantly reinforce the message that knowledge management is key to how you work in your department.

Knowledge management is perceived as the work of an isolated group

In some law departments, there is no expectation for all staff to get involved in knowledge management. That law department will fail in its knowledge management efforts.

Knowledge management is perceived as an IT initiative

If knowledge management is synonymous with technology, staff think that this is just about developing databases. Although the IT department can build some of the tools to capture and disseminate knowledge, without the involvement of staff to develop content and implement non-technology processes, knowledge management will have a very limited scope, impact and life span.

In addition to identifying cultural barriers to knowledge management, you should also have a clear understanding of the knowledge management culture you want in your law department. Chapter 6 describes the target law firm knowledge management culture, which also applies to law departments and how best to address cultural barriers, namely:

- ◆ Identify cultural barriers at the strategy development stage.

- ◆ Management must be in front of, and behind, cultural change.

- ◆ Management must tell the department that knowledge management is a business imperative.

♦ Knowledge management must be made a top priority with substantial financial investment.

♦ Adopt specific initiatives to overcome cultural barriers.

Knowledge Management Technology

Chapter 7 describes the key principles you should apply as you develop your knowledge management system. One of those principles is to leverage what you already have. For a law department, this means leveraging the technology tools your department has as well as the technology systems and applications your organization has before acquiring any new systems and applications.

Implementing Knowledge Management

Implementing your law department knowledge management strategy requires your department to identify specific initiatives that enable the department to achieve its strategic goals. As you identify specific knowledge management initiatives, you should look at whether your organization has implemented knowledge management initiatives that could be adapted to meet your department's needs. You should also look at what your law firms offer. For example, can they give you access to work product repositories, professional development programs and precedents?

In Chapters 2 and 9, I described how knowledge management is not a project with a completion date. This is about adopting new ways to work that, over time, become deeply ingrained in the work processes within your department. It takes several years to achieve the desired knowledge management environment—even with a well thought through knowledge management strategy. The key is to take a phased approach, and apply business rigor to every phase and every initiative.

Take a phased approach to implementation

As knowledge management takes several years, your department should examine the recommendations within its knowledge management strategy and identify short term, mid term and long term goals.

In the short term (a period of 12 to 18 months), your department should focus on simple knowledge management initiatives that are easy to implement and provide high value to the department. This "quick win" approach is an effective way to build understanding of, and support for, knowledge management.

Simple, high value knowledge management initiatives include drafting precedents, building a repository of best practice documents, and creating a law department intranet site.

The short term goal should be to build a solid foundation for more sophisticated knowledge management in the department. By building understanding of knowledge management at its simplest level, your department will create an appetite for more complex, and higher value knowledge management initiatives. Addressing some of the basic cultural barriers to knowledge management, creating a formal organization to lead knowledge management, and looking at ways to leverage the department's technology platform, enables you to begin building support for knowledge management—and paves the way for the successful implementation of more complex, higher value knowledge management.

Many of the cultural barriers to knowledge management can be best addressed in the mid term (a period of 18 to 36 months). By this stage, the department has already seen the value of simple knowledge management. It should also see the limitations of knowledge management in the department caused by cultural barriers. Since knowledge management is no longer a theoretical concept, demonstrating the cultural barriers to knowledge management should be straightforward. It should also be relatively easy to identify how best to address these cultural barriers.

The resources required to implement knowledge management should also become clearer in the mid term. While the focus in the short term is on leadership of the knowledge management organization, in the mid term, your department should examine whether it has adequate knowledge management resources to build more complex, higher value knowledge management systems and processes.

The increased understanding of knowledge management typically leads to an increased appetite for knowledge management initiatives. This typically involves looking at more sophisticated use of a department's technology platform. In the short term, your department should be leveraging its existing technology platform. In the mid term, the limitations of your existing technology platform will be evident. This will be the appropriate stage to identify gaps in the knowledge management technology platform, and examine new systems that fill those gaps.

In the long term (a period of three to five years), your department should focus on implementing initiatives to develop sustainable best practice knowledge management. By this stage, the department should have created a culture that supports and promotes knowledge sharing. It should have built a knowledge management organization to direct and facilitate the development of knowledge management programs and systems through the department, consistent with the department's knowledge management strategy. It should have built a technology infrastructure to support capture and delivery of knowledge.

Apply business rigor to every phase and every initiative

To succeed at knowledge management, you should ensure that every knowledge management initiative meets your business and knowledge management objectives.

Before you commence any knowledge management initiative, you should draft a project plan and a business case. The project plan enables you to understand the investment and time associated with implementing the initiative. The business case allows you to articulate how the initiative meets a specific business need or business objective. You can then assess whether the predicted outcomes justify the investment in the initiative.

Conducting pilot initiatives gives the knowledge management organization the opportunity to get initiatives right. The best planned projects may sometimes miss critical barriers that only become evident during implementation. Before you roll out a knowledge management initiative across your department, you may want to begin with a small group. This enables your department to manage any issues associated with implementation with minimal disruption to the department.

Measuring the value of each initiative is fundamental to demonstrating how knowledge management drives the achievement of your department's business objectives.

Measure and Demonstrate the Value of Every Initiative

Knowledge management is all about driving the achievement of your department's business objectives. To do it well requires significant, ongoing investment by the department. Demonstrating the value of knowledge management to the department is critical to securing the support necessary to implement knowledge management initiatives. It is simply not possible to demonstrate value without first measuring value. However, this is not just about hard numbers. Value can also be measured in soft terms. The key question to ask is—how does this knowledge management initiative specifically achieve our knowledge management objectives and support the achievement of our business objectives?

Chapter 10 provides a detailed description of how to measure and demonstrate the value of knowledge management.

Introduce Knowledge Management into Your Law Department

To introduce knowledge management to your law department, follow these steps:

1. Have you learned about your organization's approach to knowledge management?

2. Have you gained law department management support for knowledge management?

3. Have you formed a knowledge management team to develop the law department knowledge management strategy?

4. Has management sent a clear message about the importance of knowledge management throughout the law department?

5. Have you understood the knowledge needs of your law department?

6. Have you drafted a knowledge management strategy?

- Have you defined the scope of knowledge?
- Have you defined the scope of knowledge management?
- Have you recommended a knowledge management organization?
- Have you identified cultural barriers that need to be addressed?
- Have you reviewed your current technology infrastructure and made recommendations to build a knowledge management system?

7. Have you defined specific knowledge management initiatives?

8. Have you looked at what your law firms can offer?

9. Have you defined short term, mid term and long term initiatives based on their value and complexity?

10. Have you applied business rigor to every phase and every initiative?

11. Have you measured and demonstrated the value of each knowledge management initiative?

Knowledge Management and the Solo Practitioner

A lawyer runs a solo practice handling a broad range of work, including real estate, trusts and estates, commercial matters, and some personal injury litigation. Though the lawyer is quite successful, he recognizes that there are a number of inefficiencies in his practice that impact his profitability. Often, when the lawyer searches for prior work product, he cannot find what he is looking for, and has to draft new documents from scratch. Typically, as he prepares a bill, and reviews the time spent on a matter, he feels he cannot justify charging the full amount to the client. Consequently, he often writes off time. The lawyer has also been feeling pressure from competitors in his neighborhood to reduce the amount he charges for routine matters. In particular, he has noticed that the law firm across the street charges a lower fee to handle the sale and purchase of residential real estate. In reaction to this, he drops his fees for this work.

With the downward pressure on fees, the lawyer knows he must find more efficient ways to work so that he can generate work in a shorter period of time, and reduce the amount of write-off time. He often talks about developing precedent documents and checklists to make his life easier, but never makes the time to develop these tools.

It is not until the lawyer faces a serious threat to his practice that he realizes he needs to change the way he works. One of his regular clients slips and falls in a subway while vacationing in another state. The client sustains serious injury and wants to sue the city in which the accident occurred. She asks the lawyer to file a notice of claim. Overwhelmed with work, the lawyer does not check the statute of limitations for filing a claim for personal injury in that city. Assuming the statute of limitations is three years (as it is in his own state), the lawyer does not immediately file the notice of claim. When the lawyer files the claim five months after the accident, he soon learns that the statute of limitations for filing a notice of claim in that city is only 90 days. Through the lawyer's lack of knowledge, the client is statute barred from filing a claim. Furious with the lawyer, the client sues him for legal malpractice.

The lawyer realizes that this could have been avoided if he had the time, and the knowledge tools, to research this issue. He realizes that knowledge management is not just about improving his profitability. It is also about protecting his livelihood.

Why Knowledge Management Is Important
to a Solo Practitioner

Practicing law is a knowledge based profession, whether for a global law firm or a solo practitioner. There is a direct link between your knowledge and your profitability. There is also a direct link between your knowledge and your risk exposure, as illustrated above. As I described in Chapter 1, knowledge management is an absolutely critical element of how you manage your business.

Much of this book has dealt with how lawyers leverage knowledge by sharing knowledge with others. As a solo practitioner, sharing knowledge with others is not your challenge. Rather, leveraging knowledge means applying your present knowledge to your future needs.

Think about how your business would benefit if you could:

♦   Stop reinventing the wheel.

♦   Eliminate low value tasks.

♦   Generate consistent work product.

♦   Improve the quality of your work.

♦   Have more time to pursue higher value work.

These are all outcomes of knowledge management.

Your focus should be on first understanding what your business objectives are, and how knowledge management can help you achieve those objectives. Next, you need to understand what you do and how you use knowledge to do it. You should define the categories of knowledge you use and examine how best to manage that knowledge. You should consider the organizational, cultural and technological elements of knowledge management. Then, you should develop a knowledge management strategy. With a well thought-out strategy, you can build systems and processes to identify, capture, retrieve and use your knowledge to meet your business objectives.

Understand What Your Business Objectives Are and How Knowledge Management Can Support Those Objectives

Knowledge management is all about finding more efficient ways to manage your practice and your business. You need to first understand your business and your business objectives. Consider:

What is your practice?

- ♦ What areas of law do you practice in?
- ♦ Is there a dominant area in which you practice?

Who are your clients?

- ♦ How many clients do you have?
- ♦ What type of clients do you have?
- ♦ What type of work do you do for your clients?
- ♦ How do you win clients?
- ♦ How do you keep clients?

Who are your competitors?

- ♦ How many competitors do you have?
- ♦ What do you know about your competitors' practices?
- ♦ What distinguishes you from your competitors?

What are your market strengths?

- ♦ What are you best known for in your market?
- ♦ What generates the most income for your practice?

♦ What is the most profitable work for your practice?

What are your market weaknesses?

♦ What are you least known for in your market?

♦ What generates the least income for your practice?

♦ What is the least profitable work for your practice?

When you have a clear understanding of your business, you are able to define your business objectives. Consider what you are trying to achieve:

♦ Improve profitability?

♦ Grow your practice?

♦ Provide a better client service?

♦ Create a more satisfying work environment?

When you have defined your business objectives, you can then connect the dots between knowledge management and achieving those business objectives. Consider:

Knowledge management can help improve profitability by improving productivity. This means eliminating low value tasks, reducing duplicative work processes and improving the quality of work.

Knowledge management can help grow your practice by improving productivity (and having a better understanding of your business). This means knowing about your clients and your market, and analyzing where your growth opportunities are.

Knowledge management can help you provide a better client service by improving the speed of delivery of legal services and the quality of your work.

Knowledge management can help you create a more satisfying work environment by eliminating low value tasks and giving you more time to pursue higher value work.

This first step—tying knowledge management to your business objectives—ensures that any investment you make in knowledge management has a direct impact on your practice and your business. Without a strong understanding of what you are trying to achieve in your business, your approach to knowledge management may not reap the many rewards it can bring to your business.

> Consider the solo practitioner described at the start of this Chapter. He takes a close look at his business, asking himself the questions listed above:

What is my practice?	Real estate, trusts and estates, commercial, personal injury litigation.
	Handling commercial matters for small business is the dominant area of practice.
Who are my clients?	88 clients
	30% private—mainly real estate, trusts and estates, personal injury litigation
	70% local businesses—mainly commercial and real estate/leasing work.
	Clients are acquired through personal recommendation.
Who are my competitors?	Clients are retained through high quality of work and competitive fees.
	Three main competitors in the neighborhood.
	Firm A focuses almost entirely on purchase and sale of real estate and charges very low fees.

	Firm B does a broad range of work and is best known for commercial work.
	Firm C focuses on personal injury litigation.
	My practice distinguishes itself from my competitors by offering a full range of services.
What are my market strengths?	I am best known for my breadth of practice, i.e., I am able to service all of my clients' needs.
	I generate the most income from commercial matters.
	My most profitable work is personal injury litigation.
What are my market weaknesses?	I am least known for, and generate the least income from, real estate work.
	The least profitable work for me is trusts and estates.

On the basis of this analysis, and as a result of the personal injury lawsuit fiasco described earlier, the lawyer defines his business objectives as follows:

♦ Improve profitability.
♦ Grow the practice in real estate and commercial work.
♦ Provide better client service.
♦ Create a more satisfying work environment.

To achieve these business objectives, the lawyer defines his knowledge management objectives as:

- ♦ Improve productivity:
  - – Eliminate low value tasks
  - – Reduce duplicative work processes
- ♦ Gain a better understanding of the business.
- ♦ Improve the speed of delivery of legal services.
- ♦ Improve the quality of legal services.
- ♦ Create more time to pursue higher value work.

Understand What You Do and How You Use Knowledge to Do It

Once you understand your business and knowledge management objectives, you should consider what you do on a daily basis and how you use knowledge to do it.

In Chapters 2 and 8, I described how larger law firms should understand their knowledge needs through a series of focus sessions. As a solo practitioner, you should ask yourself the following questions:

1. What work processes are associated with your areas of practice (e.g., document drafting, research, project management, client relationship management, etc)?

2. What knowledge do you currently use to practice law?

3. What knowledge do you currently use to manage clients and grow your business?

4. What knowledge systems do you currently use in your practice (e.g., databases, on-line services, etc.)? Consider how these systems help you in your practice.

5. What knowledge needs are not currently met in your practice? How would your practice benefit from implementing or improving systems to meet those knowledge needs?

As you consider your current work processes, you should identify:

♦   Where are the inefficiencies (or the opportunities to improve)?

♦   What do you do well and can apply to other areas of your practice?

The solo practitioner described earlier takes a close look at his work processes.

He *drafts documentation* that is largely repetitive, especially for the real estate, trusts and estates, and commercial work. He has no systematic way of drafting these documents. Sometimes, he uses prior "best practice" documents he has drafted as the basis of new documents. Often, he drafts from scratch. He has never developed generic precedent documents. He stores documents on his hard drive, under client folders, but has no standard document naming convention, so retrieving documents at a later stage is usually very time consuming.

He *conducts research* when he advises clients on the applicability of law to their particular situation. He uses a subscriber based legal research tool. He does not

---

keep a record of the questions of law he has researched, and cannot re-use his research in the future.

He *manages litigation,* ensuring that all documents are filed by their due dates. He stores documents relating to a litigation both electronically, in a database, and in hard copy in a filing cabinet. Unfortunately, this lawyer faces some issues with how he manages litigation, having missed the deadline for filing a notice of claim for his personal injury client.

He *manages his practice.* He records time in a time-keeping system and stores financial information about the practice in an electronic spreadsheet. The spreadsheet is used to record information about his clients, matters, costs and revenues.

He *keeps abreast of developments in the law and the market* through reading newspapers and periodicals and attending seminars on particular topics of interest. He is often overwhelmed with the sheer volume of knowledge he must absorb.

Define the Categories of Knowledge You Use (the Scope of Knowledge)

As you think about what categories of knowledge you use, do not limit yourself only to categories of legal knowledge. Also, do not limit yourself to knowledge on paper (explicit knowledge). In Chapter 3, I described how lawyers, in defining the scope of knowledge they use, typically place heavy emphasis on explicit legal knowledge, such as:

♦ Case law, commentary and interpretation

♦ Legislation and commentary

♦ Best practice (or model) documents

♦ Precedent (or form) documents

You also use many categories of non-legal knowledge in your practice. What do you know about your clients and the industries in which they operate? If you are a litigator, what do you know about the likely mindset of a judge, the tactics of opposing counsel and the most appropriate expert or external consultant?

You use knowledge for the practice of law. But you also use knowledge to manage your business—knowledge for the business of law. For example, you possess knowledge about:

♦ The law

♦ Your practice

♦ Clients

♦ The commercial market and specific industries

♦ Your skills and expertise

♦ Methodology and processes

♦ Past projects and lessons learned

♦ Third parties (e.g., regulators, judges, counsel, experts, external consultants)

♦ Your market position

♦ Your revenue, costs and profitability

Your knowledge may be on paper or in your computer system (explicit knowledge) or it may simply be in your head (tacit knowledge). Both are very important.

As you define the knowledge you use to do your work and achieve your business objectives, consider the tacit and explicit knowledge you use for both the practice of law and the business of law.

Chapter 3 describes these categories of knowledge in detail. As you define the broad categories of knowledge you use, you should be conscious of the value of that knowledge, since this will determine the level of effort you should dedicate to managing that knowledge. The knowledge pyramid in Chapter 3 illustrates the different levels of knowledge a lawyer uses. The concept is simple—where the knowledge you use is readily available in the public domain, you should pay less attention to managing that knowledge. Where knowledge is so unique to your practice that it differentiates your practice in its market, you should focus heavily on managing this knowledge. You should create your own version of the pyramid:

Highest
Value
Knowledge

- Precedent documents
- Client, industry and project information
- Skills and expertise
- Project methodologies
- Policies and procedures
- Easily accessible
- Searchable by categories and full text searchable
- Strictly maintained

Highly Relevant
Knowledge and
Information

- Best practice documents, e.g., transactional documents, methodologies and research
- Regularly used information indexed by subject matter
- Easily accessible
- Regularly maintained
- Searchable by categories and full text searchable

General Information and Data

- Publicly available legal, industry and client information
- Full text searchable

In Chapter 3, I described how a law firm must understand who within the firm owns the knowledge. For a solo practitioner, the simple question is *where is the knowledge located?* Understanding this will help you determine how best to manage that knowledge.

To help you determine which knowledge you use and how you should manage that knowledge, consider this adapted version of the checklist in Chapter 3.

The solo practitioner uses this checklist to define the categories of knowledge he uses, assess the value of that knowledge, describe whether it is currently tacit or explicit and determine where that knowledge is currently located.

KNOWLEDGE CATEGORY	TACIT OR EXPLICIT	VALUE (LOW, MEDIUM, HIGH)	KNOWLEDGE LOCATION
The law			
♦ Case law, commentary and interpretation	Explicit	Low	On-line services
♦ Legislation and commentary	Explicit	Low	On-line services
♦ Best practice (model) documents	Explicit	High	Computer hard drive or hard copy files
♦ Precedent (form) documents	Explicit	High	Does not exist yet
My practice	Explicit and tacit	High	Spreadsheet In my head
Clients	Tacit	High	In my head
The commercial market and specific industries	Explicit	Low	On-line services

KNOWLEDGE CATEGORY	TACIT OR EXPLICIT	VALUE (LOW, MEDIUM, HIGH)	KNOWLEDGE LOCATION
My skills and expertise	Tacit	High	In my head
Methodology and processes	Explicit	High	Does not exist yet
Past projects and lessons learned	Explicit	High	In my head
Third parties (e.g., regulators, judges, counsel, experts, external consultants)	Explicit	Medium	Contacts database
My market position	Tacit	High	In my head
My revenue, costs and profitability	Explicit	High	Spreadsheet

Examine How Best to Manage That Knowledge (the Scope of Knowledge Management)

Having identified the categories of knowledge you need to manage, your next step is to define how best to manage that knowledge. In other words, you should define the scope of your knowledge management efforts. In Chapters 1 and 4, I defined "knowledge management" as the leveraging of your firm's collective wisdom by creating processes and systems to support and facilitate the identification, capture, dissemination and use of your firm's knowledge.

For many lawyers, knowledge management is synonymous with technology. In fact, there are many knowledge management initiatives that do not involve technology at all, yet bring great value to your practice. As you define the scope of knowledge management, you should follow these four principles I described in Chapter 4:

1. Understand what knowledge you must manage before you identify the best way to manage that knowledge.

2. Don't limit your thinking on the scope of initiatives that can help you manage that knowledge.

3. Base your investment in knowledge management on the value of the knowledge to your practice and your business.

4. Begin with simple, discrete knowledge management initiatives, and, over time, draw them together into more complex knowledge management tools and processes.

From the outset, you should define the scope of knowledge management as including:

♦   Management of explicit and tacit knowledge (described earlier in this Chapter and in Chapter 3)

♦   Management of legal and non-legal knowledge (described earlier in this Chapter and in Chapter 3)

♦   Technology and non-technology systems and processes to manage knowledge (described in Chapter 4)

♦   Simple and complex means of managing knowledge (described in Chapter 4).

Chapter 4 provides examples of specific knowledge management initiatives to support the identification, capture, dissemination and use of explicit and tacit knowledge. For a solo practitioner, consider the following:

◆ Precedents

◆ Best practice document repositories

◆ Legal research tools and systems

◆ Methodologies based on common work processes

◆ Know how files

◆ Debriefing

◆ Matters/credential database

Examine How Best to Facilitate Knowledge Management

Knowledge management organization

A larger law firm requires significant dedicated resources to identify, capture and disseminate knowledge in a form that others can use. Chapter 5 describes what that law firm knowledge management organization should look like. Clearly, as a solo practitioner, you will not be building a knowledge management organization. However, you need to consider:

Do you know how best to identify, capture and disseminate your knowledge?

Do you have time to manage your knowledge?

Knowledge management culture

There are many cultural barriers, described in Chapter 6, that a law firm must overcome to build a culture of knowledge sharing among its staff. As a staff of one, knowledge sharing is not your challenge. However, you still face the biggest cultural impediment to knowledge management in a law firm—the time-based billing model. You need to consider:

How can you justify investing in more efficient ways to work if you bill by the hour?

As you answer this question, bear in mind that it is unlikely you can bill a client for every hour you spend on its matter. This is usually because the work should have been performed more efficiently. If you invest some time in developing more efficient ways to work, you may be able to reduce the amount of unproductive time you must currently write off. Ultimately, this will help increase your profitability.

Knowledge management technology

Though technology is only a part of knowledge management, it is a significant part. In Chapter 7, I described key principles relating to:

♦ The scope of your knowledge management system

♦ The knowledge management system's technology platform

♦ Capturing knowledge in your knowledge management system

♦ Disseminating knowledge via your knowledge management system.

Most of the principles described in that Chapter apply to any legal practice, from the solo practitioner to a large law firm, as follows:

1. Be clear on the scope of knowledge you plan to manage before you implement a knowledge management system.

2. Define the components of your knowledge management system based on the scope of knowledge you wish to

manage and your knowledge management and business objectives.

3. Leverage the technology systems and applications you already have.

4. Apply business rigor to implementing knowledge management technology.

5. Select technology systems and applications that integrate with others.

6. Select systems and applications that are easy to use.

7. Store each piece of knowledge only once in your systems and applications.

8. Apply standards to the capture of knowledge. Don't automatically assume that everything is worth saving. (Be aware of the "garbage in, garbage out" syndrome.)

9. Categorize knowledge according to a taxonomy. (Do not just rely on full text searching to retrieve this knowledge.)

10. Ensure that you are able to find what you are looking for, quickly and accurately, regardless of time or location.

11. Ensure that the technology source is invisible to you.

12. Create a system that will allow you to share appropriate knowledge with clients.

Develop a Knowledge Management Strategy

Once you have defined your business and knowledge management objectives, and considered the scope, organization, culture and technology elements of knowledge management, you should develop your knowledge management strategy. While your strategy will not be on the scale described in Chapter 8, the principles are the same. You should:

- Place the knowledge management strategy in the context of your business.

- Articulate the objectives and benefits of knowledge management in your practice.

- Describe your philosophy and approach to knowledge management.

- Consider knowledge management in the context of your clients.

- Describe critical success factors affecting knowledge management in your practice.

- Identify the investment required to implement knowledge management in your practice.

- Identify both hard and soft measures of the value of knowledge management.

- Define the timeline for implementing the strategy.

This is essentially about understanding that knowledge is key to your business and managing that knowledge should facilitate the achievement of your business objectives.

Implement Knowledge Management

When you are clear on your knowledge management strategy, you should begin with simple, high value knowledge management initiatives that achieve your knowledge management and business objectives. With every knowledge management activity, you should ensure that your efforts directly support a clear business need or business objective. The two key principles you should follow are:

Have a good business reason for each knowledge management initiative.

Implement knowledge management initiatives based on their value and complexity.

By following the steps below, described in detail in Chapter 9, you should succeed at implementing knowledge management initiatives that are directly tied to your business objectives:

1. Turn your knowledge management strategy into specific initiatives.

2. Develop a high level project plan for each initiative to give you a clear picture of the complexity of the initiative. The project plan should identify the time, resources, and cost associated with each initiative. Define the critical success factors affecting each initiative.

3. Draft a business case for each initiative to give you a clear picture of the value of the initiative. The business case should identify the business need, current situation and benefits associated with each initiative. Identify criteria for measuring the value of the initiative. Include the level of investment required, the critical success factors and the time frame, based on the project plan.

4. Prioritize your initiatives based on their value and complexity.

5. Take a phased approach to implementing knowledge management, defining short term, mid term and long term initiatives.

6. In the short term, focus on implementing simple initiatives that will form the basis of more sophisticated systems.

7. In the mid term, focus on implementing more complex knowledge management initiatives that build upon the work achieved during the short term.

8. In the long term, focus on developing sophisticated knowledge management systems and processes that achieve your knowledge management vision.

Having determined his business and knowledge management objectives, the solo practitioner defines his knowledge management strategy, and now wants to implement simple knowledge management initiatives that bring great value to his practice.

He identifies the following knowledge management initiatives that will help him achieve his business and knowledge management objectives:

- Developing a methodology and precedents for the purchase and sale of real estate to handle these matters more efficiently.
- Developing a methodology and precedents for the purchase and sale of small businesses to handle these matters more efficiently.
- Implementing a financial management system to better manage client, matter and financial information.
- Creating an electronic file folder structure and document naming conventions to support storage and retrieval of knowledge.

To understand the value and complexity of these initiatives, he develops a business case and a project plan for each initiative. Consider the business case and project plan for the development of a methodology and precedents for the purchase and sale of real estate.

Project name—development of methodology and precedents for purchase and sale of real estate.

Business Need	Current Situation
Build a successful, profitable real estate practice.	Competition from others has placed a downward pressure on fees, making this work unprofitable.

Project Benefits/Value	Project Investment
◆ Increases profitability of real estate work ◆ Makes process more efficient ◆ Decreases write-off time ◆ Improves the quality of work product ◆ Faster delivery of service to client ◆ Creates more consistent documentation ◆ Enables delegation to administrative staff	40 hours lawyer time to identify documents, create generic precedents and develop the methodology. 20 hours administrative staff time. IT consultant time to automate document drafting process.

Critical Success Factors	Project Timeline
Having adequate time to draft the methodology and documents. Having adequate time to maintain the methodology and documents.	Two months.

Criteria for Measuring Value

◆ Level of profitability of real estate work
◆ Consistency and quality of work product
◆ Client service delivery time

His project plan is simple:

PROJECT TASK	TIMEFRAME
Identify steps in purchase of real estate	1 day
Identify documents for basis of precedent documents	2 days
Draft precedent documents and develop checklists	4 weeks
Draft methodology steps	1 week
Automate the methodology and documents	3 weeks

He then prioritizes the initiatives based on their value and complexity.

With the downward pressure on fees for real estate work, the lawyer see the greatest value in developing a methodology and precedent documents for the purchase and sale of residential real estate. These documents are also relatively simple to draft. The lawyer therefore makes this a short term initiative.

He also realizes that creating an electronic file folder structure and document naming conventions for easy storage and retrieval of electronic documents is very simple and will also bring value to his practice. He also makes this a short term initiative.

He decides that developing the methodology and precedent documents for the purchase and sale of businesses is valuable but less so than the real estate documentation. He also knows that developing the purchase and sale of business documentation will be much easier after he has drafted the real estate documentation. He makes the purchase and sale of business documentation a mid term initiative.

He knows that implementing a better financial management system than his existing spreadsheet would bring value to the practice, but he realizes that this would be a complex initiative. Because he is able to sufficiently manage his practice with his spreadsheet, he marks this initiative as a long term initiative.

Knowledge Management and Your Clients

Knowledge management plays two key roles in your business development efforts:

- ◆ You should leverage your knowledge about your clients and their industries, as well as your market strengths and weaknesses, to determine your business development strategy.

- ◆ Your clients want to know about your approach to knowledge management and expect to derive the benefit from your knowledge management efforts.

The questions you should consider are:

How do you use your knowledge about clients to build and sustain your practice?

How do you market your knowledge management efforts to your clients?

You probably will not be offering sophisticated knowledge management based e-business solutions to your clients of the kind described in Chapter 11. However, you should demonstrate to your clients how employing smarter ways to work through knowledge management translates into improved client service.

Introduce Knowledge Management into Your Practice

To ensure that your knowledge management efforts bring value to your practice, follow these steps:

1. Have you defined your business objectives?
2. Have you defined your knowledge management objectives based on your business objectives?
3. What is the scope of knowledge you will manage?
4. What is the scope of knowledge management initiatives you will pursue?
5. What are the barriers to knowledge management you need to address?
6. Do you have the right technology platform to support knowledge management?

7. How will you leverage your knowledge management efforts with your clients?

8. What will knowledge management cost?

9. What benefits does knowledge management bring to your practice?

10. Have you developed a knowledge management strategy that aligns with your business objectives and considers the above issues?

11. Have you identified simple high value knowledge management initiatives?

12. Do you have a good business case for each knowledge management initiative?

13. Have your knowledge management initiatives brought value to your practice?

Glossary

Added services

Services offered to clients in addition to traditional legal services, such as providing business consulting services, distributing updates on the law, conducting training seminars, and offering on-line legal services.

Alternative legal services

Legal services that differ from traditional legal services, such as on-line legal services.

Best practice

An approach that has proven to achieve the desired result.

Best practice document repository

A database of documents that have been identified by staff in a law firm as valuable work product.

Best practice documents

Matter specific documents that a firm has identified as good examples of its work product and could be used again in similar fact situations. A document may be a best practice document because it is commonly used, rare and complex, or because it represents an example of excellent drafting.

Business case

A project proposal that defines the business need, the current situation and the benefits that will result from implementation. Also includes investment required, drawn from the project plan, together with critical success factors and criteria for measuring value.

Business objective

A stated goal of the firm relating ultimately to the sustainability of the firm.

Business of law

The business elements of a legal practice, such as managing client relationships, leveraging the firm's strengths, addressing the firm's weaknesses, growing the firm's revenue, reducing the firm's costs and increasing the firm's profitability.

Business rigor

Tying activities to a defined business need or the firm's business objectives. Examples of applying business rigor to knowledge management include drafting project plans and business cases before implementing an initiative and then measuring the value of that initiative once it has been implemented.

Business strategy

The direction the firm will take to achieve its business objectives.

Capture

An intention to gather the knowledge of a law firm, rather than an *ad hoc* catch-all of every piece of data or information floating around the firm.

Centralized

Management of a function brought under a single, central authority in the firm.

Client extranet

Secure web-based workspaces, accessible only by the client, the firm and other defined parties. The client extranet can be used as the principal means of delivering client specific knowledge management services and products.

Client relationship management system

A system that manages information relating to the firm's clients and other important contacts, together with information about the firm's relationship with those clients and other contacts.

Client relationship partner

A partner responsible for managing the firm's relationship with a specific client.

Collective wisdom

The combined knowledge of all staff in a firm. Beyond legal knowledge, it includes all knowledge created and used in every aspect of a legal practice and business.

Communities of practice (or communities of interest)

A loose framework that draws together lawyers who work in different offices or practice groups but share a common interest, such as a common client or project.

Core work processes

Basic work activities of lawyers (e.g., interacting with clients, drafting documents, conducting research and negotiating) and administrative staff (e.g., the marketing department preparing bids for client work and organizing client events.)

Critical success factor

A factor that will impact the success of an initiative.

Data

Unstructured, objective facts. Can be in the form of numbers, words or symbols.

Deal room

See **matter extranet.**

Debriefing

The analysis of a process at the conclusion of that process.

Decentralized

Management of a function distributed across many areas of the firm.

Disseminate

Sharing knowledge with the people who seek the knowledge.

Document profile

The attachment of metadata to a document, such as document description, author, date and key words.

E-business

The transformation of a traditional business through the use of technology.

Explicit knowledge

Formal and systematic knowledge which can be easily communicated and shared.[1]

----
[1] Nonaka, "The Knowledge Creating Company," Harv. Bus. Rev. 31 (1998).

Extranet

A secure, private network based on internet technolog to share information between the firm and select third parties.

Financial management system

A system managing information about time recorded, revenue billed, revenue recovered, costs incurred and costs paid by a firm. The system generates reports on the revenue, costs and profitability of the firm, staff members, partners, practice groups, offices, regions, clients, industries and matters.

Findings report

A document summarizing the findings of focus sessions and interviews conducted with staff about the firm's knowledge needs. The findings report typically also includes knowledge management issues and opportunities facing the firm.

Firm-wide initiative

A knowledge management initiative that affects everyone at the firm.

Focus session

A meeting of a group of people to discuss a pre-defined topic to gain a deeper understanding of the group's views on the topic.

Form library

See **precedent library.**

Hard measurement

Data, including financial data and usage data, used to measure value.

Head of knowledge management

A person responsible for knowledge management strategy, knowledge management operations, influencing change and managing knowledge management staff.

Higher value work

An activity that takes full advantage of the skill set of the person performing the activity.

Hybrid

A combination of different elements or approaches. In this book, a "hybrid approach" refers to a combination of centralized and decentralized approaches to knowledge management.

Information

Data presented in a particular context.

Information officer

A central knowledge management role, usually part of the library function, responsible for content delivery and research.

Intranet

A secure, private network within a firm, with a web browser interface, accessible only by staff and used as a means of sharing knowledge about the firm. The intranet may be a portal to other systems and applications.

Know-how file

Presentation of discrete pieces of knowledge relating to the same topic in one place.

Knowledge

Value added by people—context, experience and interpretation— to information. Knowledge is human effort applied to information.

Knowledge audit

A study of the firm's knowledge needs and its current knowledge management systems and processes.

Knowledge management

The leveraging of a firm's collective wisdom by creating processes and systems to support and facilitate the identification, capture, dissemination and use of the firm's knowledge.

Knowledge management-based product

Client tailored and generic products developed by the firm based on the knowledge management efforts of the firm. Examples include client-specific precedents, work product repositories and professional development programs, as well as on-line services.

Knowledge management committee

A forum for representatives of practice groups and administrative areas to exchange ideas about knowledge management.

Knowledge management initiative

An initiative that helps achieve the firm's knowledge management and business objectives.

Knowledge management objective

A stated purpose for pursuing knowledge management at the firm. A knowledge management objective is specific to leveraging the knowledge of the firm to support the firm's business objectives.

Knowledge management partner

The partner responsible for the firm's knowledge management efforts, reporting to the firm's management. This may be a full time role, where the partner is directly involved in the operational and strategic aspects of knowledge management, or a part time, figure-head role, where the emphasis is on influencing cultural change.

Knowledge management strategy

The blueprint for the development of knowledge management processes and tools.

Knowledge management system

The combination of technology systems and applications used to support knowledge management.

Knowledge management system developer

The person responsible for the technology elements of knowledge management, who works with IT and the knowledge management organization to select and implement technology systems and applications that address the knowledge management needs of the firm.

Knowledge management team

A team of senior people, formed when a firm first decides to focus on knowledge management and often in the absence of a head of knowledge management. The team is responsible for building awareness about knowledge management throughout the firm and drafting a knowledge management strategy.

Knowledge management technology platform

The technology infrastructure (servers, desktop computers, laptop computers, cabling, operating system, modes of access, databases, systems and applications) that supports the knowledge management efforts of the firm.

Knowledge manager

Two definitions:

1. A centralized management role, acting as deputy to the head of knowledge management and largely responsible for the day-to-day operational aspects of knowledge management.

2. A practice group role, responsible for meeting the knowledge management needs of a practice group. Often a combination of the professional support lawyer and information officer.

Leverage

Improve or enhance to derive the most benefit possible.

Low value task

A task that does not fully utilize the skill set of the person performing the task.

Matter extranet

A secure web-based workspace, accessible only by defined parties involved in a matter. A matter extranet typically has a limited life-span, established at the beginning of a matter and dismantled at the conclusion of the matter.

Matter management system

A system that manages information about a law department's matters, and tracks the progress, cost and resolution of those matters.

Matters/credentials database

A database of information relating to a law firm's past matters and acquired skills and expertise.

Metadata

Structured data about electronic or paper-based knowledge. The information stored in a document profile represents metadata.

Methodology

A defined set of tasks or steps associated with a process.

Minimum knowledge management standard

The minimum standard of knowledge management that all practice groups are required to achieve. The minimum knowledge management standard ensures that the firm takes a consistent approach to knowledge management across all practice groups.

Partner compensation model

The model used to determine the compensation of a partner.

Pilot initiative

An initiative implemented in a heavily controlled environment, usually with a small number of users, for a limited time frame, and with limited objectives. The purpose of the pilot initiative is to test and refine ideas in operation before a wider initiative is implemented.

Practice group initiative

A knowledge management initiative that directly addresses the knowledge management and business needs of a practice group.

Practice group knowledge management partner

A partner responsible for ensuring that the knowledge management needs of his practice group are met.

Precedent documents (or precedents)

Generic documents that the firm has invested in developing for use in many matters.

Precedent library

A database of precedent documents.

Professional development program

A formal training program administered by the firm. The curriculum typically includes substantive areas of law, as well as practice related topics such as matter management and client relationship management.

Professional support lawyer

A lawyer responsible for supporting the knowledge needs of a practice group, with a strong focus on content development. Responsibilities typically include drafting precedents and other work product, developing and organizing training sessions, identifying and disseminating current awareness materials, and developing content for the intranet and client publications.

Project budget

Funds set aside for the costs associated with a project.

Project plan

A defined set of tasks involved in implementing a project, including an estimate of time, resources and costs associated with the project. Also includes a definition of critical success factors.

Repository

A single storage facility, such as a database.

Silo effect

The fragmentation of knowledge resulting from the lack of interaction and integration between different parts of a law firm.

Skills and expertise locator

A database that captures the skills and expertise of staff, together with contact information.

Soft measurements

Oral and written feedback from staff or clients on desired outcomes.

Tacit knowledge

Knowledge that is highly personal, hard to formalize and difficult to communicate to others.[2]

Taxonomy

A set of categories used to classify the knowledge stored in the knowledge management system.

Technology committee

A group of law firm staff (typically chaired by a partner) who advise the firm on technology issues relating to the firm.

Technology platform

The technology infrastructure (servers, desktop computers, laptop computers, cabling, operating system, modes of access, databases, systems and applications) of the firm.

Time-based billing model

A billing model in which a law firm determines the amount of a client's fee based on the amount of time spent on the client's work.

Value-based billing model

A billing model in which a law firm determines the amount of a client's fee based on the mutually agreed value of the law firm's work for the client.

Work product repository

See **best practice document repository.**

....

2 *Id.*

Index

M N O

About the Author

Gretta Rusanow is the chief executive of Curve Consulting, with offices in Sydney and New York. She advises law firms and law departments worldwide on their knowledge management, e-business, management and technology initiatives.

Ms. Rusanow holds a BA LLB from the University of New South Wales. She can be contacted at *grettarusanow@curveconsulting.com*.

ALSO FROM ALM PUBLISHING:

Game, Set, Match: Winning the Negotiations Game
by Henry S. Kramer

The Essential Guide to the Best (and Worst) Legal Sites on the Web
by Robert J. Ambrogi, Esq.

On Trial: Lessons from a Lifetime in the Courtroom
by Henry G. Miller, Esq.

Going Public in Good Times and Bad: A Legal and Business Guide
by Robert G. Heim

Inside/Outside: How Businesses Buy Legal Services
by Larry Smith

Arbitration: Essential Concepts
by Steven C. Bennett, Esq.

Courtroom Psychology and Trial Advocacy
by Richard C. Waites, J.D., Ph.D

Negotiating and Drafting Contract Boilerplate
by Tina L. Stark

The Practice of Law School
by Christen Civiletto Carey, Esq. and Kristen David Adams

Other publications available from AMERICAN LAWYER MEDIA:

LAW JOURNAL PRESS professional legal treatises—over 100 titles available

Legal newspapers and magazines—over 20 national and regional titles available, including:

The American Lawyer
The National Law Journal
New York Law Journal

Visit us at our websites:
www.lawcatalog.com
and
www.americanlawyermedia.com